The Story of God's Chosen Family SERIES

The Story of God's Chosen Family

God Chooses a Family

Old Testament Study from

Creation to the prophet Samuel

Grade 5

Teacher's Manual

Rod and Staff Publishers, Inc.
P.O. Box 3, Hwy. 172
Crockett, Kentucky 41413
Telephone: (606) 522-4348

Acknowledgments

We give thanks first of all to God for the Holy Scriptures, "which are able to make [our students] wise unto salvation through faith which is in Christ Jesus" (2 Timothy 3:15). God's Word is the textbook for this course. The goal of this workbook is to instill in our children a deeper appreciation for God and His Word, to broaden their understanding of Bible facts, and to guide them toward competent study and use of the Bible for themselves.

A number of brethren worked together in writing and editing the material for this study guide. Others spent many hours reviewing the material and preparing the manuscript for publication. Sister Ruth Goodwin and the brethren Timothy Conley and Lester Miller drew the finished illustrations. The drawing showing the Israelites' camp (page 144) is used by permission of Eastern Mennonite University.

"Thou art worthy, O Lord, to receive glory and honour and power: for thou hast created all things, and for thy pleasure they are and were created" (Revelation 4:11).

Copyright, 1997

by

Rod and Staff Publishers, Inc.

Crockett, Kentucky 41413

Printed in U.S.A.

ISBN 978-07399-0422-0

Catalog no. 17591

Table of Contents

CHAPTER FOUR: Israel in the Wilderness

CHAPTER FIVE: Israel Conquers Canaan

CHAPTER SIX: Israel in the Days of the Judges

TEACHER'S INTRODUCTION

Rod and Staff Bible Series Outline

The Story of God's Chosen Family (Grades 5–8)

Grade 5: God Chooses a Family
   (Old Testament—Creation to the prophet Samuel)
Grade 6: God's Chosen Family as a Nation
   (Old Testament—Saul to Malachi)
Grade 7: God Visits His Chosen Family
   (New Testament—the Gospels and Acts)
Grade 8: God's Redeemed Family—the Church
   (New Testament—Romans to Revelation)

The Pupil's Book

Use: Workbook Versus Textbook

The pupil's book may be used as a consumable workbook or as a textbook. It is designed as a workbook, which allows the student to write answers in the book and to keep it after he completes the course. However, since most exercises are numbered or lettered, schools that prefer to reuse the books for several years may ask students to write their answers on paper.

Chapter and Lesson Divisions

The pupil's book is divided into six chapters. Each chapter has five lessons and a review. A chapter is intended to provide work for six weeks. Chapter tests and a final test are available in a separate booklet.

This fifth grade workbook follows a chronological sequence through the first half of the Old Testament (Creation to the prophet Samuel). The first lesson of each chapter introduces the chapter and teaches general information about the Bible. The last four lessons of the chapter follow the chronological study and direct the student to the Bible for answers. Besides teaching Bible facts, these lessons help students learn to use the Bible. They have the following pattern.

1. **Lesson Introduction**
2. **A. Answers From the Bible**—Exercises that direct the student to Bible passages for answers. This is the core section of the course and should be completed by all students.
3. **B. Bible Word Study**—Exercises that increase the student's understanding of unfamiliar words.
4. **C. Thinking About Bible Truths**—Questions for class discussion or additional assignment. They are often more challenging than the other exercises.
5. **D. Learning More About the Bible**—Drawings, maps, and background information to help students better understand Bible facts, customs, and lands.

Introductory Lessons

The first lesson in each chapter teaches information about the Bible and gives practice with using a concordance, Bible dictionary, or other Bible study help. These lessons are not essential to the chronological Bible study, but the reviews and tests do include questions on them. The introductory lessons have the following regular features.

1. **A. Answers From the Bible**—Exercises that direct students to Bible passages related to the theme of the lesson.
2. **B. Bible Study Books**—Exercises requiring the use of Bible dictionaries, concordances, and Bible atlases.

The Teacher's Book

Oral Review

These optional questions are for use during the class period. If you wish, you may duplicate the questions and hand them to the students for written work or for personal study.

In This Lesson

Scope

This section gives the Bible chapters or verses on which the lesson is based. Because of time and space limitations, the lesson covers only a few key points rather than giving a thorough coverage of the whole Bible scope. Additional facts and themes could be drawn from the scope if time permits.

Main Events

This section provides a brief outline of main events covered in the lesson. The purpose of this course is to increase the student's factual understanding of the Bible. For this reason the course follows a chronological order through the Bible, rather than following themes or character studies. The goal is to have the student gain a working knowledge of what happened in Bible stories and where those stories are found, as well as to broaden his understanding of the Bible with maps, charts, sketches, and other supplementary information.

In the introductory lessons (first lesson of each chapter), this section is titled **Main Points,** since these lessons do not follow the chronological series of events.

Objectives

This section gives a list of important facts or skills that students should learn.

Truths to Instill

While the main purpose of this course is to teach Bible facts, it also provides an excellent opportunity to instill spiritual truths. Several of the main truths in each lesson are listed for your benefit. The list is by no means exhaustive, nor should you feel it necessary to cover all the points mentioned. Rather, the list is for your benefit, to provide inspiration and a sense of direction. Teach as the Lord directs, with truths He has instilled in your heart.

Answer Key

A copy of the pupil's page is provided, with the answers given in colored ink. Teachers should use their own judgment when deciding whether an answer is correct or not. Vague or incomplete answers will not suffice. When exact answers can easily be found in the Bible, do not give credit for guesses based on the student's previous Bible knowledge. In certain cases, however, some variation is permissible. For example, the correct answer for the question, "Who created the world?" is *God,* but the answer *Jesus* should be given at least partial credit. (See John 1:3.)

The pupils are instructed to write complete answers for the questions with long blanks. A complete answer is more than one or two words. However, since schools and pupils vary, you will need to decide exactly what constitutes a complete answer. Perhaps you will want your pupils to write complete sentences for these answers. Be sure your pupils understand what you expect of them.

The pupils' wording of these answers will vary. Therefore, unless a longer answer is needed for clarity, the Answer Key gives brief answers for these. The pupils' answers should include what is given in the Answer Key.

Sometimes the Answer Key gives several options for an answer or has some other direction for the teacher to consider in relation to a question. If this requires too much space to fit in the Pupil reduction, two arrows (>>) direct you to look in the margin for the additional answers or further direction.

Notes

Along the right margins are additional directions and notes that you may find interesting and helpful in teaching. The directions are in italic type, with the first line indented. The notes are preceded by bullets.

Lesson Plans

Since this course may be used in a wide variety of situations and schedules, no detailed teaching plans have been provided for each lesson. However, many schools have Bible classes two or three times a week. You may find the following suggestions helpful.

Two-Day Plan

First Day
—Read or discuss the introduction together.
—Read at least some of the lesson verses in class.
—Assign "Answers From the Bible."

Second Day
—Discuss "Thinking About Bible Truths."
—Discuss "Learning More About the Bible."
—Assign "Bible Word Study" and "Learning More About the Bible." Also assign "Thinking About Bible Truths" if you did not complete this part in class.

Three-Day Plan

First Day
—Read or discuss the introduction together.
—Read some of the lesson verses in class.
—Assign some of "Answers From the Bible."

Second Day
—Read more of the lesson verses in class.
—Assign the rest of "Answers From the Bible."
—Assign "Bible Word Study."

Third Day
—Discuss "Thinking About Bible Truths."
—Discuss "Learning More About the Bible."
—Assign "Learning More About the Bible." Also assign "Thinking About Bible Truths" if you did not complete this part in class.

Time Line: the Human Register

Learning about the Bible stretches a child's scope of time. Suddenly "a long time" as a child sees it becomes longer and longer. Very easily it becomes too long for him to comprehend.

A child needs the help of his parents and teachers to avoid stretching his concept of time to the point where time becomes meaningless, and ancient events separate from the present to drift into the realm of mystery-shrouded legend. A child with this concept of the Bible will see its stories in an unnatural light. Even the miracles recorded in the Bible will lose their significance for him. Anything could happen, the child believes, in a world and age divorced from reality.

One purpose of this Bible course is to counteract such an idea. Children must learn to accept without question that the Creation and other Bible events are historical facts. A supplementary wall chart, The Human Register, was designed to tie a child's scope of time together. It should help children comprehend that every person, from the time of Adam to the present, lived on the earth we live on, breathed the air we breathe, drank the water we drink, and was born and died in our real, historical age. The stronger the link between Bible times and our time in a child's understanding, the better he will grasp Bible truths. The Bible will not be like a fairy tale to him. It will be like a true story told to him by his parents or grandparents about things that happened before he was born.

The Human Register may be displayed in an unbroken line along one side of your classroom. Before beginning this course, show and discuss with your students the entire scope of time. This will introduce the Human Register as a framework onto which other Bible facts learned throughout the course may be placed.

The Human Register continues to the present to show students the brevity of the modern age, to be a help in making comparisons, and to give them a realistic grasp of the length of various time periods in the

Bible. The life of Noah, for example, was as long as from the time of the Vikings to the present.

The Human Register uses pictures in an attempt to fix impressions. Symbols such as the bulrushes around Moses, the star of Bethlehem, and the Viking ship mark certain events to make them more readily identifiable.

The dates that appear on The Human Register will not agree with all other Bible chronologies. Certain periods of Bible chronology are unclear, and it does not seem possible to state with certainty exact dates in early history. The focus is not on precise chronology, but on the scope of human history.

Back to 967 B.C. (the fourth year of Solomon's reign), the dates match those generally accepted in most reference books. The 480 years of 1 Kings 6:1 are used to date the Exodus at 1447 B.C. If the 430 years of Exodus 12:40 include the time of Abraham and Isaac, as well as Jacob's sojourn in Egypt, Abraham's call was approximately 1877 B.C. The data given in Genesis 5:1–12:4 and Acts 7:4 gives approximate dates of 2304 B.C. for the Flood and 3960 B.C. for the Creation.

Some people prefer Philip Mauro's system for dating the judges and early kings. (See *The Wonders of Bible Chronology,* by Mauro.) According to this view, the 480 years of 1 Kings 6:1 include only the years when God ruled through godly men. An additional 114 years of oppression and usurpation are added to these 480 years, placing the Exodus at about 1561 B.C. and the Creation at about 4074 B.C. This harmonizes well with Acts 13:20 and with the total years for the individual judges. However, this system also raises some questions, especially in regard to Jair's judgeship and the 300 years of Judges 11:26, the lack of allowance for gaps or overlaps, and the assumption that Eli became judge immediately after forty years of Philistine oppression. The Human Register follows the more traditional interpretation of 1 Kings 6:1, even though that leaves open the question of Acts 13:20.

Bible Memorization

Bible memorization should have an important place in a Christian school. If everyone knows a passage well, reciting it together can be a pleasant, worshipful exercise. With enough practice, any class can learn to recite Bible verses fluently and clearly. It is unfortunate when students see Bible memorization as drudgery.

Hints for Bible Memorization

1. Teachers can inspire enthusiasm for memorizing by being enthusiastic themselves about learning new verses.
2. Assign a reasonable number of verses for memorization. Students should learn only as many verses as can be effectively drilled in class. Memorizing a few verses well is better than trying to learn a large number without mastering them.
3. Select verses that students can understand and relate to. Explain each passage as meaningfully as you can.
4. Have short, frequent classes for Bible memorization, possibly as the first thing after the morning devotional or after the lunch break.
5. You may wish to copy the day's assignment onto the chalkboard, writing the passage in lines like the lines of a poem. After the students have read the first lines and recited them with their eyes closed, begin erasing the lines.
6. Group memorization is a great help. It offers variety and serves as an effective stimulant. But individual testing, both oral and written, also has its place.
7. Do not assign Bible memorization as a punishment.
8. Review previously learned verses throughout the school year. During the last few weeks of the year, the entire Bible memory program could be devoted to review.
9. Students may learn to memorize a series of verses by "counting fingers," associating each verse with a finger.
10. If you are teaching more than one grade, you may wish to assign the same memory passage to everyone in the room.

Suggested Memory Passages

The following suggestions may be helpful to you in selecting Bible passages for memorization.

For each chapter in this course, three Scripture passages are given. There are also three thematic selections of verses, arranged according to the theme of the chapter being studied. From these six suggestions, which are of various lengths, choose the one you feel is best suited to your class. Divide your selected passage or theme into five weekly assignments, with modification as needed.

As much as is feasible, the thematic selections have been arranged to avoid awkward transitions of person and tense. If you use these selections, you may find it helpful to type them so that the students have them all together. Typing the verses after the following pattern will make it easier for the students to memorize them line by line.

Isaiah 37:16
O Lᴏʀᴅ of hosts, God of Israel,
that dwellest between the cherubims,
thou art the God, even thou alone,
of all the kingdoms of the earth:
thou hast made heaven and earth.

Genesis 1:21
And God created great whales,
and every living creature that moveth,
which the waters brought forth abundantly, after their kind,
and every winged fowl after his kind:
and God saw that it was good.

Choose one group of verses for each chapter.

Chapter One—The Dawn of Human History

Passage Selections
1. Psalm 90
2. John 1:1–14
3. Psalm 19

Thematic Selections: God the Creator
4. (13 verses) Isaiah 37:16; Genesis 1:21–31; Nehemiah 9:6
5. (13 verses) Psalm 24:1; Genesis 1:26–31; Isaiah 40:25, 26; Amos 4:13; 5:8; 9:6; Revelation 4:11
6. (21 verses) Hebrews 11:3; Genesis 1:21–31; Psalm 146:5, 6; Isaiah 45:6, 7, 12, 18; Romans 1:18–20

Chapter Two—The Patriarchs

Passage Selections
1. Hebrews 11:1–20
2. Genesis 22:6–18
3. Acts 7:1–19

Thematic Selections: Faith
4. (13 verses) Proverbs 3:5, 6, 24–26; James 2:18–24; 1 John 5:4
5. (16 verses) Psalm 37:3–5, 39, 40; Romans 4:3, 18–22; Jeremiah 17:7, 8; Psalm 118:8, 9, 29
6. (22 verses) Hebrews 11:1–3, 8–21; Psalm 55:22; Matthew 6:31–34

Chapter Three—God's Chosen Family in Egypt

Passage Selections
1. Hebrews 11:21–40
2. Exodus 3:1–15
3. Acts 7:20–37

Thematic Selections: The Power of God
4. (13 verses) Exodus 15:3–6, 11–13, 18, 19; Deuteronomy 3:24; Psalm 29:2–4
5. (17 verses) Exodus 15:1–13; 1 Chronicles 29:11, 12; Deuteronomy 33:26, 27a
6. (21 verses) Psalm 135:5–13; Isaiah 40:12–17; Jeremiah 10:6; Micah 1:3, 4; Nahum 1:5, 6; Matthew 19:26b

Chapter Four—Israel in the Wilderness

Passage Selections
1. Exodus 20:1–17
2. Psalms 1 and 23
3. Deuteronomy 6:1–15

Thematic Selections: The Righteousness, Holiness, and Justice of God
4. (14 verses) Ezra 9:15; Psalm 119:40, 137–144; Isaiah 56:1; Jeremiah 4:2; Daniel 9:7, 14
5. (17 verses) Psalm 33:1–5; Psalm 99; James 1:13; 1 Peter 1:15, 16
6. (20 verses) Deuteronomy 32:1–4; 1 Chronicles 16:29–34; 2 Chronicles 19:7; Psalm 11:4–6; Psalm 50:3–6; Proverbs 11:31; Proverbs 11:6

Chapter Five—Israel Conquers Canaan

Passage Selections
1. Isaiah 40:1–17
2. Joshua 1:1–9
3. Joshua 24:14–25

Thematic Selections: Triumph
4. (16 verses) Psalm 44:1–8; 2 Chronicles 16:9a; Psalm 34:7–10; Psalm 91:4; Psalm 125:1, 2
5. (18 verses) Ephesians 6:10–17; Philippians 1:6; Luke 10:19; Psalm 27:1–6; Psalm 29:10, 11
6. (19 verses) 1 Chronicles 29:11–13; 1 Chronicles 16:29–35; Romans 8:35–39; Revelation 1:8; Revelation 3:5, 21; Revelation 21:7

Chapter Six—Israel in the Days of the Judges

Passage Selections
1. Isaiah 40:18–31
2. Psalm 107:1–15
3. Judges 6:7–16

Thematic Selections: Perseverance
4. (12 verses) Proverbs 4:14–19; Hosea 12:6; Hebrews 12:2; Matthew 10:22; 2 Thessalonians 2:15; 1 Corinthians 16:13; Galatians 6:9
5. (16 verses) Joshua 23:2–11; Job 11:14, 15; 17:9; James 1:12; 5:10, 11
6. (18 verses) Joshua 24:1–3, 6–8, 11–22

Teaching Subjective Thinking Skills

What Is Subjective Thinking?

Two basic kinds of questions are used in teaching. The most common is the objective question, which asks about a fact. This type of question tests recall and research skills, but does not necessarily test understanding. For instance, an objective question might ask how many legions of angels Jesus could have called to help Him. The student can read Matthew 26:53 and answer, "Twelve legions." However, just because he has given the fact does not guarantee that he understands his answer. He may have no idea what a legion is.

The other type of question is the subjective question, which requires the student to apply facts he has learned and draw conclusions from them. A person who thinks carefully about Matthew 26:53 will realize several things that are not stated. First, he will see that Jesus submitted to the mob in the garden because He wanted to. He had the ability to overpower them, but He did not use it. Secondly, Jesus could have refused to go to Calvary. Subjective questions guide the student to make this kind of conclusions.

Subjective thinking should not be allowed to become mere fantasy. It is based on fact and stays within the bounds of logic and reason.

Suppose you are traveling down a highway in a car. As you pass a house, you see a large, angry dog chasing a man down the driveway toward his car. What happened after you were past? The objective answer is that you do not know. However, you do have some facts that help you reach a probable conclusion. The dog was angry. The man was running to get away from him. A car was waiting at the end of the drive. You know that angry dogs can be vicious. Given these facts, which of the following is the most likely conclusion to the incident?

1. The man stops at his car to pat the dog and to praise him for being a good watchdog.
2. The dog chases the man all the way to his car, biting his leg as he frantically tries to open the door.
3. Just as the dog reaches him, the man sprouts wings and soars away to safety.

The first answer is not reasonable, given the facts you know about the situation. The second one is the most likely. The third is fantastic—men do not sprout wings. Subjective reasoning is the process that helps us reach conclusions like this.

Why Do We Need to Teach Subjective Thinking?

Everyone does some subjective thinking. However, some people have not learned to think logically and subjectively at the same time. Because of this, they often jump to wild conclusions. At other times, they reach wrong conclusions because they have not taken time to learn all the related facts. Such people need training in subjective thinking.

Other people allow the reasoning process to replace faith. They decide that they will not believe anything that they cannot reason through. Since they cannot understand Bible miracles, they refuse to believe them. This is the opposite extreme from jumping to conclusions, but it is even more serious because it destroys faith in God and His Word. Such people also need training in subjective thinking.

We must teach our students to avoid these overreactions. They must learn that faith in God and the Bible is a necessary part of the reasoning process. It is a fact that God is not tied to the same limitations that we are. On the other hand, God overrules natural laws only for special purposes, and His character always limits Him from doing evil.

A person who has learned to think properly knows that what he does today will affect his future. By applying verses such as "Love not the world, neither the things that are in the world," he realizes that television, tobacco smoking, and a host of other modern evils are wrong, even though the Bible does not specifically mention them. Subjective thinking trains a person to look at life realistically, and prepares him to cope with it. As a teacher, you have an obligation to teach your students good thinking skills.

How Can We Teach Subjective Thinking?

This course includes a number of subjective questions. Since subjective thinking may be new for fifth graders, it is important to take time to introduce these questions. Otherwise, some students may blindly guess at answers without understanding how to reach a reasonable conclusion.

Most subjective questions in this course are multiple-choice exercises. This gives the student a starting point for his evaluation. Teach him to read the question carefully, taking time to understand what it is asking. Then he should evaluate each possible answer, comparing it with the facts that he knows about the situation. If he follows this process, he should usually be able to eliminate the wrong answers.

If he thinks that two answers could be right, he must ask himself, "Which of the two is the best answer?" At this age level, most of the questions have only one correct answer, but you may want to introduce the idea of "best answer" to your students. At first they may not understand how a correct answer can be the wrong one, but explain that no answer is really right if a better answer is available. This is an important skill for every Christian to learn and practice.

It may take some time for your students to develop subjective thinking skills, but do not omit those questions. Instead, discuss them together. Most students can eventually learn the necessary skills.

CHAPTER ONE

The Dawn of
Human History

Thou, even thou, art LORD alone; thou hast made heaven, the heaven of heavens, with all their host, the earth, and all things that are therein, the seas, and all that is therein, and thou preservest them all; and the host of heaven worshippeth thee.
(Nehemiah 9:6)

TIME LINE—Chapter One
From the Creation to Abraham

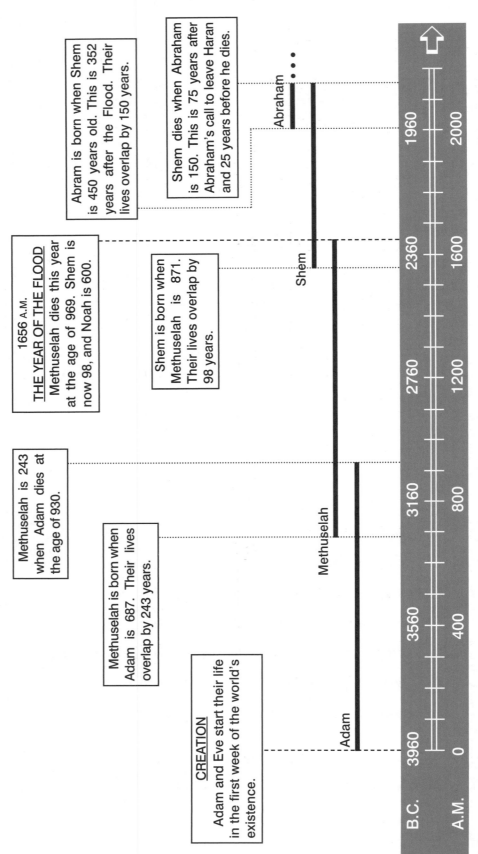

Abram is born when Shem is 450 years old. This is 352 years after the Flood. Their lives overlap by 150 years.

Shem dies when Abraham is 150. This is 75 years after Abraham's call to leave Haran and 25 years before he dies.

1656 A.M.
THE YEAR OF THE FLOOD
Methuselah dies this year at the age of 969. Shem is now 98, and Noah is 600.

Shem is born when Methuselah is 871. Their lives overlap by 98 years.

Methuselah is 243 when Adam dies at the age of 930.

Methuselah is born when Adam is 687. Their lives overlap by 243 years.

CREATION
Adam and Eve start their life in the first week of the world's existence.

Abraham

Shem

Methuselah

Adam

| B.C. | 3960 | 3560 | 3160 | 2760 | 2360 | 1960 |
| A.M. | 0 | 400 | 800 | 1200 | 1600 | 2000 |

Notes:

We do not know how well these men knew each other, but Adam could have talked with Shem, and Shem could have talked with Abraham.

All dates B.C. used in this course are approximate. Due to some unanswered questions, the exact date of Creation is difficult to determine. However, the rounded figure of 4000 B.C. should be correct within a few hundred years.

9

Lesson 1. Introduction to the Bible

The Bible is God's message to man. In this course you will be using the Bible for your textbook as you learn about things that have happened to God's people in the past.

The Bible tells us about men and women, and sometimes about children too. It shows us where people came from and what they have been doing since the world began. Each story in the Bible has lessons for us—directions about what we should do and warnings about what we should not do.

The Bible also introduces us to God Himself. What the Bible teaches about people in ancient times is important, but what it teaches about God is even more important.

We cannot see God with our eyes or talk with Him face to face. Yet through the Bible, we can learn to know God. God gave His messages to godly men, who wrote them and gave them to God's people. Later these messages were put together to form the Book we call the Bible.

Without the Bible we would not know how the earth was formed or where the first people and animals came from. Worse yet, without the Bible we would not know God, nor would we know the difference between right and wrong. We would not know what God wants us to do. Praise God for giving us the Bible, the Book that tells us how to live to please Him!

A. ANSWERS FROM THE BIBLE

★ *To complete these exercises, first study the Bible passages that are given. Fill in the short blanks with words. Whenever possible, use exact words from the Bible. Write complete answers for the questions with long blanks. For multiple choice questions, circle the letter of the correct answer.*

The Scriptures Were Inspired by God

2 Timothy 3:15–17

In these verses the Bible is called the Scriptures and the Scripture. Every verse in the Bible was inspired by God. This means that even though men wrote the words of the Bible, God told them what to write. Because of this, the Bible is the perfect Word of God.

1. According to 2 Timothy 3:15, how long had Timothy known the Scriptures? _____
   since he was a child _____

2. The Scriptures are able to make us _____ wise _____ unto salvation.

3. All Scripture is given by _____ inspiration _____ of God. This means that the men who wrote the Scriptures received their words from _____ God _____.

4. Which statement is *not* true?
   a. God inspired the Bible.
   b. The Scriptures teach us true doctrine.
   (c.) Timothy learned the Scriptures after he had grown up.

Lesson 1

In This Lesson

Main Points
- The Bible, inspired by God Himself, tells the history of man.
- God inspired the writers of the Bible to write the exact message He wanted to be recorded. God's message is without mistakes. It will stand forever.
- The word *Bible* comes from the Greek word for "book."
- Bible dictionaries help us to understand difficult words in the Bible.

Objectives
- Students should know
  —what "all scripture is given by *inspiration* of God" means. (God told men what to write.)
  —how long the Bible will stand. (forever)
  —the basic use of a Bible dictionary and how to find information in one. (See Part B.)

Truths to Instill
- We need a deep appreciation for the Bible. It is (to name a few points)
  —the most accurate history of mankind.
  —God's revelation of Himself.
  —God's revelation of His will and purpose for our lives.

2 Peter 1:20, 21

5. Who moved (directed) the men who spoke and wrote God's words? <u>the Holy Ghost (God)</u>

6. Verse 20 tells us that "no prophecy of the scripture is of any private interpretation." This means that the Bible
   - (a.) is God's message—men did not just write their own ideas.
   - b. should be read only in public meetings—never in private.
   - c. does not contain any prophecies.

The Bible Is God's Message to Us

God speaks to us from the Bible. Large parts of the Bible are the exact words that God spoke to the prophets. The New Testament records many things that Jesus said and did. The Bible also includes the words and actions of prophets, judges, kings, and other men, as well as angels and even Satan. Yet everything the Bible records is given to us by God so that we can learn from it.

Romans 15:4

7. The "things [that] were written aforetime" are the Scriptures. According to this verse, God gave us the Bible for our _____ learning _____.

Psalm 119:105

8. This verse teaches us that the Bible
   - a. can be seen in the dark.
   - (b.) shows us how to live.
   - c. will help us find the way to go if we take a trip.

John 3:16

9. God does not want man to be lost. One main purpose of the Bible is to bring the message of salvation to man. This verse tells us that God _____ loved _____ the world so much that He gave His own Son to provide a way to keep men from perishing.

The Word of God Is Eternal

Almost everything changes with time. Languages gain new words, people grow old and die, buildings age and crumble, and even the scenery around us changes. But God and His Word will never change. They are eternal.

Psalm 119:160

10. How long has the Word of God been true? _____ from the beginning _____

Isaiah 40:8

11. Many people have tried to destroy the Bible. They have burned it, they have passed laws against printing it, and they have put people in prison for owning it—but no one has been able to get rid of it. How long will the Word of God stand? _____ forever _____

- God wants us to read, hear, study, believe, and obey His Word.
- Only the Bible is completely trustworthy. Bible helps such as Bible dictionaries might contain error. We must learn to use them discriminately.

How Did the Bible Get Its Name?

The word *Bible* comes from the Greek word for *book*. The Greeks used the word *biblos* or *biblion* for a book because that was their word for papyrus. Papyrus is a lush, fast-growing reed that grows along the edges of swamps and rivers. Men made paper and books from papyrus.

In our English Bibles, the Greek words *biblos* and *biblion* are never translated as Bible. But read the verses below, which leave those words in their original language.

"The *biblos* of the generation of Jesus Christ" (Matthew 1:1).

"The *biblos* of the words of Esaias the prophet" (Luke 3:4).

"Behold, I come quickly: blessed is he that keepeth the sayings of the prophecy of this *biblion*" (Revelation 22:7).

These Greek words help us to understand how the Bible got its name.

12. Look up the above verses in your Bible and see what word is used for the italicized words. In our English Bible, the word *biblos* is translated _____book_____.

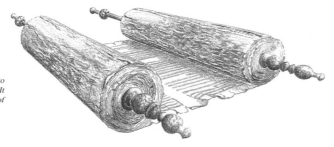

Papyrus was first used to make paper in Egypt. It grew in the wet lowlands of the Nile River delta.

How Should We Use the Bible?

The Bible is a wonderful gift from God to man. But the Bible will not do us any good unless we *use* it. The Bible tells us how we should use it so that we can benefit from our gift.

Revelation 1:3

13. This verse pronounces a blessing on those who _____read_____ the Bible, _____hear_____ its words, and keep the things that are written in it.

2 Timothy 2:15

14. If we want to have God's approval on our lives, we must _____study_____ the Bible and rightly divide (carefully use) its truths.

John 2:22

15. Like the disciples, we must remember the words of Jesus and _____believe_____ the Scriptures.

- 2 Timothy 2:15. This verse has a deeper meaning that you may want to explain to your students if you have time. The original Greek word translated *study* has the idea of diligence—that is, "be diligent to show yourself approved." This includes both studying the Scriptures and putting them into practice. To "rightly divide" means literally to "cut straight," that is, to handle rightly and teach directly and correctly.

Acts 5:29

16. We ought to _____obey_____ God (and His Word), even if rulers command us to disobey the Bible.

★ *It is very important for us to use the Bible in the ways that it tells us to. When you are sure*
you have correctly filled in the blanks for numbers 13–16, memorize the five words you
filled in.

B. BIBLE STUDY BOOKS

Men have written books to help us study the Bible. This year you will use Bible dictionaries, Bible concordances, and Bible atlases. These books can help us understand the Bible, but they are not perfect. Any book written by man may have mistakes. The Bible is the only perfect book.

Bible Dictionaries

Some Bibles have a small Bible dictionary in the back. Other Bible dictionaries are separate books. Your school
may have Bible dictionaries in its library. Bible dictionaries tell us what words mean. The Bible often mentions
ancient places, foreign plants, and other items of which we know very little. Sometimes it uses terms that we do not
use regularly. Bible dictionaries help us to understand the Bible by explaining such words.

★ *Use a Bible dictionary to do these exercises. The words in a Bible dictionary are in alphabeti-*
cal order, the same as in a regular dictionary.

1. The following words are from the chapters of Genesis that you will study in the next several lessons. Look up each word on the left. Write a phrase from the right to tell what it
means.

   a. Shinar _____a country_____   a river

   b. Euphrates _____a river_____   a country

   c. firmament _____the sky_____   the son of Seth

   d. covenant _____an agreement_____   an agreement

   e. Enos _____the son of Seth_____   the sky

2. In Bible times, people gave their children names that had special meanings. You can find the
meanings of such names in most Bible dictionaries, right after the name. Look up the following Bible names and tell what they mean.

   a. Abigail ____"my father rejoices"____

   b. Isaac ____"laughter"____

   c. Joshua ____"Jehovah is salvation"____

   d. Peter ____"a rock"____

   e. Samuel ____"asked or heard of God"____

   f. Noah ____"rest; quiet"____

Show the students a Bible
dictionary and explain how
and when to use it. Many Bible
words are also found in regu-
lar dictionaries, but sometimes
the meaning intended in the
Bible is not clearly given in
them.

Help students to use Bible
dictionaries as they encounter
new words in the Bible. Most
Bible dictionaries are written
on an adult level, with lengthy
definitions that fifth graders
may find difficult to under-
stand. They can be introduced
to its use, however, with help
from the teacher or an older
student.

Do the Bible dictionary
exercise together in class if
possible. However, the defini-
tions involved are not lengthy,
so most fifth graders should
have no difficulty with them.

As you check answers,
remember that Bible dictionar-
ies vary. Be especially aware of
this if your class has used
more than one dictionary. The
answers given in the answer
key are from the New Unger's
Bible Dictionary.

3. Sometimes you need to check the dictionary subheadings to find what you want. For example, most Bible dictionaries describe all the kinds of Bible animals under a heading such as *Animal, Animals,* or *Animal Kingdom*. Find the list of animals in your Bible dictionary. Choose two that you are unfamiliar with, and briefly describe them.

Example: coney—a rock badger   (Answers will vary.)

a. _____

b. _____

14

Lesson 2. In the Beginning

Everything in this world had a beginning. You have never seen a flower, an apple tree, or a head of cabbage that did not begin as a seed. You have never seen a boy or a girl who did not begin life as a baby. Even the earth itself had a beginning, and so did the sun, the moon, and the stars.

Everything had a beginning—except God. The Bible does not tell us how God began, because God has always been. The first verse of Genesis simply says, "In the beginning God created the heaven and the earth."

God does not expect us to understand everything about the beginning. He does not explain everything to us, because our minds are too small. But He does expect us to believe what He has told us. He gave us the Bible, which tells us everything that we need to know about the beginning.

Only God can make things begin because only He can create something out of nothing.

A. ANSWERS FROM THE BIBLE

The Bible tells us that "in six days the LORD made heaven and earth, the sea, and all that in them is, and rested the seventh day" (Exodus 20:11). In this lesson you will study each day of the first week in order.

★ *Open your Bible to the first two chapters of Genesis, and find the verses that go with each section. Whenever possible, use exact words from the Bible to fill in the short blanks. Write complete answers for the questions with long blanks. For multiple choice questions, circle the letter of the correct answer or underline the correct word in parentheses.*

The First Day

Genesis 1:1–5

1. "In the beginning God created the ____heaven____ and the ____earth____."

2. On the first day, God also created ____light____. He did this by saying, "____"Let____ ____there____ ____be____ ____light."____."

As you read more verses in this lesson, notice that God also created many other things simply by speaking.

3. God divided the light from the darkness. He called the light _____day_____, and the darkness ____night____.

The Second Day

Genesis 1:6–8

4. On the second day, God created the ____firmament____ to divide the waters that were under it from the waters that were above it.

Lesson 2

Oral Review

(The numbers in brackets tell which lessons are being reviewed.)

1. How did the men who wrote the Bible know what words to use? [1] **The Holy Spirit told the men what to write.**
2. How long had Timothy known the Scriptures? [1] **Timothy knew the Scriptures "from a child."**
3. How long will God's Word be true? [1] **forever**
4. Name five ways (from Lesson 1) that God wants us to use the Bible. [1] **read, hear, study, believe, obey**

5. Which reference book gives the meanings of difficult Bible words? [1] **Bible dictionary**

In This Lesson

Scope: Genesis 1, 2

Main Events

- God creates the world in six days and rests on the seventh. This lesson reviews what God did on each of the six days of Creation.

Objectives

- Students should know
  —what God made on each of the six days of Creation. (See Part A.)

5. The firmament is the space around the earth, sun, moon, and stars. God called the firmament _____heaven_____. Today we usually call it the (sea, <u>sky</u>, earth).

The Third Day

Genesis 1:9–13

6. On the third day, God gathered together the waters under heaven and made dry land appear. God called the dry land _____earth_____ and the waters _____seas_____.

7. God also created _____grass_____, _____herbs_____, and trees on the third day. God caused each kind of plant to produce seeds that would grow new plants after his _____kind_____.

The Fourth Day

Genesis 1:14–19

8. On the fourth day, God created the "greater light," which we call the _____sun_____, and the "lesser light," which we call the _____moon_____.

9. Then God filled the sky with more lights than any man can count. The Bible uses only five words to describe this awesome event. It says, "He _____made_____ _____the_____ _____stars_____ also."

The Fifth Day

Genesis 1:20–23

10. On the fifth day, God created moving _____creatures_____ to fill the waters and _____fowl_____ to fly in the sky. We call most of the sea animals _____fish_____ and the flying animals _____birds_____.

11. What did God mean when He told the animals, "Be fruitful and multiply"?
    a. He wanted them to eat only fruit.
    b. He wanted them to produce many more animals like themselves.
    c. He wanted them to share their food so that each would have enough.

The Sixth Day

Genesis 1:24–31

12. On the sixth day, God created land animals, including _____cattle_____, _____creeping_____ things, and _____beasts_____ of the earth. God created each after his _____kind_____.

—how God created light and many other things. (He said, "Let there be . . .")

—three ways that God created man different from the animals. (See Part A, number 13.)

—the meaning of the word *sanctify*. (to set apart for holy use)

—who was with God in the beginning and helped to create all things. (Jesus Christ)

Truths to Instill

• All things have their beginning in God. He brought all life and material things into being by His word. "All things were made by him; and without him was not any thing made that was made" (John 1:3).

• Only God can create. Man can only use materials that God created.

• Jesus was with God in the beginning. He was involved in the Creation: "by whom also he made the worlds" (Hebrews 1:2).

• God created a wonderful world. Why would He bother making a butterfly's wings so beautiful? Why would He make a snowflake so pretty? He cares deeply about the things He does.

• We should always honor God above His creation, a response of thankfulness and worship. (See Romans 1:20, 21.)

13. God also created man on the sixth day. Read Genesis 1:26 and 2:7 to find three ways God made man different from all other living things.

   a. Man was made in God's _____image_____.

   b. God gave man _____dominion_____ over all other creatures.

   c. God breathed into man the breath of life, and man became a _____living_____

   _____soul_____.

   Soon after creating Adam, God established the first home by creating Eve and bringing her to Adam. God planned that one man and one woman should marry and live together for life. Homes that follow God's plan are good places for children to be born and to learn about God.

14. Chapter 2 of Genesis tells more about the creation of woman.

   a. Why did God create woman (Genesis 2:18)? ___God saw that it was not good for man___

   ___to be alone. (God wanted to make a helper for man.)___

   b. Why did Adam call his wife *Woman* (Genesis 2:21–23)? _____

   ___because she was taken out of man___

The Seventh Day

Genesis 2:1–3

15. What did God do on the seventh day? ___God rested.___

   _____

16. *Sanctify* means "to set apart for holy use." When God sanctified the seventh day, He wanted people to use it

   a. to relax and get extra sleep.

   b. as a day of feasting and gladness.

   (c.) as a special day to refresh their souls.

B. BIBLE WORD STUDY

★ *Match these definitions with the Bible words on the right. Read the verses given or use a dictionary if you need help. All references are from Genesis.*

<u> f </u> 1. To make from nothing (1:1)

<u> a </u> 2. Empty; vacant (1:2)

<u> d </u> 3. The space around the earth, sun, moon, and stars (1:6)

<u> b </u> 4. To produce (1:11)

<u> e </u> 5. A likeness (1:26)

<u> c </u> 6. Control; rule (1:26)

<u> g </u> 7. To set apart for holy use (2:3)

a. void

b. yield

c. dominion

d. firmament

e. image

f. create

g. sanctify

C. THINKING ABOUT BIBLE TRUTHS

The Bible is more than a book of facts. It also gives us important ideas, or truths, that help us know how God wants us to live. As you complete the exercises in this workbook, look for more than just the facts needed to fill in the answers. Think about what the Bible means, and what lessons God wants you to learn from each passage. This section asks questions about some truths we can learn from the Bible.

1. Read Genesis 1:31. How did God feel about His creation? <u>God was pleased with His creation. (He saw that everything He had made was very good.)</u>

Jesus was not created, for He is a part of God, and was with God the Father in the beginning. The Bible tells us that God the Father, God the Son, and God the Holy Ghost are one (1 John 5:7).

2. Read John 1:1–3. The Word whom John writes about is Jesus. According to John 1:3, how many things did Jesus help create? <u>All things were made by Him.</u>

3. Probably a carpenter made the kitchen cabinets in your house, but we still say that God made everything. Explain how it can be true that both God and the carpenter made them. <u>The carpenter used wood that God had created.</u>

4. Read Revelation 4:10, 11.

   a. Why did God create all things? (See verse 11.) <u>for His pleasure</u>

   b. We should do the same thing the elders did when they realized that God created everything. What did they do? (See verse 10.) <u>The elders worshiped God.</u>

D. LEARNING MORE ABOUT THE BIBLE

Measures of Time

"And God said, Let there be lights in the firmament of the heaven to divide the day from the night; and let them be for signs, and for seasons, and for days, and years" (Genesis 1:14).

Day and Night

Day and night is the first measure of time mentioned in the Scriptures. The Jewish day began at sundown instead of at midnight. The days of Creation are described as the (1) _____evening_____ and the morning (Genesis 1:5).

Weeks

The week is not directly related to the movement of the heavenly bodies. God established it by working six days and resting the seventh day. God commanded Israel to (2) _____remember_____ the Sabbath Day, to keep it (3) _____holy_____ (Exodus 20:8). Besides resting on the seventh day, the Jews were also commanded to let the land rest the seventh (4) _____year_____ (Exodus 23:10, 11).

Months

The Jews measured their months from one new moon to the next. Each (5) _____new_____ moon was considered a solemn feast day (Psalm 81:3). They needed to add an extra month every three years or so, because the moon circles the earth about 12 1/3 times each year. Later, the Romans divided the year into twelve months that were each a little longer than the moon's cycle.

Years

A year is the time it takes the earth to travel one time around the sun. Each year is a complete cycle of seasons. Since the beginning, men have measured the length of their lives by years. God mentioned the (6) _____seasons_____ of the year in Genesis 8:22.

19

Lesson 3. Man Falls Away From God

Before Adam and Eve had their first child, one of the most terrible events in history took place. God had placed Adam and Eve in a beautiful garden called Eden, which He had filled with many kinds of pleasant trees. Four rivers flowed from the Garden of Eden. The air was filled with the sweet smells of growing things. All the birds and animals lived peacefully together.

However, Satan also spent time in the Garden of Eden. God had told Adam and Eve that they could eat fruit from any tree in the Garden except one—the tree of the knowledge of good and evil. Satan came in the form of a serpent and tempted Adam and Eve to disobey God. Satan made disobeying God look attractive. He still tries to do the same thing today, but disobedience to God is sin. Sin is always a terrible mistake, even when it seems harmless. In the end, it always brings shame, misery, and death.

Because Adam and Eve listened to the serpent, God could not let them live in the Garden of Eden anymore. Worse yet, Adam and Eve received a sinful nature and passed it on to their children. Their first son was a murderer, and everyone born since then has also been affected by sin.

Jesus, the Son of God, is the only man who never sinned. He offers the only hope for Adam and Eve's family.

A. ANSWERS FROM THE BIBLE

★ *Study the Bible passages to find answers to complete these exercises. Fill in the short blanks with exact words from the Bible. Write complete answers for the questions with long blanks. For multiple choice questions, circle the letter of the correct answer.*

The Serpent's Lie

Genesis 3:1–5

Satan did not want man to bring glory to God. He appeared in the Garden as a serpent.

1. The first thing the serpent did was to
   a. tempt Eve to eat the fruit.
   b. question God's commandment.
   c. tell Eve she would not die.

2. Next the serpent lied to Eve. He told her that if she and Adam ate the forbidden fruit, they would
   a. not die.
   b. know more than God.
   c. live in the Garden forever.

Lesson 3

Oral Review

1. How long will God's Word be true? [1] **forever**
2. Why did God give the Bible to men? [1] **God gave the Bible for our learning.**
3. What are five ways (from Lesson 1) that God wants us to use the Bible? [1] **read, hear, study, believe, obey**
4. Who was with God in the beginning and helped to create all things? [2] **Jesus Christ**
5. How did God make the light and many other things? [2] **He said, "Let there be . . ."**
6. What do we call the firmament today? [2] **the heavens, the sky, or space**
7. What did God make on the fourth day of Creation? [2] **the sun, moon, and stars**

In This Lesson

Scope: Genesis 3–5

Main Events
- Satan tempts Adam and Eve, and they fall from their innocent state.
- Adam and Eve feel ashamed of themselves and afraid of God.

Adam and Eve's Sin

Genesis 3:6–13

3. Eve saw that the tree was good for _____food_____, that it was _____pleasant_____ to the eyes, and that it was to be desired to make one _____wise_____. Both she and Adam did _____eat_____ of its fruit.

4. Why were Adam and Eve afraid when they heard God in the Garden?
   a. They feared that God would no longer want to talk with them.
   b.) They knew that they had done wrong.
   c. It was the first time God had come to the Garden.

5. What did both Adam and Eve do when God asked them about their sin?
   a. They felt sorry and repented.
   b. They said they had not eaten of the fruit.
   c.) They blamed someone else.

God's Judgment

Genesis 3:14–19

God held Adam and Eve responsible for their own sin. He pronounced judgments on them and on the serpent.

6. What curse did God place upon the serpent that has affected all snakes? _____
   God said that the serpent would have to go on its belly.

7. God said that Eve would
   a.) bring forth children in sorrow.
   b. have only a few children.
   c. rule over her husband.

8. Because of Adam's sin, God cursed the _____ground_____. He said it would bring forth _____thorns_____ and _____thistles_____, and that someday Adam himself would return to the _____ground (dust)_____.

God's Plan to Save Man

God was very grieved when Adam and Eve sinned. He loved them and wanted to have fellowship with them. Even before Adam and Eve disobeyed, God had planned a way to bring man back to Himself. In the verses below, God began to show how He would do this.

Genesis 3:15

While cursing the serpent, God gave a special promise to man. The seed, or descendant, that He speaks of in this verse is Jesus.

9. God said that the seed of the woman (Jesus) "shall bruise thy [Satan's] _____head_____, and thou shalt bruise his _____heel_____."

- God tells Adam and Eve what the consequences of their sin will be, and He removes them from Eden.
- God begins to reveal His plan to save fallen man (Genesis 3:15).
- Cain becomes envious of his brother Abel and kills him.

Objectives
- Students should know
  —the lie Satan told Eve. (that she would not die if she ate the forbidden fruit)
  —where Adam and Eve needed to go after they disobeyed God. (out of the Garden of Eden)
  —in which chapter of Genesis the story of Adam and Eve's sin is found. (Genesis 3)
  —who belongs to Adam and Eve's family. (everyone)
  —why all men need to die. (because all men have received Adam's sinful nature and have sinned)
  —why God did not accept Cain's sacrifice. (Cain did not do what was right. He did not honor God by offering the best that he had.)
  —why Cain killed Abel. (He was envious when God accepted Abel's righteous works and rejected his own evil works.)

10. What did this promise mean?

    ⓐ Someday Jesus would conquer Satan and deliver men from his control.

    b. Someday Jesus would bruise and kill all snakes.

    c. The seeds that the woman planted would bring forth thistles.

Genesis 3:21

11. The aprons of fig leaves did not satisfy God. He killed animals and used their
_____<u>skins</u>_____ to clothe Adam and Eve.

    By doing this, God showed that He expects us to keep our bodies well covered. Later God told man that only a sacrifice of blood can cover sin.

Genesis 3:22–24

    God wanted man to enjoy fruit from the tree of life again someday, but He knew that sinful men were not fit for holy things. God reserved the tree of life for those whom Jesus would cleanse from sin.

12. What reason did God give for keeping man out of Eden?

    a. God did not want him to eat more of the same fruit.

    b. God did not want the serpent to have another chance to deceive man.

    ⓒ God did not want sinful man to eat of the tree of life.

13. How did God keep man out of Eden? _____

    <u>God placed cherubim and a flaming sword at the east of the Garden.</u>

14. When will Christians be able to eat of the tree of life? (See Revelation 22:1, 2.) _____

    <u>when they get to heaven</u>

- God provided the first blood sacrifice by killing animals to clothe Adam and Eve.

F
I
G
S

Besides the tree of life and the tree of the knowledge of good and evil, the only specific tree the Bible mentions as having grown in the Garden of Eden was the fig tree. Adam and Eve used the large fig leaves in their attempt to cover themselves.

Figs stay hidden among the foliage of small, bushy trees until they are almost ripe. The figs are purplish to greenish yellow. The flowers of some varieties are hidden inside their fruit. Some varieties with hidden flowers bear mature fruit only after a tiny insect called a fig wasp crawls through a small hole in the fruit and pollinates the flowers.

Figs served many useful purposes. They were a common food in Bible times. People dried them, pressed them into cakes, or juiced them for wine.

Who was healed of a boil after a lump (poultice) of figs was placed on it? (2 Kings 20:5–7).

Truths to Instill

- Adam and Eve's disobedience brought sin and death into the world. Because Adam and Eve are the ancestors of all people, we have all received their nature and the effect of their sin.
- Disobedience brings separation from God. It makes people ashamed of themselves and afraid of God. In contrast, obedience brings trust and security.
- Envy is always destructive. It makes people want to harm and destroy the object of their envy. It moved Cain to kill his own brother, even though he gained nothing by doing so. Envy is really hatred.

Adam and Eve's Children

Adam and Eve's first sons were Cain and Abel. After these boys were grown, they each brought an offering to the LORD. The LORD accepted Abel's offering, but He rejected Cain's. God requires true worship.

Genesis 4:1–8, 25

15. Copy the sentence in these verses that tells us Abel offered the best that he had. _____
    "And Abel, he also brought of the firstlings of his flock and of the fat thereof."

    _____

16. Copy the sentence in these verses that tells us God would have accepted Cain if Cain had
    done what was right. ___"If thou doest well, shalt thou not be accepted?"___

    _____

17. Write Cain, Abel, or Seth after the sentence which describes that person the *best*. Explain
    why you chose the name you did. Use each name once. The students' explanations may vary.

    a. My parents were very sad because of me, but I could not help it. _____
       Abel; He was killed by Cain.

    b. I was born at a time when my parents were very sad. _____
       Seth; He was born after Abel was killed.

    c. I became a very unhappy person, and it was all my fault. _____
       Cain; He was cursed because he had killed Abel.

The Families of Cain and Seth

After Cain killed Abel, Adam and Eve had another godly son, named Seth. Cain's descendants followed his evil ways, but some of Seth's descendants followed the LORD.

Genesis 4:23

18. Lamech was an ungodly descendant of Cain. He married two wives and ___killed (slew)___
    a young man.

Genesis 4:26

19. What did men begin to do in the days of Enos, the son of Seth? _____
    Men began to call upon the Name of the LORD.

Where Is It Found?

20. The story of Adam and Eve's sin is found in
    a. Genesis 1.   b. Genesis 2.   (c.) Genesis 3.   d. Genesis 4.

21. The story of Cain and Abel is found in
    a. Genesis 1.   b. Genesis 2.   c. Genesis 3.   (d.) Genesis 4.

B. BIBLE WORD STUDY

★ *Write a word from the verse given to fit each definition. All references are from Genesis.*

_____subtil_____ 1. Sly; crafty; cunning (3:1)

_____beguiled_____ 2. Deceived (3:13)

_____enmity_____ 3. Hatred; opposition (3:15)

_____cherubims_____ 4. Angels (3:24)

_____respect_____ 5. Favor; high regard (4:4)

_____wroth_____ 6. Angry (4:5)

_____countenance_____ 7. The expression of one's face (4:5)

- Number 1. The modern spelling is *subtle.*

- Number 4. The modern plural of *cherub* is *cherubim.*

C. THINKING ABOUT BIBLE TRUTHS

The things that we do affect other people. When we do right, we are a blessing to others; but when we do wrong, others often need to suffer. Adam and Eve brought suffering to everyone. Jesus brings peace and joy to everyone who believes in Him.

1. Read Romans 5:12. How did Adam's sin affect all men?
   a. All men have heard about Adam's sin, and this makes them sad.
   b. Because of Adam's sin, all men must die, even if they have not sinned themselves.
   ⓒ All men must die because all men have received Adam's sinful nature and have sinned.

2. Read Hebrews 2:14, 15. These verses tell why Jesus allowed His body to die, even though He had not sinned. Whose power did Jesus destroy when He died and rose again? _the devil's_

Adam and Eve were not the only ones who needed to choose between good and evil. Their first two sons made their own choices. Everyone born since then has either turned back to God or gone further away from Him.

3. Hebrews 11:4 says, "By faith Abel offered unto God a more excellent sacrifice than Cain." This shows that
   a. Abel's excellent sacrifice helped him to believe in God.
   ⓑ Abel believed in God and honored Him by offering an excellent sacrifice.
   c. Cain gave a better sacrifice, but Abel had more faith.

4. Read 1 John 3:11, 12. Why did Cain kill Abel?
   ⓐ He was envious when God accepted Abel's righteous works and rejected his own evil works.
   b. He thought that his brother was evil and needed to be punished.
   c. He had received a sinful nature from his parents and could not help what he did.

Enoch was a righteous man in Seth's family line. Because of Enoch's faithfulness, God took him from the earth in an unusual way. By doing this, God showed that He wants the righteous to live with Him.

5. Read Genesis 5:21–24. What did Enoch do that prepared him for the special privilege of being taken from earth without dying? _Enoch walked with God._

D. LEARNING MORE ABOUT THE BIBLE

The Family Tree of Adam and Eve

The Bible names three sons of Adam: Cain, Abel, and Seth. This family tree shows the main family lines that descended from Adam and Eve. Most of the men on this chart had other sons and daughters who are not named in the Bible.

After Cain cut off Abel's branch, Seth took Abel's place as a righteous descendant. Although the Flood destroyed most of Seth's descendants, Noah and his sons kept the family alive. Everyone born since the Flood is from Seth's branch.

Cain's descendants seemed to prosper for a time in spite of their wickedness, but God used the Flood to cut off Cain's branch.

★ *Using Genesis 4:17–22 and 5:6–32, write the missing names on the branches of this family tree.*

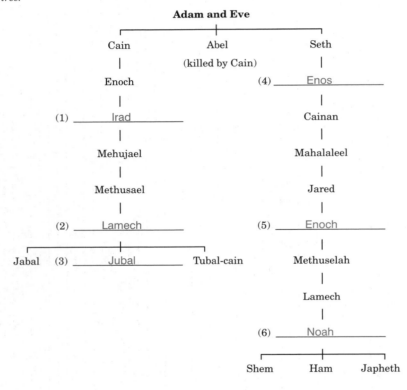

Adam and Eve

Cain — Abel — Seth

Cain
|
Enoch
|
(1) _____ Irad _____
|
Mehujael
|
Methusael
|
(2) _____ Lamech _____

Jabal   (3) _____ Jubal _____   Tubal-cain

Abel
(killed by Cain)

Seth
|
(4) _____ Enos _____
|
Cainan
|
Mahalaleel
|
Jared
|
(5) _____ Enoch _____
|
Methuselah
|
Lamech
|
(6) _____ Noah _____

Shem   Ham   Japheth

25

Lesson 4. God Destroys the Earth

When God had finished creating the heaven and the earth and everything in them, He was pleased with His work. The Bible says, "God saw every thing that he had made, and, behold, it was very good" (Genesis 1:31). But after Adam and Eve sinned, God could no longer say that everything was very good.

We have seen that Cain and his descendants were ungodly. Seth's family started out better, but before long the children of the godly began marrying the ungodly. The world grew more and more wicked, until God felt sorry that He had created man. He said, "I will destroy man whom I have created from the face of the earth" (Genesis 6:7).

In the entire world, God found only one righteous family left. This was Noah's family. God warned Noah that He would destroy the earth with a flood, and told him how he and his family could be saved.

In this lesson you will study what happened to most of Adam's family when they disobeyed God, and what happened to Noah's family when he followed God's commands. All people who now live on the earth come from Noah's family.

A. ANSWERS FROM THE BIBLE

★ *Study the Bible passages to find answers to complete these exercises. Fill in the short blanks with exact words from the Bible. Write complete answers for the questions with long blanks. For multiple choice questions, circle the letter of the correct answer.*

God Sees Man's Wickedness

Genesis 6:5–9

The ungodly men who lived just before the Flood had forgotten God, but God still knew all about them. He was grieved when He saw their wickedness. But God's all-seeing eyes saw something else too. God saw Noah, and He was pleased with Noah's life.

1. God saw that the _____wickedness_____ of man was great, and that their thoughts were only _____evil_____ continually.

2. In verse 6 the word *repented* means "saddened." What other word in this verse shows how sad God felt about sinful man? _____grieved_____

3. Verse 8 states that Noah found grace in the eyes of the Lord. What does this verse mean?
   a. Noah did not see how wicked everyone else had become.
   (b.) God was pleased with Noah because he was living right.
   c. Noah saw God's eyes when God talked with Him.

4. a. The Bible speaks well of Noah. It says that he was a _____just_____ man and _____perfect_____ in his generations.

   b. Copy the part of verse 9 which shows that Noah was a friend of God. _____
   "Noah walked with God."_____

Lesson 4

Oral Review

1. How much of the Bible was inspired by God? [1] **all of the Bible**
2. Where can we find the meanings of difficult Bible words? [1] **in a Bible dictionary**
3. What did God make on the sixth day? [2] **land animals and man**
4. What did God create on the fifth day? [2] **sea animals and birds**
5. What lie did Satan tell Eve? [3] **that she would not die if she ate the forbidden fruit**
6. How did Adam and Eve feel after they had disobeyed God? [3] **They felt afraid.**
7. Which son of Adam and Eve had some godly descendants? [3] **Seth**

In This Lesson

Scope: Genesis 6, 7

Main Events
- Mankind becomes increasingly wicked. God decides to destroy the earth with a flood.
- God tells Noah how to build an ark to save his family.
- Noah obeys all God's commands.

God's Plan for an Ark of Safety

God knew that it was time to bring judgment upon sinful man. However, before God destroyed the earth, He planned a way for Noah and his family to be saved.

Genesis 6:13–17

5. Why did God tell Noah to build an ark? _____

   God planned to destroy the earth with a flood, and He wanted Noah to be saved.

6. How did Noah know how to build the ark? _____

   God told him how.

Genesis 6:18–22

7. List the people God planned to save in the ark. _____

   Noah, his sons, his wife, and his sons' wives

8. God also wanted to preserve each kind of animal. He told Noah to take

   _____ two _____ of each kind into the ark. In Genesis 7:2, God told Noah to take

   _____ seven _____ of each kind of clean animal.

9. Which group of animals could survive outside the ark during the Flood? (Think about the

   days of Creation.) __ fish (sea animals) _____

10. How was Noah to prepare for feeding his family and the animals in the ark? _____

    Noah was to take food for his family and for the animals.

11. Copy the verse that tells how well Noah followed God's commands. _____

    "Thus did Noah; according to all that God commanded him, so did he."

    _____

God Sends the Flood

Noah and his sons worked hard for many years to build the huge ark. After it was finished, they gathered food for themselves and for the animals. Then the animals entered the ark, two by two, and Noah and his family left their old home behind as they boarded. Their ungodly neighbors still refused to believe that God would destroy the world with a flood.

Genesis 7:11–24

12. Noah was _____ 600 _____ years old when God sent the Flood.

13. From what two places did the water come? _____

    from the fountains of the great deep and from the sky

14. How long did it rain? _____

    forty days and forty nights

15. The water rose until it was _____ 15 _____ cubits higher than the highest moun-

    tains (about 22 ½ feet).

- Flood waters rise high enough to cover all mountains and to drown all the people and land animals that were not in the ark.
- Noah saves his family by obeying God's command.

Objectives

- Students should know
  —how many days and nights it rained during the Flood. (forty)
  —how high the water rose during the Flood. (15 cubits [about 22 ½ feet] higher than the highest mountains)
  —who was saved and who perished in the Flood. (Noah, his sons, his wife, and his sons' wives were saved; everyone else perished.)

—which chapter in Genesis tells how Noah built an ark. (Genesis 6)
—why God felt sorry He had made man. (Man's wickedness was great, and his thoughts were only evil.)
—how Noah proved his faith in God. (See Part C, number 2.)

Truths to Instill

- Wickedness always brings judgment. God is longsuffering, but the wages of sin is always death.
- Noah obeyed, even though he could not have understood how a flood could happen, since it had never rained. Why did he obey? Because he had

16. The Flood destroyed every living substance upon the face of the ground, both _____man_____, and _____cattle_____, and the _____creeping_____ things, and the _____fowl_____ of the heaven.

17. Only _____Noah_____ remained alive, and they that were with him _____in the ark_____.

Where Is It Found?

18. The story of the Flood is found in
   a. Genesis 3.   b. Genesis 4–6.   (c.) Genesis 7, 8.   d. Genesis 9–11.

B. BIBLE WORD STUDY

★ *Write a word from the verse given to fit each definition. All references are from Genesis.*

_____grace_____ 1. Favor (6:8)

_____corrupt_____ 2. Evil; defiled; spoiled (6:11)

_____gopher_____ 3. A kind of tree growing in the Middle East (6:14)

_____pitch_____ 4. Tar; asphalt (6:14)

_____cubit_____ 5. An ancient unit of measure equal to about 18 inches (6:15)

_____deep_____ 6. The sea; ocean (7:11)

C. THINKING ABOUT BIBLE TRUTHS

1. Read Genesis 6:13 again. How does this verse show that Adam's descendants had moved to many parts of the earth before the Flood? _____
   God said that the earth was filled with violence through them.

   Several New Testament writers speak of Noah as a great man of faith.

2. Read Hebrews 11:7. When God said a flood was coming, Noah showed that he believed God by obeying Him. Which three statements below tell how Noah proved his faith in God?
   (a.) Noah listened to God's warning, even though the whole earth had never been flooded before.
   (b.) Noah built an ark because he loved his family and wanted them to be saved.
   c. Noah was glad that only his family would be left after the Flood.
   (d.) Noah lived a holy life, even though the people around him did not like to be reminded of their sins.

more faith in what God said than in what he could understand. We too must obey and do what is right, even though we do not understand everything.

- God's word about the coming destruction of the earth by fire is as certain as His word about destroying it by water. See 2 Peter 3:3–7.
- We want to be ready when Jesus comes. We do not want to make the mistake people did in Noah's time—becoming so involved with living our own lives that obeying God seems foolish.
- All people who have lived since the Flood are descendants of Noah's family.

3. Read Luke 17:26, 27. These verses tell us that when the Flood came, the people were eating and drinking and getting married. We know that these things are not wrong if they are done properly. They are necessary things for people to do. Then what are these verses saying?

a. The people did not listen to the warnings that Noah gave. They kept on living as if nothing were going to happen.

b. When judgment is coming, God does not want people to eat and drink, or to get married.

c. The people wanted to repent, but they thought that God would not listen to their prayers, even if they fasted.

4. Read 2 Peter 3:5–7. These verses remind us that God created the earth simply by speaking the word. Since God created the earth by speaking, He can also destroy the earth by His word.

a. When men became too ungodly, God commanded that the earth be overflowed with _____ water _____.

b. God promised that He would never again destroy the earth with water, but He warns that someday He will destroy it by _____ fire _____.

5. Because Noah obeyed God and prepared for the Flood, he and his family were saved. How does God want people to prepare for the coming Judgment? (See 2 Peter 3:11–13.)

God wants people to live holy lives and to look for His coming.

**C
Y
P
R
E
S
S**

Cypress trees are evergreens that grow in the moderately warm regions of Asia, Europe, and North America. The common or Italian cypress is native to the Mediterranean region.

Cypress trees give off an aroma. The wood is yellow or reddish, moderately hard, and light. Because cypress wood contains much resin, it resists rotting even when submerged in water for a long time.

Many scholars believe that the Hebrew word *gopher* in Genesis 6:14 refers to cypress. What was this wood used for?

D. LEARNING MORE ABOUT THE BIBLE

Noah's Ark

★ *In Genesis 6:14–16, God told Noah how to build the ark. Read these verses and the other verses given below for help to fill in the blanks.*

1656 A.M.   1657 A.M.

God told Noah to build the ark of gopher (cypress) wood, and to daub it with (1) ___pitch___ to make it watertight.

Inside the ark, Noah built (2) _3_ stories.

Noah and his family lived in the ark for one year and ten days. Noah was (3) _600_ years old when he entered the ark (Genesis 7:11).

Height: (4) _30_ cubits (45 feet)

Width: (5) _50_ cubits (75 feet)

Length: (6) _300_ cubits (450 feet)

Rain fell upon the earth for (7) _40_ days and (8) _40_ nights (Genesis 7:12).

At its highest, the Flood covered the mountains with (9) _15 cubits_ (about 22 ½ feet) of water (Genesis 7:20).

After the Flood, the ark rested on the mountains of (10) ___Ararat___ (Genesis 8:4).

The waters flooded the earth completely for 150 days. Imagine sailing on a shoreless sea for five months!

During all this time in the ark, Noah did not lose faith in God.

30

Lesson 5. God Restores the Earth

Sin had reaped its awful harvest. The great Flood had destroyed the world, and only the people and animals inside the ark were still alive. For months Noah and his family remained in the ark, with the sounds and smells of the animals all around them.

The ark drifted on a shoreless sea until the waters began to go down. Finally it came to rest "upon the mountains of Ararat." Even then, Noah had to wait until it was safe to leave the ark.

In this lesson you will see how God remembered Noah and those that were with him. God caused the waters to go down so that Noah and his family and the animals could again live on the earth. Noah was so glad that he offered a sacrifice to the LORD. His offering pleased God, and God made a covenant with Noah's family and the animals. Noah's family started out again on a fresh, new earth; but all too soon, sin once more corrupted the world.

A. ANSWERS FROM THE BIBLE

★ *Study the Bible passages to find answers to complete these exercises. Fill in the short blanks with exact words from the Bible. Write complete answers for the questions with long blanks. For multiple choice questions, circle the letter of the correct answer.*

God Remembers Noah

The Bible tells us that after the Flood had destroyed all life on the earth, "God remembered Noah, and every living thing, and all the cattle that was with him in the ark" (Genesis 8:1). God always remembers, even when people forget. God caused the Flood waters to rise, and when it was time, He caused them to go down again.

Genesis 8:1–3

1. What did God do that shows He had not forgotten Noah and those with him in the ark? ___
   God made a wind to pass over the earth and caused the waters to go down.

The ark came to rest "upon the mountains of Ararat" five months after the rain had started. During the next seven months, Noah and his family waited for the waters to dry up.

Genesis 8:6–12

2. The first bird Noah released from the ark was a _____ raven _____. It went forth _____ to _____ and _____ fro _____, until the waters were _____ dried _____ _____ up _____ from off the earth.

3. Next, Noah sent out a dove
   a. to find the raven.
   b. to build a nest for its young.
   c. to see if it could find a place to rest.

Lesson 5

Oral Review
1. Name the things God made on each day of Creation. [2] *First day*: light (also heaven and earth); *Second*: firmament; *Third*: dry land, seas, and plants; *Fourth*: sun, moon, and stars; *Fifth*: sea animals and birds; *Sixth*: land animals and man
2. How did God create light and many other things? [2] **He said, "Let there be . . ."**
3. When did God rest? [2] **on the seventh day**
4. What lie did Satan tell Eve? [3] **He said that she would not die if she ate of the forbidden fruit.**
5. Where did God send Adam and Eve after they disobeyed Him? [3] **out of the Garden of Eden**
6. Why did God save Noah and his family from the Flood? [4] **Noah found grace in God's eyes and obeyed all of God's commands.**
7. Which chapter in Genesis tells how Noah built an ark? [4] **chapter 6**

In This Lesson

Scope: Genesis 8–11

Main Events
- God remembers Noah and his family after the Flood.

4. Seven days later, Noah sent out the dove again. It returned with an olive leaf in its mouth. What did Noah know from this? _____

 Noah knew that the waters had gone down (abated).

5. Did the dove return after Noah sent it out the third time? ___ no ___

God Makes a Covenant

Genesis 8:18–22

6. The first thing Noah did after he left the ark was to build an ____ altar ____. On it he offered ____ burnt ____ ____ offerings ____.

7. God accepted Noah's sacrifice. He said in His heart, "I will not again ____ curse ____ the ____ ground ____ any more for man's sake; . . . neither will I again smite any more ____ every ____ ____ thing ____ ____ living ____."

8. God promised that while the earth remains, ____ seedtime ____ and harvest, cold and ____ heat ____, ____ summer ____ and ____ winter ____, and day and night will not cease.

Genesis 9:8–13

God made a covenant, or binding agreement, with Noah, his sons, and their descendants. He also made it with every living creature that came out of the ark.

9. What did God promise that He would never do again? _____

 God promised that He would never again destroy the earth with a flood.

10. What was the sign (or token) of God's promise? __ the rainbow __

God Confuses the Language

Genesis 11:1–9

God had destroyed all the wicked men in the Flood, but Noah and his sons still had the sinful nature they had received from Adam. Soon wickedness was spreading over the earth again.

11. What two things did Noah's descendants begin to build on the plain of Shinar? _____

 a city and a great tower

12. What two reasons did they give for their building projects? __ They wanted to make a name for themselves, and they wanted to keep from being scattered to other places.

_____

13. The LORD did not approve of this, because the people were becoming
 a. angry. (b.) proud. c. discouraged. d. fearful.

14. The word *Babel* means "confusion." Why was this a fitting name for the place where men began building this tower? __ God confused the language of the people and caused confusion among them.

- Noah leaves the ark after sending out a raven and a dove.
- God makes a covenant that He will never again destroy the earth with a flood, and He gives the rainbow as a token of His promise.
- Noah's descendants rise up in pride and begin to build a great tower.
- God confuses the language and scatters the people to other parts of the world.

Objectives

- Students should know
 —the meaning of *covenant*. (a binding agreement)
 —what Noah did first after he left the ark. (built an altar)

 —what God sent as a token of His covenant with Noah. (the rainbow)
 —the meaning of *Babel*. (confusion)
 —in which chapter of Genesis the story of the Tower of Babel is found. (Genesis 11)
 —what covenant God made with Noah. (He would never again destroy the earth with a flood.)
 —why men decided to build the Tower of Babel. (to make a name for themselves and to keep from being scattered)
 —why God was displeased with the building of the Tower of Babel. (The people were becoming proud.)

15. What did the LORD do to the people after they stopped building the tower? _____

    He scattered the people abroad upon the face of all the earth.

Where Is It Found?

16. The story of God's promise to mankind after the Flood is found in
    a. Genesis 3.   b. Genesis 6.   c. Genesis 7.   (d.) Genesis 9.

17. The story of the Tower of Babel is found in
    a. Genesis 10.   (b.) Genesis 11.   c. Genesis 12.   d. Genesis 13.

B. BIBLE WORD STUDY

★ *Match these definitions with the Bible words on the right. Read the verses given or use a dictionary if you need help. All references are from Genesis. Notice that one word in Genesis 8:1 has about the same meaning as a different word in Genesis 8:3.*

_b_   1. Went down; settled down (8:1)   a. abated

_a_   2. Decreased; reduced (8:3)   b. assuaged

_f_   3. A binding agreement (9:9)   c. Babel

_h_   4. A sign or symbol (9:12)   d. bow

_g_   5. Never-ending (9:12)   e. confound

_d_   6. A rainbow (9:13)   f. covenant

_e_   7. To confuse or perplex (11:7)   g. perpetual

_c_   8. A place of noise and confusion (11:9) h. token

C. THINKING ABOUT BIBLE TRUTHS

1. Compare Genesis 7:11 with 8:13, 14. About how long were Noah and his family in the ark?

    about one year

2. God made a solemn agreement, or covenant, with Noah. Throughout the Bible, we find other covenants that God made. Read the verses below and fill in the blanks.

    a. Genesis 12:1–3. God made this covenant with __Abram (Abraham)__. He promised to

    _____bless_____ those who blessed him and _____curse_____ those who

    cursed him.

    b. 2 Samuel 7:8, 16. God made this covenant with _____David_____. God had taken

    the kingdom away from Saul, but God said that He would establish David's kingdom

    _____for_____ _____ever_____.

Truths to Instill

- Every rainbow reminds us of the steadfastness of God's promises.
- Where people obey God, and where His law prevails, there is order. Disobedience brings disorder and disintegration.
- Pride at Babel brought confusion of the language and the division of people into nations. At Pentecost the opposite happened. Dying to self and being filled with the Holy Spirit caused people of different languages to understand each other. Together, they formed a "holy nation."

c. John 3:16. God made this important covenant with ___whoever believes in Jesus___. God promised that such people should not _____perish_____, but have _____everlasting_____ _____life_____.

3. The rainbow covenant that God made with Noah was for all of Noah's descendants, including us. What should we remember when we see a rainbow?
   a. If men become too wicked, God might send another flood to destroy the whole earth again.
   (b.) God always keeps His promises, and He will never again destroy the whole earth with a flood.
   c. Those who drown in floods today must not be descendants of Noah.

4. God scattered people over the face of all the earth and changed their language. He also changed their appearance. We do not know whether God did this quickly, or over a period of time; but today we can see different kinds of people living in different places. We say these people are of different races. In what ways are people from all over the earth alike? (Sample answers) All people of the earth are descendants of Noah. All have inherited Adam's sinful nature and have sinned, and all may be saved by receiving Christ as their Lord and Saviour.

The Rainbow

Oh, come, see the rainbow!
A span of bright hues,
Greeting in splendor
Our wondering views.

Then pause to remember
His promise secure
That harvests shall fail not
While earth may endure.

And worship the Artist
Beyond the bright blue;
Such grand architecture,
God only can do!

And see in each rainbow
Hope's emblem bright;
Some day our faith shall be
Glorious sight!

—Ada Wine

D. LEARNING MORE ABOUT THE BIBLE

Noah's Family

1. What did God tell Adam, as well as Noah and his sons, to do? (Compare Genesis 9:1 with Genesis 1:28.)   "Be fruitful, and multiply, and replenish the earth."

Many books of the Bible contain genealogies (jee nee AHL uh jeez). A genealogy is a list that names the people in a family from one generation to another. For example, the New Testament begins with a genealogy that goes from Abraham to Jesus (Matthew 1:2–16).

2. A genealogy in Genesis 11:10–27 records some of the descendants of Noah's son Shem. Fill in the missing names on this part of Noah's family tree.

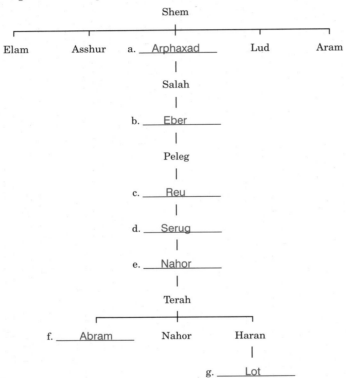

Shem

Elam   Asshur   a. Arphaxad   Lud   Aram

Salah

b. Eber

Peleg

c. Reu

d. Serug

e. Nahor

Terah

f. Abram   Nahor   Haran

g. Lot

The Tower of Babel

We do not know for sure exactly where the Tower of Babel was built or what it looked like. The people who remained in Shinar after God confused the language built other towers in all their main cities. These towers, called ziggurats (ZIHG uh rats), had flat tops where people offered sacrifices to their gods.

The people whom God scattered to other parts of the world also built similar pyramids and idol temples. Remains of these towers can still be seen in Egypt, Mexico, Central America, and Peru. Probably all these were based on the original Tower of Babel.

This sketch shows how some people think the Tower of Babel might have looked.

Discuss this with the students; show photographs of pyramid structures from various countries.

- This information was taken from the George Smith tablet, Nabopolassar's cylinders, and Herodotus's account of his travels in Babylon. See also "Babel, Tower of" in *Unger's Bible Dictionary*.

36

Chapter One Review

A. ORAL REVIEW

★ *Be sure you know the answers to these questions. Give as many answers as you can without looking back in your book. If you need help, you may check the Bible reference or the lesson given in brackets.*

Who

1. Who made all things? [Genesis 1:31]   God
2. Who tempted Adam and Eve to disobey God? [Genesis 3:1–5]   Satan (the serpent)
3. Who has been affected by Adam and Eve's sin? [Romans 5:12]   all people
4. Who was saved in the ark? [Genesis 6:18; 7:23]   Noah, his wife, his sons, and his sons' wives

Where

5. Where did men build the Tower of Babel? [Genesis 11:2]   on the plain of Shinar
6. Where can we find the meanings of difficult Bible words? [Lesson 1]   in a Bible dictionary

What   >>

7. What did God make on each of the six days of Creation? [Genesis 1]
8. What is the firmament? [Lesson 2]
9. What did Timothy know as a child? [2 Timothy 3:15]

When

10. When did God rest from His work of creating the world? [Genesis 2:2]   on the seventh day
11. When did God scatter man over the face of all the earth? [Genesis 11:9]

       after He confused the language at the Tower of Babel

Why   >>

12. Why did God give the Bible to men? [Romans 15:4]
13. Why must all men die? [Romans 5:12]
14. Why did Cain kill Abel? [1 John 3:11, 12; Lesson 3]
15. Why did God destroy the earth with a flood? [Genesis 6:5–7]
16. Why did men start to build the Tower of Babel? [Genesis 11:4]

How   >>

17. How long will God's Word stand? [Isaiah 40:8]
18. How did God keep man out of Eden? [Genesis 3:24]
19. How long did it rain during the Flood? [Genesis 7:12]
20. How high did the water rise during the Flood? [Genesis 7:19, 20]
21. How did Timothy become wise? [2 Timothy 3:15]

7. First day: light (also heaven and earth); Second: firmament; Third: dry land, seas, and plants; Fourth: sun, moon, and stars; Fifth: sea animals and birds; Sixth: land animals and man
8. the sky
9. the Holy Scriptures

12. for our learning
13. All men have sinned, and sin brings death.
14. Cain was envious when God accepted Abel's righteous works and rejected his own evil works.
15. because of man's wickedness
16. to make a name for themselves; to avoid being scattered over the earth
17. forever
18. with cherubim and a flaming sword
19. forty days and forty nights
20. 15 cubits (about 22½ feet) above the mountain peaks
21. through his knowledge of the Scriptures

Chapter One Review

This section includes an oral review and a written review. The oral review may be used either as a self-study guide or as an oral review in class. Encourage students to remember as many facts as possible without looking back. If they need help, they may check the verse or lesson given in brackets. A good understanding of the concepts covered in the review will help prepare the pupils for the test.

B. WRITTEN REVIEW

★ *Write answers to these questions. If you need help, use the Bible reference or the lesson given in brackets.*

Who

1. Who was with God in the beginning and helped to create all things? [John 1:1–3]
   _____ Jesus _____

2. Who perished in the Flood? [Genesis 7:23] _____
   all the people and land animals that were not in the ark

What

3. What lie did Satan tell Eve? [Genesis 3:4] _____
   "Ye shall not surely die."

4. What did God use to clothe Adam and Eve? [Lesson 3] _____
   animal skins

5. What chapter in Genesis tells about Adam and Eve's sin? [Lesson 3] ____ chapter 3 ____

6. What does the word *sanctify* mean? [Lesson 2] _____
   to set apart for holy use

7. What does the word *covenant* mean? [Lesson 5] _____
   a binding agreement

8. What did God curse because of man's sin? [Genesis 3:17] _____
   the ground

9. What covenant did God make with Noah? [Genesis 9:11] _____
   that the earth would never again be destroyed by a flood

10. What chapter in Genesis tells how Noah built an ark? [Lesson 4] _____ chapter 6 _____

Why

11. Why were Adam and Eve afraid of God? [Genesis 3:8–11; Lesson 3] _____
    because they had disobeyed Him

12. Why was the LORD displeased with what was happening on the plain of Shinar? [Genesis 11:5, 6; Lesson 5] _____
    The people were becoming proud.

How

13. How does God want us to use the Bible? Give five ways. [Lesson 1] _____ read _____ ,
_____ hear _____ , _____ study _____ , _____ believe _____ , and
_____ obey _____

14. How did the men who wrote the Bible know what to write? [2 Timothy 3:16; 2 Peter 1:21]
    The Holy Spirit told men what to write. (God inspired them.)

15. How did God create light and many other things? [Genesis 1:3; Lesson 2] _____
    by saying, "Let there be . . ."

16. How did Abel show that he had faith in God? [Hebrews 11:4; Lesson 3] _____
    Abel offered a better sacrifice than Cain's. *or* Abel offered the best that he had.

17. How do we know that Noah had faith in God? [Hebrews 11:7; Genesis 6:22] _____
    Noah built the ark just as God had commanded. (He obeyed God.)

Bible Outline

★ *So far this year, you have studied stories from the first eleven chapters of Genesis. Match the chapters with the correct descriptions.*

  c   18. Genesis 1, 2   a. Adam and Eve's family

  e   19. Genesis 3   b. Noah's family after the Flood

  a   20. Genesis 4, 5   c. the Creation

  d   21. Genesis 6–8   d. the Flood

  b   22. Genesis 9–11   e. Adam and Eve's sin

CHAPTER TWO

The Patriarchs

Blessed is the man that trusteth in the LORD, and whose hope the LORD is. For he shall be as a tree planted by the waters, and that spreadeth out her roots by the river, and shall not see when heat cometh, but her leaf shall be green; and shall not be careful in the year of drought, neither shall cease from yielding fruit.

(Jeremiah 17:7, 8)

TIME LINE—Chapter Two
The Patriarchs

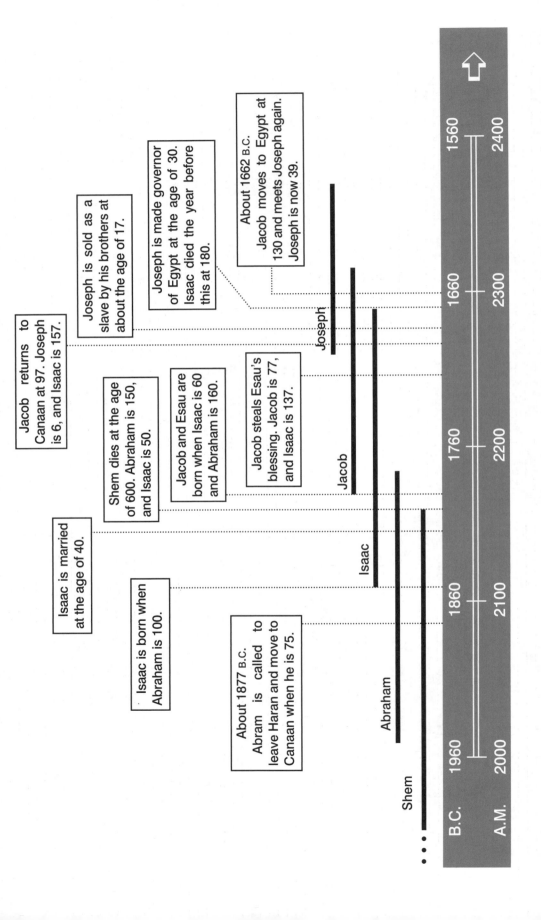

Jacob returns to Canaan at 97. Joseph is 6, and Isaac is 157.

Joseph is sold as a slave by his brothers at about the age of 17.

Joseph is made governor of Egypt at the age of 30. Isaac died the year before this at 180.

About 1662 B.C. Jacob moves to Egypt at 130 and meets Joseph again. Joseph is now 39.

Shem dies at the age of 600. Abraham is 150, and Isaac is 50.

Jacob and Esau are born when Isaac is 60 and Abraham is 160.

Jacob steals Esau's blessing. Jacob is 77, and Isaac is 137.

Isaac is married at the age of 40.

Isaac is born when Abraham is 100.

About 1877 B.C. Abram is called to leave Haran and move to Canaan when he is 75.

Joseph

Jacob

Isaac

Abraham

Shem

| B.C. | 1960 | 1760 | 1660 | 1560 |
| A.M. | 2000 | 2100 | 2200 | 2300 | 2400 |

41

Lesson 6. Dating Bible Events

So far you have studied the first eleven chapters of the Bible. You have followed the history of the world from the Creation to the Flood. But when did all this happen? When was the Creation? How old was the world when God destroyed it with the Flood? We can find answers to many interesting questions like these by studying the Bible.

For example, Noah's son Shem was Abraham's great-great-great-great-great-great-great-grandfather! Did you know that Shem was still living when Abraham was born? It is possible that Shem and Abraham talked with each other. Abraham was almost 150 years old when Shem died.

How old do you think the earth is today? By reading the Bible carefully and making some calculations, people have come within several hundred years of the world's exact age. They could come even closer, but they are not quite sure what the Bible means by some of the figures it gives.

In this lesson you will study some of these questions and a few others as well.

Some concepts in this lesson may be difficult for fifth grade students. You may want to do some of the exercises together in class to make sure the students understand them.

Be sure the students understand the time lines. Note that time-line scales vary according to how long a span they cover.

A. ANSWERS FROM THE BIBLE

From Creation to the Flood

Before the Flood, people lived much longer than they do today. Adam lived for more than half the time between the Creation and the Flood.

1. The lines on Chart 1 show when each man lived and how long he lived. Find the total number of years each man lived by reading the Bible references, and write the numbers in the blanks. Several have been done for you.

Chart 1

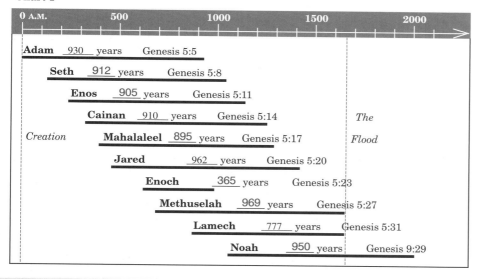

Lesson 6

Oral Review

(The numbers in brackets tell which lessons are being reviewed.)

1. Who was with God in the beginning and helped to create all things? [2] **Jesus Christ**
2. Name the things God created on each day of Creation. [2] *First day*: light (also heaven and earth); *Second*: firmament; *Third*: dry land, seas, and plants; *Fourth*: sun, moon, and stars; *Fifth*: sea animals and birds; *Sixth*: land animals and man

3. Why did Cain kill Abel? [3] **He was envious of Abel.**
4. Why did God destroy the earth with a flood? [4] **The people had become exceedingly wicked.**
5. Who perished in the Flood? [4] **everyone except Noah and his family**
6. How long did it rain during the Flood? [4] **forty days and forty nights**
7. How did Noah prove that he had faith in God? [4] **He obeyed all of God's commandments.**
8. What does the word *covenant* mean? [5] **a binding agreement**

★ *Use Chart 1 to answer questions 2–4.*

2. Who lived the most years? _____Methuselah_____

3. You probably noticed that Enoch's life was much shorter than the other men named on Chart 1. Genesis 5:24 says, "Enoch walked with God: and he was not; for God took him." This means that
   a. Enoch was killed by the evil men of his time.
   (b) Enoch did not need to die, because God took him from the earth in a special way.
   c. Enoch left his home and friends so that he could serve God better.

4. How many of the men listed were born before Adam died? To find out, hold a ruler straight up and down across the lines, placing the edge at the end of Adam's life. Write the names of all the men whom Adam could have seen. _____

   Seth, Enos, Cainan, Mahalaleel, Jared, Enoch, Methuselah, Lamech

5. God created Adam on the sixth day of Creation. Seth was born when Adam was 130 years old, and Enos was born when Seth was 105 years old. By adding these two figures together, we can see that Enos was born 235 years after the Creation. Complete this exercise to find the dates relating to Noah's life.

   a. The figures in Chart 2 are from Genesis 5. They tell how old each man was when his son was born. Add them together to find how many years passed between the Creation and Noah's birth.

   b. Noah was 600 years old when the Flood began. How many years passed between the Creation and the Flood? (Add 600 to the total years in Chart 2.) __1,656__ years

Chart 2

Adam (at Seth's birth)	130
Seth (at Enos's birth)	105
Enos (at Cainan's birth)	90
Cainan (at Mahalaleel's birth)	70
Mahalaleel (at Jared's birth)	65
Jared (at Enoch's birth)	162
Enoch (at Methuselah's birth)	65
Methuselah (at Lamech's birth)	187
Lamech (at Noah's birth)	+ 182
Years from Creation to Noah's birth:	1,056 years

Labeling Dates in History

6. When years are counted from the Creation, as in the exercise above, the dates are labeled with the abbreviation A.M. This means "in the year of the world." Seth was born 130 years after the Creation, so we say that Seth was born in the year A.M. 130. (These letters are usually written before the number rather than after.) According to Chart 2, Noah was born in A.M. __1056__.

• The abbreviation A.M. stands for the Latin words *anno mundi* (in the year of the world). A.D. stands for the Latin words *anno Domini* (in the year of our Lord).

In This Lesson

Main Points
• The figures in the Bible show that the earth is approximately 6,000 years old.
• Because of uncertainty about certain periods, time lines based on the Bible vary slightly. On all those that closely follow the Bible, however, the Creation is dated within several hundred years of 4000 B.C.
• After the Flood, man's average life span shortened drastically.
• Dates counted from Creation are labeled A.M., which means "in the year of the world." Dates counted from Christ's birth are labeled B.C. (before Christ) or A.D. (in the year of our Lord).
• Concordances can help us find certain words in the Bible.

Objectives
• Students should know
   —how Bible dates are determined for the periods before and just after the Flood. (See Part A, number 5.)
   —the approximate age of the earth. (6,000 years)
   —the meaning and use of A.M., B.C., and A.D. (See Part A, numbers 6–8)
   —how to the use a concordance. (See Part B.)

7. Instead of counting years from the Creation, we usually start counting from Jesus' birth. When years are counted in this way, events that took place before Jesus' birth are labeled B.C., meaning *Before Christ*. If an event took place 500 years before Jesus was born, it happened in the year 500 B.C. (These letters always come after the number, never before.) You might be interested in knowing that the man who started this system made a little mistake. Jesus was probably born about 5 years before the man thought He was. This means that Jesus was born about the year ____5____ B.C., instead of the year A.D. 1 as you would expect.

8. When years are counted after Jesus' birth, the dates are labeled with the abbreviation A.D. This means "in the year of our Lord." If something happened 750 years after Jesus' birth, it happened in the year A.D. 750. (These letters are usually written before the number rather than after.) You were born in A.D. _____. (We usually omit the label A.D., since all recent dates are after Christ.)   (Individual answers)

★ *Be sure to memorize the meanings of all three time labels given in numbers 6–8, and know when to use them.*

From the Flood to Abraham

The lines on Chart 3 represent the number of years each person lived and when they lived. Even after the Flood, people lived longer than we do today. But they did not live as long as the men before the Flood did. Noah lived much longer than the other men on this chart.

Chart 3

1000 A.M.	1200	1400	1600	1800	2000	2200

Noah	Genesis 9:29	950 years
	Genesis 11:10, 11	**Shem** 600 years
	Genesis 11:12, 13	**Arphaxad** 438 years
	Genesis 11:14, 15	**Salah** 433 years
	Genesis 11:16, 17	**Eber** 464 years
	Genesis 11:18, 19	**Peleg** 239 years
	Genesis 11:20, 21	*The* **Reu** 239 years
	Genesis 11:22, 23	*Flood* **Serug** 230 years
	Genesis 11:24, 25	**Nahor** 148 years
	Genesis 11:32	**Terah** 205 years
	Genesis 25:7	**Abraham** 175 years

Truths to Instill

- The universe is very young compared with eternity. Most students know someone between eighty and one hundred years old. Sixty to seventy-five such life spans, placed end to end, would reach all the way back to the Creation. The planet Pluto, which takes about 248 years to make one orbit around the sun, has completed only about twenty-four circuits (assuming its rate of speed has remained constant).
- Careful Bible study involves comparing Scripture with Scripture.

★ *Use Chart 3 to answer questions 9–12.*

9. The world after the Flood was very different from the world before the Flood. Many people have wondered why people lived longer before than after the Flood, but no one knows for sure.

   a. How much longer did Noah live than Shem did? (Subtract Shem's age from Noah's age.)

   ___350___ years

   b. How much longer did Noah live than Abraham did? (Subtract Abraham's age from Noah's age.) ___775___ years

10. Charts can show interesting facts that you might not notice otherwise. If you look at Chart 3 carefully, you will see that the three men born after Shem each lived over 400 years. Then the life span suddenly shortened to less than 250 years. Apparently something happened that made people start to die younger. Who was the first man shown on Chart 3 to live less than 250 years? _____Peleg_____

    The Bible does not tell us for sure why this man and his descendants did not live as long as their forefathers, but something very serious must have happened to make such a big difference. Can you think of an event that took place soon after the Flood that might have been serious enough to do this? (Hint: It scattered people all over the world.) _____

    the confusion of languages at the Tower of Babel _____

11. Which man listed on Chart 3 died last? (Hold a ruler straight up and down, and see which line is closest to the right edge of the chart.) ___Eber >>_____

12. Which man listed on Chart 3 was born soon after Noah died? ___Abraham_____

Eber died about four years after Abraham. Since this is difficult to see on the chart, you may want to give credit for Abraham.

Figuring Bible Dates

Sometimes we must compare different verses to learn the correct date for a Bible event. For example, Genesis 11:26 could give the impression that Abram's father, Terah, was 70 years old when Abram, Nahor, and Haran were born. However, Abram, Nahor, and Haran were probably not all born the same year. This verse likely means that Terah was 70 when he *started* having children.

Genesis 11:32 says that Terah was 205 years old when he died. According to Acts 7:4, Abram lived in Haran until Terah died, and Abram was 75 years old when he left Haran (Genesis 12:4).

13. If Abram left Haran the year that Terah died, how old was Terah when Abram was born?

    (Subtract Abram's age when he left Haran from Terah's age when he died.) ___130___ years

You can see that it would be a mistake to read Genesis 11:26 and say that Terah was 70 years old when Abram was born—even though you might think that if you read this verse alone. We must be careful when we figure Bible dates because sometimes we might miscalculate them without careful study. At other times, the Bible does not give enough information to show exactly when an event took place. Then we must be satisfied with approximate dates.

Using a Time Line

Many people have tried to make complete time lines from the Creation to Christ's birth or to the present, but all of these are based on some guesswork. However, all time lines that closely follow the Bible place the date of the Creation within a few hundred years of 4000 B.C. (about 6,000 years ago).

14. This simple time line shows the years from the Creation to the present and gives the approximate dates of a few important events. In the blanks, write the year that you were born and your name, and then answer questions 15 and 16.

Chart 4

3960 B.C.	3000 B.C.	2000 B.C.	1000 B.C.	1 B.C. / A.D. 1	A.D. 1000	A.D. 2000

3960 B.C.	2304 B.C.		5 B.C.	A.D. _>>_
Creation	*The Flood*	1877 B.C.	*Birth of Christ*	I, ___>>___
		Abraham enters Canaan		*was born.*

Individual answers.

15. How many years passed between the Creation and the year Abraham entered Canaan? (Subtract the date Abraham entered Canaan from the date of Creation.) __2,083__ years

16. About how many years passed between the Creation and the year you were born? (Add the year B.C. of Creation to the year A.D. when you were born.) ___>>___ years

Individual answers. Remind students that the figure is approximate.

O God, our help in ages past, our hope for years to come,
Our shelter from the stormy blast, and our eternal home!

Before the hills in order stood, or earth received her frame,
From everlasting Thou art God; to endless years the same.

Time, like an ever-rolling stream, bears all its sons away;
They fly, forgotten, as a dream dies at the opening day.

A thousand ages, in Thy sight, are like an evening gone;
Short as the watch that ends the night, before the rising sun.

O God, our help in ages past, our hope for years to come;
Be Thou our guide while life shall last, and our eternal home!

B. BIBLE STUDY BOOKS

Bible Concordances

Have you seen a Bible concordance? A Bible concordance works like an index to the Bible. It lists words used in the Bible and tells where in the Bible to find them. Many Bibles have a small concordance near the back. These small Bible concordances are handy to use. You do not need a separate book, and you do not need to look through as many words and references as you would in a large concordance.

Sometimes you may need to find a word or reference that is not found in a small concordance. Large Bible concordances can help you find these words. The largest Bible concordances list every reference for every word in the Bible.

★ *Find the following names in a concordance, and copy the first verse listed for each. Include the references with the verses. The first one is done for you. Read these steps carefully, and then do the rest yourself.*

Step 1. Look up the name *Shem* in your concordance. The words are listed in alphabetical order, just as they would be in a dictionary. They are usually in boldface so that you can see them more easily.

Step 2. Be sure that you have the right word. The word *Shema* is also in this section, but you do not want to look up *Shema*. You are looking for *Shem*.

Step 3. Find the first verse listed after the name *Shem*. You will see a phrase from the verse, with the letter *S* in it. This letter *S* stands for the name *Shem*. Before the phrase you will see a reference.

Step 4. Look up this reference in your Bible.

Step 5. Copy the verse and the reference.

```
Shelomoth (shel'-o-moth)  See also SHELOMITH.
1Ch 24:22 S': of the sons of S'; Jahath.        8013
shelter
Job 24: 8 embrace the rock for want of a s'. 4268
Ps 61: 3 thou hast been a s' for me, and a    "
Shelumiel (she-lu'-me-el)                        8017
Nu  1: 6 S' the son of Zurishaddai,
    2:12 shall be S' the son of Zurishaddai.     "
    7:36 fifth day S' the son of Zurishaddai,    "
    41 of S' the son of Zurishaddai.             "
   10:19 was S' the son of Zurishaddai.          "
Shem (shem)  See also SEM.
Ge  5:32 Noah begat S', Ham, and Japheth.8035
    6:10 Noah begat three sons, S', Ham,         "
    7:13 same day entered Noah, and S',          "
    9:18 that went forth of the ark, were S',    "
    23 S' and Japheth took a garment,            "
    26 Blessed be the Lord God of S';            "
    27 he shall dwell in the tents of S';        "
   10: 1 the sons of Noah; S', Ham, and          "
    21 Unto S' also, the father of all the       "
    22 children of S'; Elam, and Asshur,         "
    31 the sons of S', after their families,     "
   11:10 These are the generations of S':        "
    10 S' was an hundred years old, and          "
    11 S' lived after he begat Arphaxad          "
1Ch  1: 4 Noah, S', Ham, and Japheth.           "
    17 The sons of S'; Elam, and Asshur,         "
    24 S', Arphaxad, Shelah,                      "
Shema (she'-mah)  See also SHEMAIAH; SHIMHI.
Jos 15:26 Amam, and S', and Moladah,      8087
1Ch  2:43 and Tappuah, and Rekem, and S'.
    44 And S' begat Raham, the father of         "
    5: 8 Bela the son of Azaz, the son of S' .   "
    8:13 Beriah also, and S', who were           "
Ne  8: 4 him stood Mattithiah, and S', and      "
Shemaah (shem'-a-ah)
1Ch 12: 3 the sons of S' the Gebeathite;   8093
```

1. Shem *"And Noah was five hundred years old: and Noah begat Shem, Ham, and Japheth" (Genesis 5:32).*

2. Methuselah
    "And Enoch lived sixty and five years, and begat Methuselah" (Genesis 5:21).

3. Abram
    "And Terah lived seventy years, and begat Abram, Nahor, and Haran" (Genesis 11:26).

★ *Using a concordance and your Bible, find and copy a verse and reference that answers the following question.*

4. Which Bible verse tells us that God changed Abram's name to Abraham? (Hint: Look for the first time Abraham is used, or one of the last times Abram is used.) _____

  "Neither shall thy name any more be called Abram, but thy name shall be Abraham; for a father of many nations have I made thee" (Genesis 17:5).

★ *In this chapter you will be studying about Abraham. Some items that Abraham would have used while he lived in Canaan are listed below. Find these words in your concordance, and copy the first reference given for each. Do not copy the verse.*

5. Camels _____ Genesis 12:16 _____

6. Money _____ Genesis 17:12 _____

7. Milk _____ Genesis 18:8 _____

8. Knife _____ Genesis 22:6 _____

48

Lesson 7. Abraham—Father of the Faithful

Noah's descendants soon forgot the lesson of the Flood. Before long they were almost as wicked as the people before the Flood had been. After the Flood, God had commanded Noah's family to spread out and repopulate the earth. But they decided that they would rather live in one place, so the people built themselves a large tower on the plain of Shinar. In Chapter 1, you saw how God defeated their plans by confusing their language and scattering them.

As these people moved to different parts of the world, they developed different ways of living. Some supported themselves by hunting or fishing, while others tended flocks of sheep. Some people made houses out of earth or wood, while others lived in tents made of animal skins. They traveled far and wide, and they built great cities. But of all the people on the earth, only a few were interested in obeying God.

You remember Adam and Eve's family. Out of that large family, God saved only Noah, his wife, his sons, and their wives. Following the Flood, Noah's family also grew and became large. Like Adam's family, Noah's descendants became sinful and disobedient. Therefore God called a faithful man, Abram, to come out from among them to be saved.

In this lesson you will see how Abram, whom God later called Abraham, became the father of the faithful.

A. ANSWERS FROM THE BIBLE

★ *Study the Bible passages given. Fill in the short blanks with words, using exact words from the Bible whenever possible. Write complete answers for the questions with long blanks. For multiple choice questions, circle the letter of the correct answer or underline the correct word in parentheses.*

The LORD Calls Abram

God was grieved by the great sins of Noah's descendants. Most of them served false gods. But in the city of Ur, God saw a man named Abram, who still served Him even though his relatives worshiped idols. God chose Abram to be the father of His special "chosen family."

Genesis 11:31, 32

1. Abram's father was _____ Terah _____.

2. Abram married _____ Sarai _____, his half-sister. She had the same father as he did, but a different mother.

3. Abram's first home was in __Ur of the Chaldees__.

God's call to Abram is first mentioned in Genesis 12. But according to Acts 7:2, 3, God appeared to Abram *before* the journey described in Genesis 11:31. God told Abram to leave the place where he had been born, and Abram's father apparently decided to move with him.

Lesson 7

Oral Review

1. What are five ways that God wants us to use the Bible? [1] **read, hear, study, believe, obey**
2. Why did God give the Bible to man? [1] **for our learning (so that man can know God's will)**
3. How did God make the light and many other things? [2] **He said, "Let there be . . ."**
4. How high did the Flood waters rise above the highest mountains? [4] **15 cubits (about 22½ feet)**
5. What covenant did God make with Noah? [5] **He promised that He would never destroy the whole earth with a flood again.**
6. Why did men start to build the Tower of Babel? [5] **to make a name for themselves, and to keep from being scattered**
7. About how many years have passed since the Creation? [6] **about 6,000**
8. What do the abbreviations *A.M.*, *B.C.*, and *A.D.* mean when they are used with dates? [6] **A.M.—in the year of the world; B.C.—before Christ; A.D.—in the year of our Lord**

4. Abram, his wife, his father, and his nephew Lot all moved to _____Haran_____, where they stayed until _____Terah_____ died.

Genesis 12:1–5

These verses record God's call to Abram. It is not clear whether they refer to God's first call before Abram left Ur, or whether God appeared to Abram a second time after his father died in Haran. We do know that Abram did what God asked him to do. Apparently some others in his father's family also moved to Haran with Abram, but only Lot went with Abram and his family when they left Haran.

5. God gave Abram clear instructions when He called him. What three things did Abram need to give up to follow God? a. _____his country_____ b. _his kindred (relatives)_ c. _his father's house_

6. Where did God tell Abram to go? _____

"unto a land that I will shew thee" _____

7. Did Abram know where this place was? (See Hebrews 11:8.) ____no____

8. Which of the following sentences tells why Abram left his home, even though he did not know where God would lead him?
   a. Abram did not care where he lived.
   b. Abram believed that God would lead him back to Ur.
   (c.) Abram had faith that God would always lead him right.

Abram in Egypt

When Abram reached Canaan, God appeared to him again and promised to give the land of Canaan to his descendants.

Genesis 12:10–13

Abraham was a man of faith. He did what God told him to do, without questioning or complaining. But Abraham was not perfect. These verses tell of a time when he allowed fear to overpower his faith.

9. Abram went to Egypt because of a _____famine_____ in the land of Canaan.

10. Although Sarai was at least sixty-five years old by this time, she was still a very beautiful woman. Abram asked Sarai to tell the Egyptians that she was his _____sister_____ so that they would not _____kill_____ him in order to marry her.

Genesis 12:14–20

11. Who spoke highly of Abram's wife to Pharaoh? _____the princes_____

12. What happened to Sarai? _____

Sarai was taken into Pharaoh's house. _____

13. What did God do to the Egyptians because of Sarai? _____

God plagued Pharaoh and his house with great plagues. _____

• Apparently Terah's whole family, including Abram's brother Nahor, moved from Ur to Haran. Some of Nahor's descendants remained in the area for at least several generations. There Abraham's servant met Rebekah, a granddaughter of Nahor, and there Jacob married two great-granddaughters of Nahor.

In This Lesson

Scope: Genesis 12–14

Main Events

• God calls Abram out of his homeland and promises to give the land of Canaan to his family.
• Abram believes God and obeys Him.
• Abram travels to Egypt because of a famine. There he allows fear to overpower his faith.
• Abram allows Lot to take his choice of the land.
• God renews His covenant with Abraham and promises that his seed will be "as the dust of the earth."

Objectives

• Students should know
  —what city Abram originally came from. (Ur of the Chaldees)
  —how Abram was related to Terah and to Lot. (Abram was Terah's son and Lot's uncle.)
  —why Abram's move to Canaan was a move of faith. (He did not know where God would lead him.)
  —why Abram went to Egypt, and why he was afraid to tell the truth about his wife. (There was a famine in Canaan. He was afraid the Egyptians would kill him in order to marry her.)

14. What did Pharaoh do to Abram after Abram's untruth became known? _____

   Pharaoh rebuked Abram and sent Abram and Sarai away._____

   _____

Abram and Lot

Genesis 13:1, 2, 5–13

The Bible calls both Abram and Lot righteous men. However, these verses show a weakness in Lot that would one day ruin his family.

15. Why could Abram and Lot not continue living at the same place? The herdsmen of Abram

   and Lot began quarreling because there was not enough land for all the flocks and herds.

16. How do we know that Abram was an unselfish man? _____

   Abram gave Lot the first choice of land._____

17. Why did Lot choose the plain of Jordan? _____

   The plain of Jordan was well watered. It had the best land. Lot wanted the best for himself.

   _____

God's Promise to Abram

Genesis 13:14–17

The selfishness of one man can never change God's plan. God renewed His promise to Abram in these verses. Perhaps He wanted to reassure Abram that He would keep His promise, no matter what Lot did.

18. God asked Abram to look in every direction. He promised that He would give all the

   _____land_____ that Abram could see, to him and his seed _____forever_____ .

19. Read verse 16 carefully. God promised Abram that his seed would be "as the dust of the earth." This means that
   a. Abram's descendants would be impossible to count because there would be so many of them.
   b. Abram's descendants would be lowly people who would never become very important.
   c. Abram's descendants would be farmers, working with the dust of the earth for a living.

Where Is It Found?

20. The story of God calling Abram out of Ur is found in
   a. Genesis 10.   b. Genesis 12.   c. Genesis 13.   d. Genesis 14.

21. The story of Lot choosing the best land is found in
   a. Genesis 10.   b. Genesis 12.   c. Genesis 13.   d. Genesis 14.

—the story of Lot choosing the best land. (See Part A, numbers 15–17.)
—why God compared Abram's descendants to the dust of the earth. (His descendants would be impossible to count because there would be so many of them.)

Truths to Instill
- God called Abraham for much the same purpose that He had called Noah—to save a faithful remnant. In response to God's call, Abraham set an outstanding example of faith. To this day, his obedient faithfulness is held forth as a pattern for us to follow.

- In an age when people are demanding their rights, we should consider Abraham's treatment of Lot. As the elder and the leader, Abraham had every right to choose first. But rather than acting on his "rights," Abraham acted on what was "right" and gave preference to Lot. Children have many opportunities to practice this principle, "in honour preferring one another" (Romans 12:10).

B. BIBLE WORD STUDY

★ *Write a word from the verse given to fit each definition. All references are from Genesis.*

____kindred____   1. Relatives (12:1)

____substance____   2. Belongings; wealth (12:5)

____sojourn____   3. To stay for a short time (12:10)

____famine____   4. Extreme lack of food (12:10)

____strife____   5. Conflict; quarreling; fighting (13:7)

____herdmen____   6. Men in charge of cattle (13:7)

____seed____   7. Children; descendants (13:15, 16)

- Number 6. The modern word is *herdsmen.*

C. THINKING ABOUT BIBLE TRUTHS

We can learn many truths from Abraham's life. His godly example is still worth following today, even though he lived almost four thousand years ago.

Joshua 24:2

Like Noah, Abraham was righteous when most of those around him were ungodly. There may have been a few other God-fearing people in his time, such as Melchizedek (Genesis 14:18), but most of the people on earth did not serve the true God.

1. According to this verse, even Terah, the father of Abraham, served _____other_____

_____gods_____. Probably most of his family also did.

2. Earlier in this lesson, you read about God's call to Abram, in Genesis 12:1. In light of this verse in Joshua, give a good reason why God wanted Abram to move away from his father's house. ____Abram's relatives worshiped idols. God wanted Abram to worship Him.____

_____

3. How can families follow the good example of Abraham today?
   a. They should be ready to follow God's leading if He calls them to leave their homes and friends to take the Gospel to other places.
   b. If the church they attend does not obey the Bible, they should be ready to leave their family and friends to join a church that does.
   c. They should be ready to follow God's plan for them, even if they do not know why God wants them to do what He asks of them.
   (d.) All the choices above are correct.

Galatians 3:9, 14

Abraham's descendants were not the only ones who received a blessing through him. In Genesis 12:3, God promised Abraham that "all families of the earth" would be blessed through him.

4. Only people who have _____faith_____ are blessed with Abraham.

5. The blessing of Abraham comes on the Gentiles through _____Jesus_____

_____Christ_____.

- There is an old tradition that Melchizedek, the king and priest of Salem, was Shem. (See *Halley's Bible Handbook.*) Although this is possible, it cannot be proven. Bible dates do indicate that Shem was still alive in Abraham's time. Depending on where these men lived, Adam could have talked with Methuselah, Methuselah could have talked with Shem, and Shem could have talked with Abraham.

- The word *flood* in Joshua 24:2 means *river,* and refers to either the Jordan River or the Euphrates River—not to the Flood of Noah's time. In other words, Terah and his ancestors lived on the other side of the river from where Joshua was when he said this.

D. LEARNING MORE ABOUT THE BIBLE

The Patriarchs' Tents

"By faith (1) _____Abraham_____, when he was called to go out, . . . obeyed; and he went out, not knowing whither he went. By faith he sojourned in the land of promise, as in a strange country, dwelling in tabernacles [tents] with (2) _____Isaac_____ and (3) _____Jacob_____, the heirs with him of the same promise: for he looked for a city which hath foundations, whose builder and maker is God" (Hebrews 11:8–10).

Tents in Bible times were made of goats' hair. People draped the cloth over poles and ropes, and then pegged it down at the ends to keep it from blowing away.

Side curtains and partitions in the tent were sometimes made from worn roof coverings. They separated the women's room from the open area where guests were entertained.

Rugs covered the sand floor of the tent. Around the tent poles stood food containers, pots, and water jugs. Families slept on mats that they rolled up and laid aside during the day.

Each of (4) _____Jacob_____'s four wives had her own tent (Genesis 31:33).

Strong rope, a wooden mallet, and tent nails belonged to the patriarchs' households.

Cloth for tent making was woven on looms stretched out on the ground.

The (5) __tabernacle__ was a large tent where the Israelites worshiped God (Exodus 39:33).

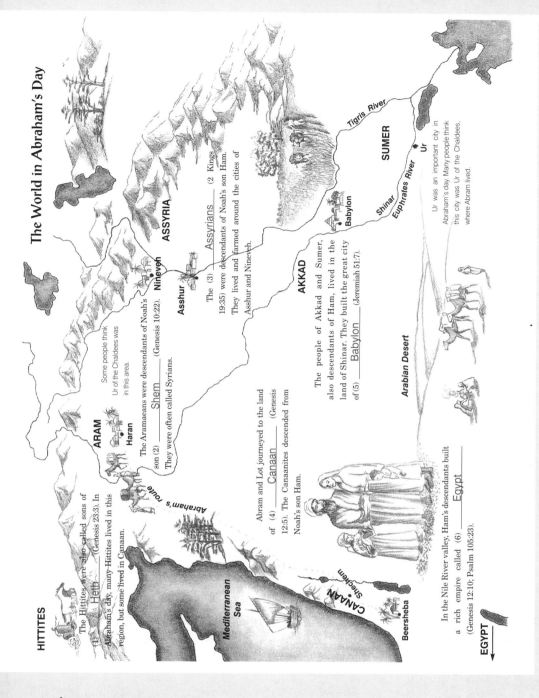

The World in Abraham's Day

HITTITES

(1) The Hittites were also called sons of _____ Heth _____ (Genesis 23:3). In Abraham's day, many Hittites lived in this region, but some lived in Canaan.

ARAM

Haran

The Aramaeans were descendants of Noah's son (2) _____ Shem _____ (Genesis 10:22). They were often called Syrians.

Some people think Ur of the Chaldees was in this area.

Abraham's route

Mediterranean Sea

CANAAN
Shechem
Beersheba

Abram and Lot journeyed to the land of (4) _____ Canaan _____ (Genesis 12:5). The Canaanites descended from Noah's son Ham.

ASSYRIA
Nineveh
Asshur

The (3) _____ Assyrians _____ (2 Kings 19:35) were descendants of Noah's son Ham. They lived and farmed around the cities of Asshur and Nineveh.

Tigris River

SUMER

AKKAD
Babylon

The people of Akkad and Sumer, also descendants of Ham, lived in the land of Shinar. They built the great city of (5) _____ Babylon _____ (Jeremiah 51:7).

Shinar

Euphrates River

Ur

Ur was an important city in Abraham's day. Many people think this city was Ur of the Chaldees, where Abram lived.

Arabian Desert

EGYPT

In the Nile River valley, Ham's descendants built a rich empire called (6) _____ Egypt _____ (Genesis 12:10; Psalm 105:23).

- The Bible always calls Abram's hometown "Ur of the Chaldees." This may indicate that Abram's hometown was not the famous Ur located in the southern Euphrates valley. Barry Beitzel, in his *Moody Atlas of Bible Lands,* gives arguments in favor of a northern Ur. However, most sources still consider it more likely that Abram lived in the traditional Ur.

54

Lesson 8. Abraham's Family

In the last lesson, you learned about God's promise that Abram would become the father of God's chosen family. God had promised him more descendants than anyone could count. But Abram and his wife were growing old, and they had no children at all! How could Abram become the father of so many people if he had no children? How could his descendants become as many as the stars if he had no sons?

Abram and Sarai wondered about these things. They knew God would keep His promises, but they did not understand how. Each year it seemed less likely that they would have a child. Finally, in desperation, Sarai decided that maybe her servant Hagar could be the mother of the promised son.

Hagar had a son, but he was not the promised one. God told Abraham that Sarah would still have a son of her own, even though she was old. Sarah laughed when she heard this. But when Abraham was one hundred years old and Sarah was ninety, they had their first baby! They called him Isaac, the name God had chosen for him. They were filled with joy.

God had been testing Abraham's faith during the long years he had waited for his promised son. But God planned another test for Abraham that was even harder. Do you know what God asked Abraham to do with Isaac? You will read about this and other things that happened in Abraham's family as you study this lesson.

A. ANSWERS FROM THE BIBLE

God Renews His Promise

Genesis 15:1–6

In these verses, it appears that Abram had started to doubt that God's promise would be fulfilled. The "word of the LORD" came to Abram in a vision to confirm His promise and to renew Abram's faith.

1. God told Abram that He was his _____shield_____ and his "exceeding great _____reward_____."

2. Abram wondered how the LORD would make him the father of many people, because
   a. he had no heir to take over his goods after he died.
   b. he had no children of his own.
   c. it had been so long since the LORD had last appeared to him.

3. The LORD told Abram that he would have a child of his own to be his heir. He told Abram that his descendants would be as many as the _____stars_____.

4. Abram was counted righteous by God because he ___believed in the LORD___
   _____.

Lesson 8

Oral Review
1. How did the men who wrote the Bible know what words to use? [1] **The Holy Spirit told men what to write.**
2. Why was God pleased with Abel's sacrifice and not Cain's? [3] **Abel showed his faith in God by the more excellent sacrifice he offered.**
3. What is the token of God's covenant with Noah? [5] **the rainbow**
4. From what point do we start counting dates labeled *A.M.*? [6] **from the Creation**
5. From what point do we start counting dates labeled *B.C.* and *A.D.*? [6] **from the birth of Christ**

6. What can we use to find the reference of a Bible verse? [6] **a concordance**
7. Who was Abram's nephew? Who was Abram's father? [7] **Lot; Terah**
8. Where was Abram's first home? [7] **in Ur of the Chaldees**

In This Lesson

Scope: Genesis 15–22

Main Events
- God renews His promise to give Abram innumerable descendants.
- Hagar bears Abram a son, Ishmael.

Hagar and Ishmael

Genesis 16:1–6, 15, 16

Finally Sarai grew tired of waiting on God. She thought of a way that Abram and she could have a child without waiting any longer. However, when people take their own way rather than God's way, it leads to trouble. Sarai's plan caused many problems for everyone involved.

5. Sarai persuaded Abram to take Hagar, her Egyptian   handmaid (maid) , to be his

       wife   . She thought that if Abram and Hagar had a son, she could claim

   him as her own.

6. Sarai's plan worked. But because of it, Hagar   despised   Sarai. This upset

   Sarai so much that she dealt   hardly   with Hagar.

Hagar fled from Sarai into the wilderness, but an angel found her and sent her home again. He told her to submit herself to Sarai. He also promised her that she would have a son who would be a wild man.

7. Abram called Hagar's son   Ishmael   . This name means "God will hear."

Sarai's plan caused more problems. You will learn about some of these in the next lesson. Even today, descendants of Ishmael (Arabs) are bitter enemies of the descendants of Isaac and Jacob (Jews).

8. How old was Abram when Hagar's son was born?   eighty-six years

God Talks to Abraham

Thirteen years after the birth of Ishmael, the LORD appeared to Abram again. This time, after renewing the covenant, God told him that the child of promise would be born within a year. Finally, the long years of waiting were almost over!

Genesis 17:1–5, 15, 16

9. God changed Abram's name to   Abraham   and Sarai's name to   Sarah   .

10. God told Abraham that Sarah would be a   mother   of   nations   .

Genesis 18:1, 2, 9–15

Soon after this, Abraham and Sarah received a visit from the LORD. He had come to see Sodom and Gomorrah, the wicked cities of the plain where Lot lived. The LORD decided to destroy those cities by raining fire and brimstone upon them, but He saved Lot and his daughters.

11. During this visit, the LORD again told Abraham that Sarah would have a son. When Sarah

    heard the LORD's message, she   laughed   within herself. She thought that she

    was much too   old   to have a child.

12. God knew Sarah's thoughts and rebuked her for not believing His words. She needed to

    learn that nothing was too   hard   for the LORD to do.

- In those times, it was common for a wife to give her maid to her husband. (Rachel and Leah did the same.) In fact, that was expected of her if she did not have a son herself. But in following this custom, these women brought many problems on themselves and their families.

If any of your students have time for extra work, assign them to research why God changed these names as He did. Have them look up the meanings of the old and new names in a good Bible dictionary and give a report to the class on likely reasons for the change.

- God changes Abram's name to Abraham and Sarai's name to Sarah.
- Isaac is born to Abraham and Sarah.
- God tests Abraham by asking him to offer Isaac.

Objectives
- Students should know
  —what God promised Abraham about his descendants. (They would be many, as the stars of the heaven, and as the sand of the seashore.)
  —who was Abraham's oldest son. (Ishmael)
  —what Sarah did when she heard that she would have a son. (She laughed.)

—the meaning of *heir*. (a person who receives property after the owner dies)
—why Abraham went to Mount Moriah, and what God provided as a substitute for Isaac. (to offer Isaac as a sacrifice; a ram)

Truths to Instill
- Abram believed God and was counted righteous. His faith is revealed in the following ways, as given in Hebrews 11:8–19.
  —When God promised Abram a strange land, he went to find it even though he was not sure where it was and though he had no prior claim to it.

The Child of Promise

Genesis 21:1–3

God fulfilled His promise exactly when He had planned. God knows the best time for everything. We do not always understand God's ways, but they are always best.

13. Isaac was born at the _____ set _____ _____ time _____ that God had revealed to Abraham.

Genesis 22:1–17

Abraham loved Isaac very much. Did he love Isaac more than he loved God? Would he be willing to give up his beloved son at God's request? God had another test for Abraham.

14. God tested Abraham by telling him to _____ offer _____ Isaac as a _____ burnt _____ _____ offering _____ on a mountain in the land of Moriah.

15. Abraham could have made excuses and asked many questions. He could even have refused to obey God. Instead, he rose up _____ early _____ in the morning to do what God had commanded.

16. God did not stop Abraham until he took his _____ knife _____ to _____ slay _____ Isaac. Then an angel called to Abraham from _____ heaven _____, "Lay not thine hand upon the lad, . . . for now I know that thou _____ fearest _____ _____ God _____."

17. God provided a _____ ram _____ to take Isaac's place.

18. Before Abraham and Isaac returned home, God renewed His promise to Abraham again. This time He compared Abraham's descendants to the _____ stars _____ of the heaven and the _____ sand _____ upon the seashore.

Where Is It Found?

19. The story of Abraham offering Isaac is found in
    a. Genesis 18.   b. Genesis 20.   c. Genesis 21.   (d.) Genesis 22.

B. BIBLE WORD STUDY

★ *Write a word from the verse given to fit each definition. All references are from Genesis.*

_____ heir _____ 1. A person who receives the property of someone who dies (15:3)

_____ righteousness _____ 2. The condition of being right; virtue (15:6)

_____ handmaid _____ 3. A girl or woman who is a servant (16:1)

_____ despised _____ 4. Held in low esteem (16:5)

_____ hardly _____ 5. Harshly; severely (16:6)

_____ thicket _____ 6. A thick growth of shrubs or trees (22:13)

- God considered Abraham's offering complete (Hebrews 11:17), even though He stopped Abraham from killing his son.

- The Hebrew word translated *steward* in Genesis 15:2 implies "possessor," or "heir." The word *steward* is not included in this section, because a steward is normally not an heir.

—He remained in this land as a stranger for the rest of his long life. He lived fifteen years after his grandsons were born, "dwelling in [tents] with Isaac and Jacob, the heirs with him of the same promise"—yet never receiving any land from God.

—Abraham and Sarah received strength through faith to bear a son, even though they were nearly one hundred years old.

—Abraham sacrificed Isaac, even after God had told him that Isaac would be his heir. He believed that God could raise his son from the dead.

C. THINKING ABOUT BIBLE TRUTHS

Hebrews 11:11, 17–19

Even though Abraham and Sarah made some mistakes, they are outstanding examples for us to follow. In these verses, God commends them for their faith in Him.

1. What does it mean to have faith in God? Cross out the statement that gives a *wrong* answer for this question.
   a. A person with faith in God will do whatever God asks of him, even if he does not understand why God wants him to do it.
   b. A person with faith in God will continue to believe God's promises, even if they seem impossible.
   c. ~~A person with faith in God will always move away from his own home and country, as Abraham did.~~
   d. A person with faith in God will accept hard things without becoming upset, because he knows God has a reason for them.

2. Sarah proved her faith in God by
   (a.) believing that God would be faithful and give her a child as He had promised.
   b. laughing when God said that she would have a child in her old age.
   c. giving her maid, Hagar, to Abraham as a wife so that Hagar could bear a child for her.
   d. all the ways given above.

3. Abraham proved his faith in God by
   a. taking Hagar for his wife when Sarah suggested it.
   (b.) believing that God would keep His promise to make him a father of many nations, even if he offered up his only son as a burnt offering.
   c. pretending that Sarah was only his sister and not his wife.
   d. all the ways given above.

★ *How well did you read the verses for the exercises that you did about the life of Abraham? Match the following characters from the story of Abraham with their descriptions. Do as many as you can without looking back in your workbook or using your Bible.*

g 4. I married one of my father's sons.   a. Abraham
f 5. I traveled with my uncle to a strange land.   b. Eliezer
b 6. My home was in Damascus.   c. Hagar
c 7. My husband married me because his wife wanted him to.   d. Isaac
a 8. God asked me to leave my home and travel to a new land.   e. Ishmael
h 9. My son worshiped a different God than I did.   f. Lot
e 10. My mother was the servant of a rich man's wife.   g. Sarah
d 11. My mother laughed when she heard that I would be born.   h. Terah

This exercise brings out some details that the student may have missed as he read the Bible accounts. It also serves as a brief review of Abraham's life. You may want to do it together in class.

58 Chapter Two The Patriarchs

D. LEARNING MORE ABOUT THE BIBLE

God's Children of Promise

Before God created the earth, He knew that man would sin and would need a Redeemer to save him. So God planned a family line that He could use to bring the Redeemer, Jesus Christ, into the world.

In each generation after Adam, another person was born into the line of people through whom the Redeemer would someday come. This person was the child of promise. Each child of promise brought the coming of Jesus one generation closer.

★ *Through the maze below, find God's children of promise from Adam to Isaac. List the names you need to cross over, and be prepared to read them in class.*

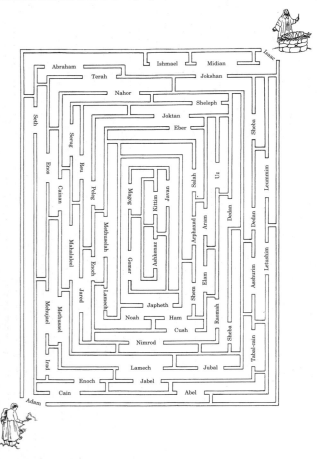

1. _____Adam_____
2. _____Seth_____
3. _____Enos_____
4. _____Cainan_____
5. _____Mahalaleel_____
6. _____Jared_____
7. _____Enoch_____
8. _____Methuselah_____
9. _____Lamech_____
10. _____Noah_____
11. _____Shem_____
12. _____Arphaxad_____
13. _____Salah_____
14. _____Eber_____
15. _____Peleg_____
16. _____Reu_____
17. _____Serug_____
18. _____Nahor_____
19. _____Terah_____
20. _____Abraham_____
21. _____Isaac_____

Lesson 9. Isaac Serves God

As you remember, Abraham and Sarah waited many years before God blessed them with a child of their own. Yet when God appeared and told them that their son would soon be born, Sarah laughed. She thought she was too old to have children. But God's word is always true, and Sarah did indeed have a son. They called him Isaac, which means "laughter."

Isaac, the son of promise, received many blessings. As you learned in the last lesson, God spared his life on the mountain of sacrifice, after it seemed certain that he would die. God gave him a beautiful wife named Rebekah, whom he loved very much. God also blessed Isaac with many possessions—great flocks of sheep and goats, and many servants to take care of them.

But Isaac had to learn that blessings sometimes require patience and that they are often mixed with sorrow. He was forty years old when he married, and he had to wait twenty years before his twin boys, Jacob and Esau, were born. These sons disappointed Isaac in the last years of his life. Jacob lied to him and then left home for many years. Esau married ungodly women.

The Bible tells about some events in Isaac's long life in southern Canaan. Isaac called upon the Name of the LORD, as his father Abraham had done. Even his enemies saw that the LORD was with him.

A. ANSWERS FROM THE BIBLE

Hagar and Ishmael Cast Out

Ishmael was about fourteen years older than his brother Isaac. He was probably fifteen to eighteen years old when this incident took place.

Genesis 21:9–21

1. What did Sarah see that caused her to ask Abraham to cast out Hagar and Ishmael? _____
   She saw Ishmael mocking.

2. This seemed like a harsh thing for Sarah to demand, and Abraham was very unhappy about it. However, God told him to do what Sarah wanted. Which of these sentences tells why God approved of casting out Hagar and Ishmael?
   a. God planned that Isaac, not Ishmael, should be Abraham's heir.
   b. God wanted to punish Ishmael for mocking Isaac.
   c. God did not love Hagar and Ishmael.

3. God promised that he would make a _____ nation _____ of Ishmael because he was Abraham's _____ seed _____.

4. God watched over Ishmael in the wilderness. He grew up and became an _____ archer _____.

- The customs of the East did not allow a father to cast out the son of a secondary wife if his primary wife bore him an heir. Sarah asked Abraham to do something that even his heathen neighbors would not have done. However, God allowed this to clearly show that Isaac was the son of promise.

Lesson 9

Oral Review

1. Why did God destroy the earth with a flood? [4] **People had become exceedingly wicked.**

2. What is the meaning of the word *covenant*? [5] **a binding agreement**

3. About how many years have passed since the Creation? [6] **about 6,000**

4. What did God compare Abram's descendants to? [7, 8] **the dust of the earth, the stars of the heaven, the sand of the seashore**

5. How did Abraham show that he had faith in God? [8] **Abraham left his home without knowing where God would lead him. Abraham believed God's promise before he had a son. Abraham was willing to sacrifice his promised son.**

6. What did Sarah do when God said she would have a son? [8] **She laughed.**

7. What did God supply as a sacrifice to take Isaac's place? [8] **a ram**

8. What is the meaning of the word *heir*? [8] **a person who receives the property of someone who dies**

60   Chapter Two   The Patriarchs

A Wife for Isaac

Abraham knew that Isaac needed a good wife so that the line of promise could continue with God's blessing. He planned carefully because he wanted to find the wife whom God had chosen for Isaac.

Genesis 24:1–7

5. Abraham asked his most trusted servant to find a wife for his son. He told him not to take a

   daughter of the _____Canaanites_____ as a wife for Isaac.

6. Abraham warned his servant that he must not take Isaac back to Haran. From this list, choose the *two best* reasons why Abraham did not want his son to move there.
   - (a.) The people of Haran were idol worshipers, and Isaac might have forgotten the true God if he had lived with them.
   - b. Abraham did not want Isaac to move away, because he wanted Isaac to care for him in his old age.
   - (c.) Abraham did not want Isaac to forget that God had promised to give Canaan to Abraham's descendants.
   - d. Abraham needed Isaac in Canaan to help him herd his sheep.

Genesis 24:10–14

Abraham's servant needed to travel about 500 miles to reach Haran. For those traveling by camel, this journey probably took two or three weeks, and maybe even longer.

7. The servant came into the city of _____Nahor_____, who lived in Mesopotamia.

8. The servant wanted to be sure that he found the woman whom *God* wanted to be Isaac's wife. He stopped at the well and asked God for further guidance. What sign did the servant ask the LORD to give him so that he would know which woman was the right one? _____
   He asked God to send a woman who would draw water for him and for his camels.

   _____

Genesis 24:15–20

9. How soon did the LORD answer the servant's prayer? _____
   _while the servant was still speaking_____

10. The name of the woman the LORD had chosen for Isaac was _____Rebekah_____.

It is hard for us to imagine the change that took place in this woman's life. One evening she went to draw water with no idea that something unusual was about to happen. Before the next day was over, she was on her way to Canaan to be the wife of a man whom she had never seen. As far as she knew, she would never see her family again.

11. Isaac's wife was the daughter of _____Bethuel_____. Her grandfather was
    _____Nahor_____, Abraham's brother. This means that her father was Isaac's first cousin.

- A full-grown camel would generally drink five or more gallons of water, so Rebekah probably had to draw at least fifty gallons of water for the ten camels.

In This Lesson

Scope: Genesis 21:8–21, Genesis 24–26

Main Events

- Abraham sends Hagar and Ishmael away.
- Abraham sends his oldest servant to find a wife for Isaac.
- Isaac and Rebekah have twin sons, Esau and Jacob.
- Isaac worships God and receives the same promise God had made to Abraham.

Objectives

- Students should know
  - —why Sarah wanted to send Hagar and Ishmael away. (She saw Ishmael mocking Isaac.)
  - —the story of how God provided a wife for Isaac. (See Part A, numbers 5–11.)
  - —what God told Rebekah about her twins before they were born. (They would become two manner of people, and the elder would serve the younger.)
  - —how the herdsmen of Gerar treated Isaac, and how he responded. (They took two wells that he had dug. He let the herdsmen have them.)

Isaac—a Man of Peace

The next several chapters of Genesis tell mainly about Isaac and his family. Abraham lived another thirty-five years and had six more sons, but the Bible does not say much about these last years of Abraham's life. Isaac was now responsible for passing on God's covenant to the next generation.

Genesis 25:19–26

12. Isaac was _____forty_____ years old when he married Rebekah.

13. For twenty years, Isaac and Rebekah did not have any children. But Isaac prayed to God, and God gave them twin sons. Their names were _____Esau_____ and _____Jacob_____.

14. Even before they were born, God told Rebekah that her two sons would be two different "manner of people." What did this mean?
    a. One boy would be rude and the other one mannerly.
    (b.) The descendants of the two boys would become two completely different nations.
    c. One boy would be tall and slender, while the other would be short and plump.

15. God also told Rebekah that the _____elder_____ would serve the _____younger_____.

Genesis 26:1–5

In these verses, we see the first recorded covenant that God made with Isaac. God confirmed the promise that He had first made to Abraham.

16. God's promise to Isaac had a condition attached to it. Isaac was to "___sojourn (dwell)___ in this land" (meaning the land of Canaan). God told him not to go to the land of _____Egypt_____.

17. Isaac benefited from the faithfulness of his father Abraham. God gave him the same promise He had made to Abraham because Abraham had _____obeyed_____ His voice and kept His commandments.

Genesis 26:17–25

18. How did Isaac show that he was a man of peace? _____
    Isaac let the herdsmen of Gerar take two wells that he had dug._____

    _____

19. a. Where did Isaac worship God? ___at Beersheba_____
    b. How did he worship? ___He built an altar and called upon the name of the Lord.___

    _____

Where Is It Found?

20. The story of Abraham's servant seeking a wife for Isaac is found in
    a. Genesis 13.   b. Genesis 18.   (c.) Genesis 24.   d. Genesis 26.

Truths to Instill

- Mocking is never right. Teasing can be a form of mockery. Mockery and the Golden Rule are opposites.
- We need to depend on God when making important decisions in life. In this story we see confidence and trust in God's leading—in Abraham as he trusted God to direct his servant, in Isaac as he allowed the matter to rest in the servant's hands, in the servant as he asked God to reveal His will, and in Rebekah as she saw God's work and believed in it. The result was a beautiful marriage.
- Isaac left a good example of living peaceably with all men.

B. BIBLE WORD STUDY

★ *Match these definitions with the Bible words on the right. Read the verses given or use a dictionary if you need help. All references are from Genesis.*

<table>
<tr><td>c</td><td>1. A female slave (21:10)</td><td>a. barren</td></tr>
<tr><td>d</td><td>2. The distance an arrow can be shot with a bow (21:16)</td><td>b. threescore</td></tr>
<tr><td>f</td><td>3. A person who uses a bow and arrow (21:20)</td><td>c. bondwoman</td></tr>
<tr><td>a</td><td>4. Having no children (25:21)</td><td>d. bowshot</td></tr>
<tr><td>b</td><td>5. Sixty (25:26)</td><td>e. oath</td></tr>
<tr><td>e</td><td>6. A solemn statement or promise (26:3)</td><td>f. archer</td></tr>
</table>

C. THINKING ABOUT BIBLE TRUTHS

Galatians 4:22–24, 28

In these verses, the apostle Paul uses the story of Isaac and Ishmael as an allegory (a parable) to teach an important lesson.

1. In verse 24, Paul says the two sons were like the two _____covenants_____. Ishmael was the son of a slave, but Isaac was free. In the same way, those who lived under the Old Testament Law could never be as free as those who live under the blessings of the New Testament.

2. According to verse 28, we can be the children of _____promise_____. This means that we can claim God's promise and blessing if we believe and obey God as Abraham and Isaac did.

Genesis 26:26–31

Earlier in this chapter, the Philistines asked Isaac to move away because of how the LORD was blessing him. They also quarreled about some wells that he had dug, and took the wells away from him. Now in these verses Abimelech, the king of the Philistines, came to Isaac to make a covenant of peace with him.

3. According to verse 28, why did the Philistines want to make peace with Isaac after they had caused so much trouble for him? ___They saw that the LORD was with Isaac.___

4. The Bible says, "When a man's ways please the LORD, he maketh even his enemies to be at peace with him" (Proverbs 16:7). In a short paragraph, explain how Isaac's life demonstrates this verse.

___(Individual work. The paragraph should contain the thought that the Philistines, who had been Isaac's enemies, came to make peace with Isaac, whose ways pleased the LORD.)___

★ *In some ways, Isaac's life was similar to Jesus' life. Because of this, we say that Isaac was a type of Christ. Match each event in Christ's life with an event in Isaac's life.*

___d___ 5. Isaac's birth was a miracle, since Sarah was too old to have a child.

___a___ 6. Isaac was the only son of Abraham and Sarah.

___c___ 7. Isaac was willing to let his father offer him as a sacrifice.

___b___ 8. Isaac came back to his family unharmed after the ram was offered in his place.

a. Jesus is the only begotten Son of God.

b. Jesus rose from the dead and appeared to His disciples for forty days after He had offered His life as a sacrifice for sin.

c. Jesus was willing to give His life as a sacrifice for the sins of the world at God's command.

d. Jesus' birth was a miracle, since He had no earthly father.

L E N T I L S

Among the ruins of ancient Sumeria, archaeologists found a pot of lentils. These ancient vegetables might have been harvested before Abraham was born.

Known as the poor man's meat, lentils grow with little attention. The plants resemble pea plants. The seeds are very nourishing. People of Bible times took parched lentils with them on long trips because they did not easily spoil. Farmers around the Mediterranean Sea still raise many acres of lentils.

Lentils cooked with meat and herbs make a delicious stew. Who traded his most valuable possession for a pot of lentil stew? (Genesis 25:32–34).

D. LEARNING MORE ABOUT THE BIBLE

Ishmael

Ishmael was (1) _____Abraham_____'s oldest son (Genesis 25:12). His mother, Hagar, was a (2) _____bond_____ woman (Genesis 21:10). After Ishmael (3) _____mocked_____ his brother (Genesis 21:9), Hagar took him out into the desert, where he almost died of thirst. But God heard Ishmael's voice and sent an angel to show his mother a (4) _____well_____ (Genesis 21:19).

God was with Ishmael in the desert, and he grew up to be an (5) _____archer_____ (Genesis 21:20). He had twelve sons, whose names were

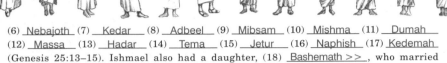

(6) _Nebajoth_ (7) _Kedar_ (8) _Adbeel_ (9) _Mibsam_ (10) _Mishma_ (11) _Dumah_ (12) _Massa_ (13) _Hadar_ (14) _Tema_ (15) _Jetur_ (16) _Naphish_ (17) _Kedemah_ (Genesis 25:13–15). Ishmael also had a daughter, (18) _Bashemath >>_, who married (19) _Esau_ (Genesis 36:2, 3).

God had said that Ishmael would be a wild man. He also said that his hand would be against (20) _____every man_____, and (21) _____every man_____'s hand against him (Genesis 16:12).

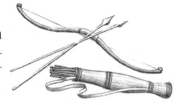

Apparently Ishmael's daughter had two names. Compare Genesis 28:9 with Genesis 36:2, 3. Mahalath *should also be considered correct.*

Even today, many of Ishmael's descendants live in tents in the desert. Blowing sand, robbers, long dry periods, and warfare make their lives difficult. One descendant of Ishmael, named Mohammed, wrote the Koran, a religious book that talks about God, Adam and Eve, Noah, Abraham, Moses, and Jesus. But the Koran also includes untruths and false doctrines. Ishmael's large family, the Arabs of the Middle East, follow the teachings of the Koran today. They call their religion Islam (ihs LAHM).

ISAAC

★ *Write the words that go in the blanks.*

Isaac lived in the southern part of Canaan. He was a shepherd, and he lived in tents with his family and servants. Isaac did not travel far as his father, Abraham, did. Isaac was buried at Hebron after he died.

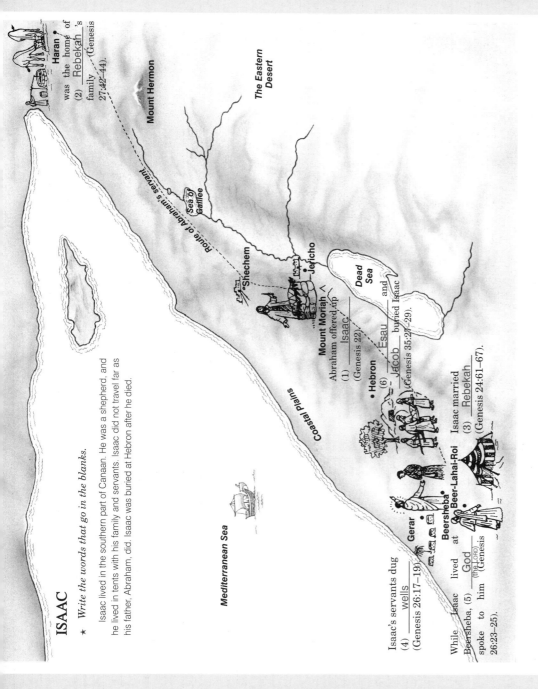

Haran was the home of (2) _Rebekah's_ family (Genesis 27:42–44).

Mount Hermon

The Eastern Desert

Route of Abraham's servant

(Sea of) Galilee

Shechem

Jericho

Dead Sea

Mount Moriah — Abraham offered up (1) _Isaac_ (Genesis 22).

Hebron

(6) _Jacob_ and Esau buried Isaac (Genesis 35:27–29).

Isaac married (3) _Rebekah_ (Genesis 24:61–67).

Coastal plains

Mediterranean Sea

Gerar

Beersheba

Beer-Lahai-Roi

Isaac's servants dug (4) _wells_ (Genesis 26:17–19).

While Isaac lived at Beersheba, (5) _God_ (the LORD) spoke to him (Genesis 26:23–25).

66

Lesson 10. Jacob Learns to Walk With God

In the last lesson, you saw that Isaac and Rebekah had twin sons. Even before Rebekah's sons were born, God showed her that they would be very different from each other. The older twin, Esau, became a hunter when he grew up. His father loved him because of the meat that he brought home for him to eat. Jacob, the younger, became a shepherd and was his mother's favorite.

One day when Esau came back from hunting, he was very hungry. Jacob persuaded him to trade his birthright for some pottage. This incident shows the characters of these two brothers. Esau despised his birthright and gave up God's promise without a second thought, just because he was hungry. Jacob wanted the birthright, but he was also a crafty person, ready to take advantage of others' weaknesses. Both of the brothers had to suffer later in life because of their choices.

This was not the last time that Jacob cheated his brother. Later, with his mother's help, Jacob deceived his father and received the blessing that Isaac wanted to give Esau. He deceived other people too. But other people also deceived Jacob. His uncle even deceived him into marrying a woman he did not want.

In spite of his crafty ways, Jacob was better suited to receive the blessing than Esau was. Jacob knew that the birthright and the blessing were very important. He also chose better wives than Esau did. The Bible tells the story of how Jacob learned to fear God and walk with Him. Through Jacob, God fulfilled His promise to make Abraham's descendants as many as the stars of heaven.

A. ANSWERS FROM THE BIBLE

Jacob—the Deceiver

Jacob's name means "supplanter." A supplanter is a person who takes the place of another person by tricking him. Jacob lived up to his name, as we can see in these Scripture passages.

Genesis 25:27–34

These verses show what kind of persons Jacob and Esau had grown up to be. It was not right for Jacob to take advantage of his brother, but Esau's careless attitude was even worse.

1. Because Esau was born before Jacob, it was his right to receive the birthright and the promise that God had given to Isaac and Abraham. However, verse 34 says that Esau _____despised_____ his birthright. Apparently he was not interested in God's promises.

2. Jacob wanted the birthright, though the Bible does not say why. He must have realized that it was valuable. Perhaps his mother had told him that God had said his older brother would serve him. But Jacob should have let God give him the birthright in His own way. Instead, he took advantage of Esau's weakness and persuaded him to _____sell_____ his birthright for some bread and _____pottage_____.

- In a discussion with the students, it may be pointed out that Esau did not place a high enough value on the privileges that could have been his. Today many people despise an eternal inheritance for a few years of pleasure in this world.

Lesson 10

Oral Review
1. Where did God send Adam and Eve after they disobeyed Him? [3] **out of the Garden of Eden**
2. What do the abbreviations *A.M.*, *B.C.*, and *A.D.* mean when they are used with dates? [6] **A.M.—in the year of the world; B.C.—before Christ; A.D.—in the year of our Lord**
3. Where did Abram go during a famine? [7] **to Egypt**
4. What did God ask Abraham to do to show his love to God? [8] **to offer Isaac as a burnt sacrifice**
5. Why did Sarah want to send Hagar and Ishmael away? [9] **Sarah saw Ishmael mocking Isaac.**
6. Why did Abraham not want his servant to take Isaac back to Haran? [9] **Isaac was to receive the promise of the land of Canaan, and Abraham's relatives at Haran worshiped idols.**
7. How did Isaac show that he was a man of peace? [9] **Isaac let the herdsmen of Gerar have his wells instead of fighting over them.**
8. What two things did God tell Rebekah about her sons before they were born? [9] **They would become two manner of people, and the elder would serve the younger.**

Genesis 27:1–5

It seems that Isaac also made some mistakes. He allowed Esau to choose his own ungodly wives. He did not find a wife for Jacob, as his father, Abraham, had done for him. In these verses, he decided that he would give the covenant blessing to Esau in return for a good meal. Apparently he did not ask God if this was the right thing to do. Perhaps he had forgotten that God had said the elder would serve the younger.

It is interesting to note that Jacob and Esau were about seventy-seven years old at this time and that Isaac lived another forty-three years afterward.

3. Isaac wanted Esau to hunt for some _____venison_____ and make him a good meal with it. Then he would _____bless_____ Esau. This meant that Esau would receive the covenant promise in spite of his agreement with Jacob years before.

Genesis 27:6–29

Jacob was not the only deceiver in Isaac's family. Rebekah overheard Isaac when he was telling his plans to Esau. She wanted Jacob to receive the blessing, so she called Jacob and told him how to trick Isaac, who was blind. Jacob brought her two small goats, and she prepared them like venison. Then Jacob went to Isaac, his father.

4. Why was Isaac suspicious of Jacob? _____
   Jacob's voice sounded different from Esau's voice.

5. List four things Jacob did to deceive his father.   (Answers may vary somewhat.)

   a.   He put on Esau's clothes.

   b.   He wore goatskin on his hands and neck.

   c.   He took goat meat instead of venison.

   d.   He told his father lies.

Genesis 27:30–34, 37

After Isaac had blessed Jacob, Esau returned from his hunt and brought venison to his father. But he was too late.

6. When Isaac realized what had happened, he _____trembled_____ greatly.

7. True or false: Isaac could take back the blessing he had given to Jacob and give it to Esau.
   __false__

Isaac's family was torn apart by this incident. After Esau learned that Jacob had cheated him, he threatened to kill Jacob. Rebekah decided that Jacob should leave home for a while. But instead of telling Isaac her real reason for wanting Jacob to go, she suggested that they send Jacob to her brother Laban to find a wife.

Jacob Meets God

Genesis 28:10–13, 16–18

Jacob was about seventy-seven years old when he left home. His father had taught him some things about God, but he still had much to learn. One night soon after he left home, Jacob had an experience that began to change his life.

- Deceptiveness seemed to be a family trait among Rebekah's family. Laban was no better than Jacob and Rebekah; and his daughters, especially Rachel, showed the same tendency.

In This Lesson

Scope: Genesis 25:27–34; 26:34–35:29

Main Events

- Esau sells his birthright to Jacob.
- Rebekah helps Jacob deceive his father to gain the blessing of the first-born son.
- Jacob flees to Padan-aram to avoid his brother's anger.
- God appears to Jacob in a vision at Bethel.
- Jacob marries two wives and has a large family.
- Jacob wrestles with a heavenly messenger and receives a new name from God.
- Jacob meets Esau peaceably and then returns to Canaan.

Objectives

- Students should know
  —the meaning of *birthright*. (the special rights of the oldest son in a family. See Part D for what these special rights included.)
  —how Jacob obtained Esau's birthright. (He persuaded Esau to sell it for some bread and pottage.)
  —what Jacob saw at Bethel. (a ladder that reached to heaven, with angels going up and down on it and God standing at the top)
  —the story of Jacob's marriage to two wives. (See Part A, numbers 11–13.)
  —why God changed Jacob's name. (Jacob had changed; his old name did not describe him anymore.)

8. In his vision, Jacob saw _____angels_____ going up and down a _____ladder_____ that reached to _____heaven_____. At the top stood the _____LORD_____.

9. Which of the following gives a good reason why the LORD told Jacob that He was the God of Abraham and Isaac?
   a. When Isaac had blessed Jacob, Jacob received the covenant promises that God had given to Abraham and Isaac.
   b. Jacob worshiped many different gods, so he needed to know which god was speaking to him.
   c. Because Abraham and Isaac had been very good men, God could overlook Jacob's sins.

10. Jacob was afraid when God talked to him. What was one good reason for his fear?
    a. He was afraid the ladder would fall on him.
    b. He had never heard about God before.
    c. He realized his own sinfulness while he was in God's holy presence.

Jacob Is Deceived

Genesis 29:21–26

Jacob's uncle was happy to see him, and Jacob decided to stay and work for him. He promised Laban that he would work for seven years without any wages if he could marry Rachel, Laban's younger daughter.

11. The time came for Jacob to claim his wife. Since brides always veiled their faces on their wedding day, Jacob did not see who his wife was until the next _____morning_____. Then he discovered that he had married _____Leah_____.

12. What excuse did Laban give Jacob for the trick he had played on him? _Laban said that in his country, a younger daughter must not be given before the first-born._

13. Laban promised Jacob that he could marry Rachel too, if he agreed to work for him another _____seven_____ years. So a week later Jacob married Rachel as well.

Jacob Returns Home

The LORD blessed Jacob with many children, many animals, and great riches. When he had finished working fourteen years for his wives, he stayed six more years and worked for wages. However, Laban and Jacob did not get along well. While Jacob was thinking about what to do next, God spoke to him again.

Genesis 31:11, 13

14. God reminded Jacob that He was the God of _____Bethel_____. He told Jacob to _____return_____ to the land of his fathers (Canaan).

—the meaning of *Jacob* and *Israel*. (*Jacob* means "heel catcher; supplanter." *Israel* means "having power with God.")

Truths to Instill
- Children should understand that the deception Jacob practiced in his early life is not an example for them to follow. Jacob obviously did wrong in this, but he is also listed among the men of faith in Hebrews 11. It seems that after his struggle at the brook Penuel, Jacob depended more heavily on God. His faith is seen in the following:
  —His desire to return to the Land of Promise
  —His persistence in seeking a blessing from God
  —His trust in God when facing Esau
  —His putting away the family idols at Bethel
  —His blessing Joseph's sons in Egypt, in confidence that their descendants would someday inherit the Land of Promise.

Jacob left in secret, but Laban went after Jacob and caught up with him. They both complained that the other had done wrong, but they agreed to part in peace.

Now Jacob had to face his biggest fear. Was Esau still angry with him? Would he try to kill him? His worries increased when he heard that Esau was coming with four hundred men. For the first time, we read that Jacob cried to God for help instead of trying to plan his own way out of his problem. That night God sent a heavenly messenger to him.

Genesis 32:24–30

15. Jacob and the man wrestled until morning. Jacob refused to let the messenger go until the

    messenger had _____blessed_____ him.

16. God gave Jacob a new name. From now on his name would be _____Israel_____. This

    shows that God saw a change in Jacob's life. Instead of being a deceiver, he was as a

    _____prince_____ who had power with God.

Through this experience, it seems Jacob learned to serve God better. We do not read that he deceived anyone after this.

Genesis 33:1–4

Before his night of wrestling, Jacob had decided to try to make peace with Esau by sending him some gifts. He had also divided his servants and animals into two groups, in hope that if Esau attacked one group, the other would escape. In the morning, he divided his family into three groups. Now, walking with a limp, Jacob went ahead of his family to meet Esau.

17. How do we know that Esau had decided to forgive Jacob? _____
    Esau ran to meet Jacob, embraced him, fell on his neck, and kissed him.

Jacob and Esau lived in peace the rest of their lives. Jacob settled in Canaan, but for a number of years he did not return to Bethel, where he had first met God. Finally, after Jacob faced new problems, God called him back to Bethel.

Genesis 35:1–3

18. Which sentence tells why Jacob told his family to put away their false gods before they went
    to Bethel?
    a. He thought the images were too heavy to take along with them.
    b. He was afraid that enemies might steal the images.
    c. He knew that God would not bless his family if they had false gods.

Where Is It Found?

19. The story of Jacob deceiving Isaac is found in
    a. Genesis 22.   b. Genesis 24.   c. Genesis 26.   d. Genesis 27.

20. The story of Jacob's night of wrestling is found in
    a. Genesis 28.   b. Genesis 31.   c. Genesis 32.   d. Genesis 35

- Some people think that the "man" with whom Jacob wrestled was Jesus Himself, in a preincarnation appearance. Jacob recognized that he had had a close encounter with God (verses 28 and 30), but the "man" refused to reveal his name. He is called an angel in Hosea 12:4.

B. BIBLE WORD STUDY

★ *Match these definitions with the Bible words on the right. Read the verses given or use a dictionary if you need help. All references are from Genesis.*

_c_ 1. Skillful; clever (25:27)	a. lentils
_f_ 2. Deer meat (25:28)	b. vow
_g_ 3. A soup or stew (25:29)	c. cunning
_h_ 4. The special rights of the oldest son in a family (25:31)	d. savoury
_a_ 5. A vegetable similar to peas or beans (25:34)	e. raiment
_d_ 6. Tasty; flavorful (27:4)	f. venison
_e_ 7. Clothing (27:27)	g. pottage
_b_ 8. A solemn promise (28:20)	h. birthright

C. THINKING ABOUT BIBLE TRUTHS

The Law of Sowing and Reaping

The Bible says, "Whatsoever a man soweth, that shall he also reap" (Galatians 6:7). Jacob had deceived other people. He in turn was deceived by his uncle Laban and later by his own sons.

Near the end of his life, Jacob said that his days had been "few and evil" (Genesis 47:9). If Jacob had treated others better when he was younger, he probably would have reaped less trouble later.

★ *These passages list a few of the things Jacob reaped. Describe one sorrow for each reference.*

1. Genesis 27:41 __Esau hated him and wanted to kill him.__
2. Genesis 29:25 __Laban deceived him by giving him Leah instead of Rachel.__
3. Genesis 31:7 __Laban changed his wages ten times.__
4. Genesis 32:6, 7 __He was very fearful about meeting Esau again.__
5. Genesis 37:31–34 __His sons sold Joseph and pretended that he had been killed.__

The Deceiver Becomes a Prince

Jacob had some serious faults in his younger years. His lies and deception made problems for him and for those around him. But little by little, God changed Jacob from a man who cheated others to a prince who had power with God.

Genesis 32:26–28

★ *Find the meanings of Jacob's names in a Bible dictionary.*

6. Jacob: __heel catcher; supplanter__
7. Israel: __having power with God__

8. God changed Jacob's name because
    a. Jacob promised that he would never again deceive anyone.
    b. Jacob had changed so much that his old name no longer described him.
    c. Jacob now looked like a good man instead of a deceiver.

D. LEARNING MORE ABOUT THE BIBLE

The Birthright of the First-born Son

When a father died, his belongings were divided among his sons.

The first-born son in the family received twice as much as the other sons. He became the family leader after his father's death, and he took care of his mother and his unmarried sisters.

The younger sons in the family received half as much as the first-born. They often worked for him, and they had to obey him when he made important decisions.

After the children of Israel left Egypt, God said that every first-born son belonged to Him. The parents had to pay money to redeem (buy back) their first-born son. The price they paid to God to redeem their son was five shekels (Numbers 18:16).

Jacob's Family

Jacob had two wives, (1) _____Leah_____ and (2) _____Rachel_____, and two servant women, (3) _____Zilpah >>_____ and (4) _____Bilhah >>_____, who were the mothers of his children. Can you write the correct names in the blanks below? Study Genesis 35:23–26 and 30:20, 21 if necessary.

Zilpah and Bilhah, along with their children, could be transposed.

(1) __Leah__

(5) _Reuben_ (6) _Simeon_ (7) _Levi_ (8) _Judah_   (2) _Rachel_

(11) _Dinah_ (10) _Zebulun_ (9) _Issachar_ (13) _Benjamin_ (12) _Joseph_

(3) __Zilpah__   (4) __Bilhah__

(14) _Gad_   (15) _Asher_   (16) _Dan_   (17) _Naphtali_

Chapter Two Review

A. ORAL REVIEW

★ *Be sure you know the answers to these questions. Give as many answers as you can without looking back in your book.*

★ *In the first two sections, give a name for each description. If you need help, match with the lists on the right. To study for the test, cover the lists on the right.*

Who

1. Abram's father	Terah	Lot
2. Abram's nephew	Lot	Sarai
3. Abram's first wife	Sarai	Hagar
4. Ishmael's mother	Hagar	Terah
5. Wrestled until he received a blessing	Jacob	Esau
6. Despised his birthright	Esau	Laban
7. Jacob's first wife	Leah	Jacob
8. Jacob's favorite wife	Rachel	Rachel
9. Jacob's father-in-law	Laban	Leah

Where

10. Where Abram first lived	Ur of the Chaldees	Plain of Jordan
11. Where Abram went during a famine	Egypt	Egypt
12. Where Lot chose to live	Plain of Jordan	Ur of the Chaldees
13. Where Ishmael lived after he grew up	The wilderness	Haran
14. Where Rebekah first lived	Haran	Bethel
15. Where Jacob saw a vision of angels on a ladder	Bethel	The wilderness

★ *If you need help with the sections below, use the Bible reference or the lesson given in brackets.*

What >>

16. What is the starting point for A.M. dates? For B.C. and A.D. dates? [Lesson 6]
17. What can we use to find Bible verses that contain certain words? [Lesson 6]
18. What were the patriarchs' tents made of? [Lesson 7]
19. What did Sarah do when God said she would have a son? [Genesis 18:12]
20. What was Ishmael's skill when he grew up? [Genesis 21:20]
21. What did Jacob give to Esau for his birthright? [Genesis 25:34]

16. the Creation; the birth of Christ
17. a concordance
18. goat-hair cloth
19. She laughed.
20. He became an archer.
21. a bowl of pottage (and bread)

74   Chapter Two   The Patriarchs

Why >>

22. Why did Abram tell Pharaoh that Sarai was his sister? [Genesis 12:13]
23. Why did Lot choose to live near Sodom? [Genesis 13:10]
24. Why did Sarah want to send Hagar and Ishmael away? [Genesis 21:9, 10]
25. Why did Jacob flee to Haran? [Genesis 27:42, 43; Lesson 10]

How >>

26. About how many years has it been since the Creation? [Lesson 6]
27. How did God supply a sacrifice to take Isaac's place? [Genesis 22:13]

22. Abram was afraid Pharaoh would kill him and take Sarai.
23. Lot saw that it was well watered and had the best land.
24. Sarah saw Ishmael mocking Isaac.
25. Esau wanted to kill Jacob for stealing the blessing.
26. about 6,000 years
27. God provided a ram that was caught in a thicket.

B. WRITTEN REVIEW

★ *Write answers to these questions. If you need help, use the Bible reference or the lesson given in brackets.*

Where

1. Where was the LORD when Jacob saw his vision of angels on a ladder? [Genesis 28:13] ____
   above the ladder

What

2. What do the abbreviations A.M., B.C., and A.D. mean when used with dates? [Lesson 6]

   A.M. __in the year of the world__

   B.C. __before Christ__

   A.D. __in the year of our Lord__

3. What did Abraham do with his son that showed he had faith in God? [Hebrews 11:17–19] ___
   He prepared to offer him as a burnt sacrifice.

4. What did Rebekah do for Abraham's oldest servant? [Genesis 24:17–20] _____
   She gave water to him and his camels.

5. What trouble did the herdsmen of Gerar cause Isaac? [Genesis 26:20] _____
   They strove with Isaac's herdsmen for his wells.

6. What sorrows did Jacob reap after he cheated his brother and deceived his father? Give at least two specific answers. [Lesson 10] __(Any two) He had to run away from home to escape Esau's anger. Laban gave him Leah instead of Rachel. Laban changed his wages ten times. He feared meeting Esau again. His older sons sold Joseph and pretended that he was dead.

7. What is the meaning of *Jacob* and *Israel*? [Lesson 10]

Jacob: ___heel catcher; supplanter___

Israel: ___having power with God___

Why

8. Why did Abraham not want his servant to take Isaac back to Haran? (Give two reasons.) [Genesis 24:7; Lesson 9] ___Abraham's relatives at Haran, who worshiped idols, might have caused Isaac to forget the true God. Abraham did not want Isaac to forget that God had promised to give Canaan to Abraham's descendants.___

9. Why did God change Jacob's name? [Lesson 10] ___Jacob had changed so much that his old name no longer described him.___

How

10. How did God show Abraham what a great number of descendants he would have? Give more than one comparison if you can. [Lessons 7, 8] ___God showed Abraham the stars and told him that his descendants would also be too numerous to count. He compared Abraham's descendants to the dust of the earth and the sand upon the seashore.___

11. How did Rebekah know that her younger son would become greater than her older son? [Genesis 25:23] ___Before they were born, God told her that the elder would serve the younger.___

12. What four things did Jacob do to deceive his father into blessing him? [Genesis 27:14–27; Lesson 10] ___(Answers may vary somewhat.) Jacob put on Esau's clothes, wore goat skin on his hands and neck, took goat meat instead of venison, and told his father lies.___

Bible Outline

★ *Match these chapters with the events they record. The headings in your Bible may give you help if you need it.*

___c___ 13. Genesis 12–15   a. Ishmael is born; Isaac is promised.

___a___ 14. Genesis 16, 17   b. Jacob flees to Haran, marries wives, and has children.

___g___ 15. Genesis 18–20   c. Abram moves to Canaan; God promises him the land.

___e___ 16. Genesis 21–23   d. Isaac marries Rebekah; Jacob receives the birthright and

___d___ 17. Genesis 24–27   the blessing.

___b___ 18. Genesis 28–30   e. Isaac is born; Abraham is tested; Sarah dies.

___f___ 19. Genesis 31–36   f. Jacob returns to Canaan and meets Esau.

                                 g. Sodom is destroyed; Abram lives at Gerar.

CHAPTER THREE

God's Chosen
Family in Egypt

Who is like unto thee,
O LORD,
among the gods?
who is like thee,
glorious in holiness,
fearful in praises,
doing wonders?
Thou in thy mercy
hast led forth
the people which thou
hast redeemed:
thou hast guided them
in thy strength
unto thy holy
habitation.
(Exodus 15:11, 13)

TIME LINE—Chapter Three
The Israelites in Egypt

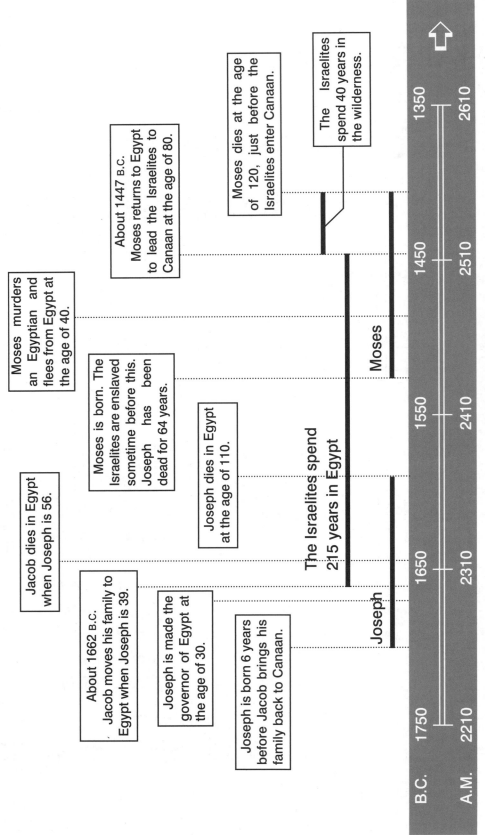

Jacob dies in Egypt when Joseph is 56.

Moses murders an Egyptian and flees from Egypt at the age of 40.

Moses is born. The Israelites are enslaved sometime before this. Joseph has been dead for 64 years.

About 1447 B.C. Moses returns to Egypt to lead the Israelites to Canaan at the age of 80.

Moses dies at the age of 120, just before the Israelites enter Canaan.

The Israelites spend 40 years in the wilderness.

Joseph dies in Egypt at the age of 110.

The Israelites spend 215 years in Egypt

About 1662 B.C. Jacob moves his family to Egypt when Joseph is 39.

Joseph is made the governor of Egypt at the age of 30.

Joseph is born 6 years before Jacob brings his family back to Canaan.

Moses

Joseph

| B.C. | 1750 | | 1650 | | 1550 | | 1450 | | 1350 |
| A.M. | 2210 | | 2310 | | 2410 | | 2510 | | 2610 |

NOTE: Exodus 12:40 and Galatians 3:17 refer to a 430-year period of sojourning. On this time line, the 215 years that Abraham, Isaac, and Jacob sojourned in Canaan are included in this 430-year period. Some time lines allot 430 years for Israel in Egypt and an additional 215 years for the patriarchs in Canaan.

79

Lesson 11. Geography of Bible Lands

So far in this course, you have studied some important events that took place from the Creation to the time of Jacob. You have seen how God chose a special family, and have learned about some people who were a part of it. In this lesson, you will study more about the lands where these people lived.

Most Bible events took place in the Middle East, an area between the Persian Gulf and Egypt. The Garden of Eden was probably somewhere in this region. After the Flood, Noah's descendants settled here first. For some reason, God has paid special attention to the Middle East.

Much of the Middle East has a very warm, dry climate. In Bible times, over half of it was desert. Some dry lands, such as Egypt and Mesopotamia, lay along large rivers that provided water for irrigation. Only a small part of the Middle East receives enough rainfall to raise crops without irrigation.

God gave His people the land of Canaan. He described it as a land flowing with milk and honey. Canaan could not be irrigated easily, but most of it usually received enough rain for crops to be grown. God had special reasons for wanting His people to live in Canaan, rather than in Egypt or Mesopotamia.

A. ANSWERS FROM THE BIBLE

Water—the Lifeblood of the Middle East

Many parts of the Middle East receive little rain. Farmers in these areas must irrigate their crops so that they will grow. Because of this, many of the early settlements in Bible lands were beside rivers or close to springs of water.

★ *For numbers 1–4 below, fill in the blanks from the references given. Then find the number of each exercise on Map 1, and write the name of the river on the blank beside it.*

Check the map work on Map 1

1. The **Nile River** flowed through Egypt. It flooded every year, and the Egyptians used the flood water to irrigate their farms. This river is often referred to in the Bible, but never by the name we use. Usually it is simply called the _____ river _____ (Genesis 41:1–3).

2. The _____ Jordan _____ **River** flowed through Canaan. This river was not used very much for irrigation, because it was too low in a valley. Lot decided to live on the _____ plain _____ beside this river (Genesis 13:11).

3. The **River** _____ Euphrates _____ flowed through Mesopotamia. In Genesis 15:18, God promised Abraham that He would give his seed all the land from the river of Egypt to this river. It was also referred to as the (<u>great</u>, long) river. (Underline the correct word.)

4. The **Tigris River** is east of the river described in number 3. In Daniel 10:4 it is referred to as "the _____ great _____ river, which is _____ Hiddekel _____." The city of Nineveh, where Jonah preached, was close to this river.

- The Nile River is not the same as the River of Egypt, which the Bible refers to a number of times. The River of Egypt was probably the stream now called *Wadi el-Arish*.
- The Jordan River is never referred to as the River of Jordan or the Jordan River in the Old Testament. The Old Testament writers simply refer to it as *Jordan*, often omitting even the article. They take for granted that the reader knows it is a river.

Lesson 11

Oral Review

(The numbers in brackets tell which lessons are being reviewed.)

1. Name the things God created on each day of Creation. [2] *First day*: light (also heaven and earth); *Second*: firmament; *Third*: dry land, seas, and plants; *Fourth*: sun, moon, and stars; *Fifth*: sea animals and birds; *Sixth*: land animals and man

2. Why did God save Noah and his family from the Flood? [4] **Noah found grace in God's eyes and obeyed all of God's commands.**

3. Why did Lot choose to live near Sodom? [7] **He liked the well-watered land.**

4. What did God compare Abraham's descendants to? [7, 8] **the dust of the earth, the stars of the heaven, the sand of the seashore**

5. What did Rebekah do for Abraham's oldest servant? [9] **She gave water to him and his camels.**

6. Who sold his birthright for a bowl of soup? [10] **Esau**

7. What did Jacob see in his vision at Bethel? [10] **He saw angels going up and down a ladder that reached to heaven, and the LORD standing above.**

8. Who was Jacob's father-in-law? [10] **Laban**

Deuteronomy 11:10–12

The land of Canaan did not have any large rivers like the Nile that could be used for irrigation. In these verses, Moses was telling the Israelites how their new land would be different from the land of Egypt, where they had been slaves.

5. Canaan was a land that the (a) _____LORD_____ took care of. It received its water from the (b) _____rain_____ of _____heaven_____.

According to these verses, how had the Israelites watered their crops and gardens in Egypt?

(c) __with their feet_____

_____

Deuteronomy 33:28

6. At certain times of the year, water was so scarce in Canaan that even the _____dew_____ of heaven was an important blessing from God. A few crops, such as grapes and figs, needed this form of moisture in order to ripen.

God wanted His people to depend on Him. In Egypt they had almost forgotten Him, but in Canaan they needed to depend on God's blessing for their needs. When they strayed from Him, He sometimes withheld the rain. This served to remind them that they needed God and helped to bring them back to Him.

Mountains, Seas, and Deserts of the Middle East

Travelers found it difficult to cross the mountains and deserts of Bible lands. Those traveling east or west through Canaan were hindered by the Mediterranean Sea to the west, a vast desert to the east, and a mountain range through the middle. For this reason, the main roads through Canaan ran north and south. These were part of the great routes that connected Egypt and Mesopotamia. Most travelers avoided the great barren deserts, even if that meant a much longer journey.

★ *Fill in the blanks, using the reference given with each exercise. You will find these exercise numbers on Map 1 too. Write the name of the mountain, sea, or desert on the blank after the number on the map.*   Check the map work on Map 1

7. On **Mount** _____Carmel_____ (1 Kings 18:19), Elijah called down fire from heaven in front of King Ahab.

8. **Mount** _____Hermon_____ (Deuteronomy 3:8) is the highest mountain in Canaan.

9. The kings of _____Arabia_____ (Jeremiah 25:24) lived in the **Eastern Desert**. It is sometimes called the Arabian Desert or the Syrian Desert, but the Bible does not call it by name.

10. The **Sea of** _____Galilee_____ (Matthew 4:18) is the world's lowest freshwater lake. It lies about 700 feet below sea level. In the Old Testament it is called the sea of Chinnereth.

11. The **Dead Sea**, lying 1,300 feet below sea level, is the lowest spot on earth. Sometimes it was called the _____salt_____ sea (Genesis 14:3).

• How did the Egyptians water their land with their feet? Sometimes they used foot-powered water pumps. They also used their feet to push aside the soil so that the water from the ditches could flow into their fields. This could also refer to carrying water for irrigating.

• See "Jordan Rift Valley" in *The Moody Atlas of Bible Lands*. This is the deepest rift on earth; the surface of the Dead Sea is 1,300 feet below sea level, and it is an additional 24,000 feet down to bedrock! By comparison, Death Valley in California is less than 300 feet below sea level.

In This Lesson

Main Points
• Most Bible events took place in the Middle East, an area between the Persian Gulf and Egypt.
• Since much of the Middle East is dry, settlements often developed near rivers or other sources of water. Well-known rivers in the Middle East include the Nile, the Jordan, the Euphrates, and the Tigris (Hiddekel).
• Canaan usually received enough rainfall for raising crops without irrigation.
• A few natural features of the Middle East are Mount Carmel, Mount Hermon, the Eastern Desert, the Sea of Galilee, and the Dead Sea.

• Haran, Shechem, and Bethel were important stops in Abram's journeys. He probably visited On, an Egyptian city, when he traveled to Egypt to escape a famine.
• Bible atlases provide maps and other information about Bible lands.

Objectives
• Students should be able to label the following features on a map of Bible lands:
  —The Nile, Jordan, Euphrates, and Tigris rivers
  —Mount Carmel and Mount Hermon
  —The Eastern Desert, the Sea of Galilee, and the Dead Sea
  —Haran, Shechem, and Bethel

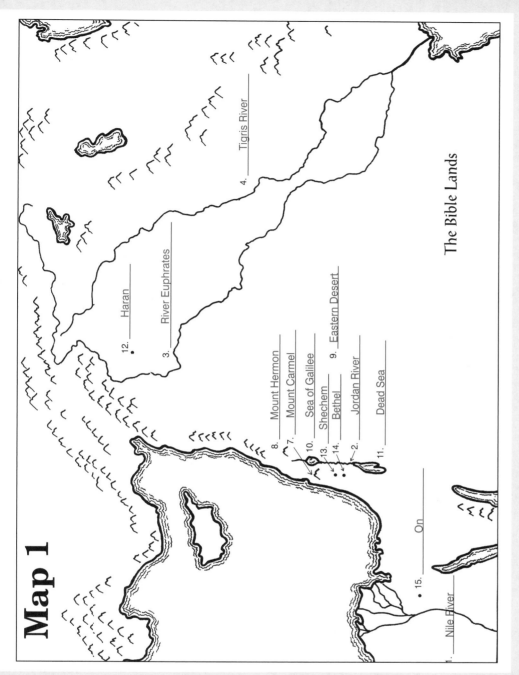

Map 1

The Bible Lands

Tigris River

4. _____

River Euphrates

Haran

12. •

3. _____

Mount Hermon

Mount Carmel

Sea of Galilee

Shechem

Bethel

Eastern Desert

Jordan River

Dead Sea

8. _____

7.

10.

13.

14.

9. _____

2. _____

11. _____

On

15. •

Nile River

- Students should be able to find simple facts by using a map.

Truths to Instill

- God prepared and chose a land "flowing with milk and honey" for His people. As long as they served Him, He blessed their land with rain. When they turned from Him, He sometimes used famine to bring them back.

Cities of the Middle East

Cities grow for a number of reasons. People of Bible times often lived in cities for protection. They built cities near good sources of water, like a river, or close to an important place, such as a harbor or a mine. Sometimes they built walled cities on the borders of their countries to help keep out enemies.

Not everyone lived in cities. As you saw in Chapter 2, God called Abraham to leave the cities and live as a wandering shepherd in the land of Canaan.

★   *Label the following cities on Map 1 beside the correct numbers.*   Check the labels on Map 1.

12. **Haran**. Abram started for Canaan from this city after the death of his father, Terah. When Jacob fled from Esau, he came here and lived with his uncle Laban for twenty years.

13. **Shechem**. Here God first promised the land of Canaan to Abram. Later, Jacob lived here for some years after returning from Haran.

14. **Bethel**. Jacob had his first encounter with God here, and later he brought his whole family back to this place. Abram also built an altar here when he first entered Canaan.

15. **On**. Joseph's father-in-law was the priest of this Egyptian city. It is probably where Abram went when he fled to Egypt to escape a famine. Today this city is called Heliopolis.

★   *Use a colored pencil to mark Abram's journeys from Haran to On, in Egypt. Abram traveled to each city in the order that they are given in numbers 12–15 above.*
The colored line should follow the cities in the order they are given in numbers 12–15.
A great ancient city named Ur was located near the place where the Euphrates and Tigris rivers meet. Most people believe that this city was the Ur of the Chaldees where Abram had lived. However, some people think that Ur of the Chaldees was another Ur, located northeast of Haran.

- See the discussion in *The Moody Atlas of Bible Lands*. Note, however, that the matter is still open to question. A definite location for a second Ur has not been established.

Rainfall in Bible Lands

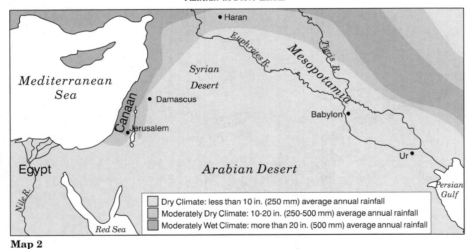

Map 2

B. BIBLE STUDY BOOKS

Bible Atlases—Maps for Bible Study

The Bible tells us what happened long ago. It tells us when and how things happened. But to understand the Bible well, we sometimes need to know more about where things happened. For example, the Bible speaks of the Israelites living in Goshen, of Solomon being visited by the queen of Sheba, and of Nehemiah serving the king of Persia at Shushan. Where were Goshen, Sheba, and Shushan? Where was Jericho, where the walls fell down; and where was Bethel, where Jacob dreamed about angels on a ladder? What kinds of people lived in these places? You may not be able to answer these questions now, but by studying maps of Bible lands, you can find the answers one by one.

This Bible workbook has some maps for you to use while studying this course. Many Bibles have a few maps in the back. Additional maps can be found in Bible atlases. Your school library may have one of these map books.

Some maps give information about the physical features of the land. They show rivers and mountains. Some maps show the population, languages, or religions of an area. Still other maps show where certain things happened and how cities, countries, and roads changed over the years.

★ *Map 3, on the following page, shows the southern part of Canaan. Use it to do these exercises.*

1. The large sea west of Canaan is the _____Mediterranean_____ Sea. (In early Bible times, it was called the Great Sea.)

2. The Dead Sea is (north, south, <u>east,</u> west) of the Mediterranean Sea.

3. The Jordan River flows south into the _____Dead_____ Sea.

4. Abraham was living at Beersheba when God told him to offer his son as a sacrifice. He took Isaac north to _____Mount_____ _____Moriah_____, which is located between Bethlehem and Bethel. Many years later, Solomon built a temple on this mountain.

5. Both Abraham and Isaac visited _____Gerar_____, a Philistine city not far from the Mediterranean Sea.

6. Abraham died and was buried near _____Hebron_____, a city southwest of Bethlehem and northeast of Beersheba.

7. The city of _____Bethel_____ was between Shechem and Mount Moriah. Here Jacob dreamed of a ladder whose top reached to heaven.

8. Jacob wrestled with a heavenly messenger at _____Penuel_____, just before he crossed the Jabbok River.

9. Jacob's wife Rachel was buried near _____Bethlehem_____, a city just south of Mount Moriah.

10. While Jacob lived at Hebron, he sent his son Joseph to _____Shechem_____, a city between the Jabbok River and the Mediterranean Sea. From there, Joseph traveled (<u>north,</u> east) to Dothan, where his brothers sold him as a slave.

• This section provides additional practice in using a map, and it introduces Bible atlases. The concept and use of map grids is taught in Lesson 21.

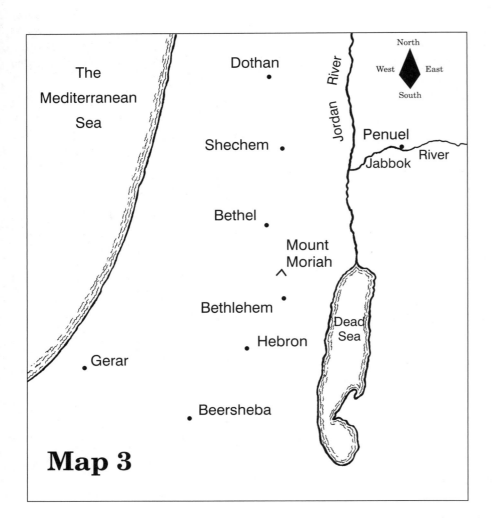

Map 3

85

Lesson 12. Joseph Endures Trials

Of all his sons, Jacob loved Joseph the best. Joseph was the oldest son of Rachel, Jacob's favorite wife. To show his love for Joseph, Jacob gave him a special coat.

However, being the best-loved son also brought trials to Joseph. His brothers became jealous when they saw that their father loved him more than them. They hated Joseph when he told Jacob about their evil deeds. When they had a chance, they sold him as a slave.

Being a slave was far different from being a favorite son. Slaves had hard lives and worked without being paid. They had to do whatever their masters told them to do. Slaves had no rights, and even when their owners mistreated them, nobody helped them.

Joseph could have become bitter toward his brothers, toward the Egyptians, and toward God. Instead, he did his best for his master, Potiphar. When Potiphar saw that the LORD was with Joseph, he placed him in charge of his whole house. But Potiphar's wife was a wicked woman who tried to persuade Joseph to sin. When he refused, she lied about him to Potiphar, and Joseph was cast into prison.

A prisoner's life was even worse than a slave's. Joseph lived in prison for years, with no one to help him get out. But God had great plans for Joseph. In one day, Pharaoh promoted Joseph from being a slave in prison to being the governor of Egypt!

A. ANSWERS FROM THE BIBLE

Joseph—the Favorite Son

Genesis 37:1–4, 11

1. What special reason did the sons of Bilhah and Zilpah have for hating Joseph?
   a. Joseph told his father about the bad things that they did.
   b. Joseph told his father lies about them.
   c. Joseph refused to help them with the work.

2. What is the main reason given in these verses for the hatred that Joseph's brothers had for him?   Jacob loved Joseph more than he loved his other sons.

3. Joseph had several strange dreams while he was a teenager. He dreamed that all his brothers and his father and mother would someday bow down to him. Verses 8 and 11 tell us that Joseph's brothers _____hated_____ him and _____envied_____ him when he told them his dreams.

Lesson 12

Oral Review

1. How did God create light and many other things? [2] **He said, "Let there be . . ."**
2. What lie did Satan tell Eve? [3] **He said that she would not die if she ate the forbidden fruit.**
3. Why was God pleased with Abel's sacrifice and not Cain's? [3] **Abel showed his faith in God by the more excellent sacrifice he offered.**
4. Why did men start to build the Tower of Babel? [5] **to make a name for themselves, and to keep from being scattered abroad**
5. What can we use to find the reference for a Bible verse? [6] **a concordance**
6. What two things did God tell Rebekah about her sons before they were born? [9] **They would become two manner of people, and the elder would serve the younger.**
7. Why did God change Jacob's name to Israel? [10] **Jacob had changed so much that his old name no longer described him.**
8. What well-known river flows through Canaan? [11] **the Jordan River**

Genesis 37:12–36

Joseph's brothers hated him even more after they heard his dreams. One day while they were caring for the flock far from home, Jacob sent Joseph to see how they were doing.

4. What did Joseph's brothers plan to do with him when they saw him coming? _____

   They planned to kill him and say that a wild beast had eaten him.

5. Verse 20 gives us a hint as to why they planned to do this. Choose the best reason.
   a. They thought that they would get into trouble for moving the flock without Jacob's per-mission.
   b. They were afraid that his dreams might come true.
   c. They wanted to steal his money.

6. (a) _____Reuben_____ saved Joseph's life by persuading his brothers to
   (b) _____cast_____ Joseph into a (c) _____pit_____. He planned to come
   back later and (d) _____deliver_____ Joseph to his father. However, before he could do
   this, a band of (e) _____Ishmeelites_____ passed by. (f) _____Judah_____ suggested
              (Midianites, merchantmen)
   that they should (g) _____sell_____ Joseph to them instead of killing him.

7. Joseph's brothers knew they had done wrong. How did they deceive their father and keep
   him from learning the truth? _____

   Joseph's brothers dipped his coat in blood and told Jacob they had found it.

   _____.

Jacob thought a wild animal must have killed Joseph. He mourned for his son many days. Joseph's brothers tried to comfort their father, but they could not. They had deceived him, just as Jacob had deceived his father.

Joseph—the Slave

Genesis 39:20–23

Meanwhile, the merchants sold Joseph as a slave to an Egyptian officer named Potiphar. Potiphar was very pleased with Joseph. Because he saw that God was with Joseph, he placed him in charge of everything that he had. But Potiphar's wife lied about Joseph to Potiphar, and he put Joseph into prison. Joseph lived there for a number of years.

8. Joseph had served his father faithfully. Then he had done his best for Potiphar. Now he was in prison, even though he had done nothing wrong. While he was in prison, Joseph
   a. sat in his cell, wondering why God was so unfair to him.
   b. found ways to serve God by helping others around him.
   c. persuaded the keeper of the prison to give him special privileges.

Genesis 41:14–16

While he was in prison, Joseph met two servants of Pharaoh, the ruler of Egypt. One night these servants, a butler and a baker, each had a dream. God showed Joseph what these dreams meant. Two years later, Pharaoh also had a dream. The butler remembered Joseph and told Pharaoh how Joseph had interpreted his and the baker's dreams.

In This Lesson

Scope: Genesis 37–41

Main Events
- Joseph's brothers sell him into Egypt.
- Joseph works as a slave for Potiphar until Potiphar puts him into prison.
- God helps Joseph interpret Pharaoh's dream, and Joseph becomes the ruler of Egypt.

Objectives
- Students should know
  —what happened to Joseph when he went to see his brothers. (They cast him into a pit, and later sold him to Ishmeelites.)
  —who bought Joseph in Egypt, and why Joseph's master put him into prison. (Potiphar; because Potiphar's wife lied about Joseph)
  —whose dreams Joseph interpreted. (the butler's, the baker's, and Pharaoh's)
  —how Joseph's life became a blessing to many. (He stored up food that people could buy during the seven years of famine.)

Truths to Instill
- From his youth, Joseph left an outstanding example of faithfulness. He was faithful even when no one seemed to notice and when things seemed to get worse instead of better.

9. Before Joseph went in to Pharaoh, he _____shaved_____ himself and changed his _____raiment_____.

10. Joseph did not want Pharaoh to think that he had special abilities of his own. He told Pharaoh that _____God_____ would tell them what the dream meant.

Genesis 41:25–30

In his dream, Pharaoh saw seven fat cows (kine) and seven thin cows come out of the river. While he watched, the thin cows ate the fat cows. Then he saw seven thin ears of grain (corn) eat seven good ears of grain.

11. Pharaoh's dream meant that there would be seven years of _____plenty_____, followed by seven years of _____famine_____.

Joseph—the Ruler of Egypt

Genesis 41:37–41, 46–49

After Joseph explained the meaning of the dream, he gave Pharaoh some good advice. He told him to appoint someone to store food during the good years so that there would be food for the bad years. Pharaoh liked Joseph's plan.

12. Pharaoh saw that the _____Spirit_____ of _____God_____ was in Joseph.

13. He also realized that no one else was so _____discreet_____ and _____wise_____ as Joseph.

14. Pharaoh decided to appoint Joseph governor over all the land of _____Egypt_____.

15. For seven years, Joseph gathered _____corn (grain)_____, until he left numbering because it was _____without_____ _____number_____.

Genesis 41:56, 57

16. After the seven good years were ended, the years of famine began. People were hungry in many countries, but there was food in Egypt because Joseph had done his work well. Joseph's faithfulness was a blessing to people from other countries because they could buy _____corn (grain)_____ in _____Egypt_____.

Where Is It Found?

17. In which chapter of Genesis do we find the story of

a. Joseph being sold by his brothers? _____Genesis 37_____

b. Pharaoh's dream? _____Genesis 41_____

- Faithfulness builds confidence. Joseph's faithfulness caused a number of people to have confidence in him.
  —His father (He sent him to check on his brothers.)
  —Potiphar (He made him overseer of all that he had.)
  —The keeper of the prison (He made him director of the prison.)
  —Pharaoh (He made him ruler over all the land of Egypt.)

- Faithfulness is a blessing to others as well. Many people were blessed through Joseph's faithfulness.
  —Potiphar's house prospered.
  —The prisoners prospered.
  —The country of Egypt had food to eat during the seven years of famine.
  —Joseph's family was saved from starvation.

B. BIBLE WORD STUDY

★ *Match these definitions with the Bible words on the right. Read the verses given or use a dictionary if you need help. All references are from Genesis.*

__d__	1. A valley (37:14)	a. conspire
__a__	2. To plan secretly to do something bad (37:18)	b. discreet
__c__	3. A dark underground cell for prisoners (41:14)	c. dungeon
__g__	4. To explain the meaning of (41:15)	d. vale
__f__	5. Cows (41:26)	e. corn
__b__	6. Careful in speech and action (41:33)	f. kine
__e__	7. Wheat or other grain (41:35)	g. interpret

C. THINKING ABOUT BIBLE TRUTHS

Genesis 39:1–6

What kind of person was Joseph? Was he a spoiled child who made trouble for himself, or was he a young person who wanted to do what was right? We can learn much about a person by noticing how he acts when things go against him. Did Joseph act like a spoiled child at Potiphar's house? Did he pout when he was put in prison for no reason? Think about this as you answer the following questions.

1. What were two things Potiphar saw about Joseph that made him different from other slaves?

   a. __He saw that the LORD was with Joseph.__

   b. __He saw that the LORD made all that Joseph did to prosper.__

2. Potiphar was so pleased with Joseph's abilities and character that he made him ____overseer____ over his ____house____ and over ____all____ that he owned.

3. You have already read Genesis 39:20–23. In these verses, find the reason that the keeper of the prison placed Joseph over all the other prisoners. _____
   __The LORD gave Joseph favor in the prison keeper's sight.__

4. As you completed this lesson, you may have noticed that the Bible often says that the LORD was with Joseph. Give at least one reason why God was with Joseph in Egypt. __(Any one)__
   __Joseph was faithful to God. God had a special work for him to do. God knew that__
   Joseph had been treated wrong and that he was trying to do right. (Other answers may also be correct; be sure they are based on careful thinking.)

5. Choose the paragraph that best describes Joseph.

   (a.) **Joseph wanted to serve God.** Sometimes evil men, such as his brothers, did not like this; but at other times, people appreciated him for it. Even as a slave in Egypt, Joseph did what he knew God wanted him to do. No matter what happened to him or where he went, he tried to help others. God blessed him for his attitude.

   b. **Joseph was a spoiled child.** He knew that he was his father's favorite son. He took advantage of this to get his brothers into trouble whenever he could. When his brothers grew tired of his tattling and sold him as a slave, he managed to work his way into Potiphar's favor. He did the same to the prison keeper, and finally managed to gain Pharaoh's favor by guessing the meaning of his dream.

Psalm 105:17–22

God had a purpose in what happened to Joseph. It was wrong for Joseph's brothers to sell him, yet God brought good out of their evil deed. God never allows something to happen to us that is not for our good in some way. Like Joseph, we should keep serving God even when everything seems to be going wrong.

6. God used the trials that Joseph faced to help him become a better person. God could use Joseph as a ruler in Egypt because

   a. God saw that he had many special talents.

   b. God saw that he was getting homesick for his family.

   (c.) God saw that he was faithful, no matter what happened to him.

Father, in my life's young morning, may Thy Word direct my way;
  Let me heed each gracious warning, lest my feet should go astray;
Make me willing, make me willing, all its precepts to obey;
  Let me heed each gracious warning, lest my feet should go astray.

Father, gentle is Thy teaching; be a docile spirit mine;
  Ev'ry day thy grace beseeching, let Thy loving kindness shine
Always on me, always on me, and my heart be wholly thine.
  Ev'ry day thy grace beseeching, let Thy loving kindness shine.

Father, let me never covet things of vanity and pride;
  Teach me truth, and may I love it better than all else beside.
Blessed Bible, blessed Bible! May it be my heavenward guide.
  Teach me truth, and may I love it better than all else beside.

D. LEARNING MORE ABOUT THE BIBLE

How Old Was Joseph?

★ *By studying the Bible, we can tell how old Joseph was at various times in his life. Complete the chart below by writing Joseph's age and Jacob's age after each event.*

Event	Joseph's Age	Jacob's Age
Joseph was born at Padan-aram.	0	91
Six years later, Joseph moved to Canaan when Jacob returned to his homeland (Genesis 30:25, 26; 31:41).	6	97
Eleven years later, Joseph fed the flocks with his brothers (Genesis 37:2).	17	108
Thirteen years later, Joseph stood before Pharaoh, the king of Egypt (Genesis 41:46).	30	121
Nine years later, Joseph's father and brothers came to live in Egypt (Genesis 45:6; 47:8, 9).	39	130
Seventeen years later, Jacob died (Genesis 47:28).	56	147
Fifty-four years later, Joseph died (Genesis 50:26).	110	

LEMON OIL GRASS AND SPIKENARD

The ancient Egyptians put fragrant grasses in the tombs of their dead. One grass they used was lemon oil grass. This tropical perennial grows six feet tall. When its leaves are crushed, they give a lemon-scented oil used in flavorings. When dried, they make a fragrant tea.

Spikenard is a much smaller grassy plant. It grows in the Himalaya Mountains of northern India and Nepal. When dried, it is a fuzzy bundle about the size of a man's little finger. The fragrant oil pressed out of these dried plants was extremely scarce and extremely expensive in Bible times.

Who sprinkled Jesus' feet with oil of spikenard? (John 12:3).

Slavery in Old Testament Times

Buying and selling people as slaves was common in Old Testament times. Slaves were bought and sold like cattle, and often their lives were miserable. Some slaves were sold away from their families, and sometimes even husbands and wives were separated.

Sometimes Abraham's descendants, the Hebrews, were slaves. At other times, they owned slaves themselves. When God gave His laws to the Hebrews, He included strict commands on how they were to treat their slaves.

How Could People Become Slaves Under the Old Testament Law?

A man could sell himself to pay a debt (Leviticus 25:39–49).

A man could (1) ___sell___ his children to pay a debt (Exodus 21:7).

A child could be (2) ___born___ as a slave (Exodus 21:4).

Captives taken in war usually became slaves.

How Could People Be Freed From Slavery Under the Old Testament Law?

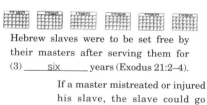

Hebrew slaves were to be set free by their masters after serving them for (3) ___six___ years (Exodus 21:2–4).

If a master mistreated or injured his slave, the slave could go (4) ___free___ (Exodus 21:26).

The relatives or friends of a slave could buy him out of slavery (Leviticus 25:48).

- While discussing this with your class, you could point out that God gave laws to protect slaves and to provide a way for them to become free. In the New Testament, the law of love instructs us to do to others as we would have them do to us.

92

Lesson 13. Joseph Returns Good for Evil

As the governor of Egypt, Joseph was a powerful man. Everyone except Pharaoh bowed to him in respect. When he gave an order, servants hurried to obey. Joseph could have demanded many things for his own pleasure. But he knew that God had not made him governor so that he could enjoy himself. Joseph needed to plan wisely and work hard, or else thousands of people would starve in the coming years of famine.

Many countries besides Egypt had famine during those seven years, but only Joseph and the Egyptians had enough food. When people in other lands heard that there was food in Egypt, they traveled there to buy grain. Joseph had to decide who could buy grain and how much they could have.

One day, Joseph saw his brothers walk into his court! Now what would Joseph do? Should he punish his brothers for the way they had treated him? Or should he forgive them and welcome them? He decided to test them and see what kind of men they were before he told them who he was.

How did Joseph test his brothers? Did they pass the tests? Had they become better men since they had sold him? You will find answers to these questions as you study this lesson.

A. ANSWERS FROM THE BIBLE

Joseph's Brothers Visit Egypt

Genesis 42:1–9

Twenty-two years had passed since Joseph's brothers had sold him into Egypt. After almost two years of famine, Jacob and his family needed food. Jacob sent ten of his sons down to Egypt.

1. Why did Jacob keep Benjamin at home? _____

   Jacob was afraid something bad would happen to Benjamin. _____

   _____.

2. Which of the following dreams did Joseph remember when he saw his brothers?
   a. The baker's and the butler's dreams that he had interpreted.
   (b.) His dreams about his brothers bowing down to him.
   c. Pharaoh's dream about seven good years and seven bad years.

3. Joseph accused his brothers of being _____ spies _____.

   Joseph put his brothers into prison for three days before talking to them again. There they experienced a little of what he had suffered as a prisoner. They did not know whether they would ever be free again.

Genesis 42:18–24

4. After Joseph released his brothers from prison, he told them to bring their _____ youngest _____ _____ brother _____ to Egypt.

Lesson 13

Oral Review

1. What did Timothy know as a child? [1] **the Scriptures**
2. How did Adam and Eve feel after they disobeyed God? Why? [3] **afraid, guilty; They knew that they had done wrong.**
3. How did Jacob deceive his father into blessing him? [10] **He put on Esau's clothes. He wore goatskin on his hands and neck. He took goat meat instead of venison. He told his father lies.**
4. What river flows through Egypt? [11] **the Nile River**
5. Which sea in Canaan is the lowest spot on earth? [11] **the Dead Sea**
6. What was the meaning of Pharaoh's dream about seven fat cows and seven thin cows? [12] **Egypt would have seven years of plenty, followed by seven years of famine.**
7. What did Joseph's brothers do to him when he came to see them? [12] **They cast him into a pit and later sold him to some Ishmeelites.**
8. What does the word *discreet* mean? [12] **careful in speech and action**

Lesson 13. Joseph Returns Good for Evil   **93**

5. Joseph's brothers felt that these bad things were happening to them because of what they had done to Joseph. This proves that

  (a.) they still felt guilty about selling Joseph.

  b. they were still angry with Joseph.

  c. they already knew who Joseph was, but they did not want him to recognize them.

6. Joseph bound _____Simeon_____ and put him into prison until his other brothers brought Benjamin.

Genesis 42:38; 43:1–14

Jacob was distressed when his sons returned from Egypt and told him what the ruler of Egypt had said.

7. What reason did Jacob give in verse 38 for not allowing Benjamin to go along to Egypt? ___ He said that he would die of sorrow if something bad happened to Benjamin. _____

  _____ .

8. Why did Jacob have to change his mind?   The famine was not over, and Jacob's family had eaten all the grain that had been bought in Egypt. _____ .

9. Jacob's son _____Judah_____ promised to bring Benjamin back to his father.

Joseph's Brothers Visit Egypt Again

Genesis 44:1, 2, 12–18; 30–34

When Jacob's sons arrived with Benjamin, they were surprised to receive a courteous welcome from the ruler of Egypt. He released Simeon from prison and even invited them to eat dinner at his house! Everything went smoothly until they were on the way home.

10. Before his brothers left Egypt, Joseph told his steward to put every man's _____money_____ in his _sack (sack's mouth)_ .

11. Which sentence explains why Joseph told the steward to put his silver cup into Benjamin's sack?

  a. Joseph wanted to show his brothers how it felt to be in trouble.

  (b.) Joseph was testing his brothers to see if they cared more about Benjamin and their father than they had cared about him.

  c. Joseph wanted to give Benjamin a valuable treasure from Egypt.

12. How did Judah prove that he and his brothers had changed since they had sold Joseph?

  a. He offered to die for his father.

  b. He offered to pay double money for the grain.

  (c.) He begged Joseph to keep him as a servant instead of Benjamin.

Joseph Makes Himself Known

Genesis 45:1–7, 13–15; 25–28

Imagine how shocked the brothers must have been to learn that the governor of Egypt was Joseph! They were terrified at the thought. What would their brother do to them now?

In This Lesson

Scope: Genesis 42–45

Main Events

- Joseph tests his brothers.
- Joseph shows his brothers that he has forgiven them.
- Joseph takes care of his father and his brothers.

Objectives

- Students should know

  —how Joseph tested his brothers. (See Part A, numbers 3–6, 10–12.)

  —how Joseph's dreams came true. (Because of the famine, his brothers came to Egypt to buy food. They bowed to the ruler, unaware that it was Joseph.)

  —why Jacob did not want Benjamin to go to Egypt. (He said that he would die of sorrow if something bad happened to Benjamin.)

  —how Joseph brought Jacob and his family to Egypt. (Joseph sent wagons to carry them.)

Truths to Instill

- Joseph set a shining example of forgiveness. When he tested his brothers, it was not to see whether he should forgive them. He had already done so; otherwise he would have tried to punish them. His testing was to see whether they were trustworthy.

94 Chapter Three God's Chosen Family in Egypt

★ *Write* true *or* false. *If a statement is false, rewrite it to make it true. The first one is done for you.* In the rewritten sentences for numbers 13–17, the corrections are in italics. The pupil's sentences may vary somewhat.

_____*False*_____ 13. Joseph's servants were with him when he made himself known to his

brothers. *Joseph was alone with his brothers when he made himself known to them.*

_____false_____ 14. Joseph scolded his brothers for selling him into Egypt. _____

Joseph *was ready to forgive* his brothers for selling him into Egypt. _____

_____true_____ 15. Joseph showed his concern for his father by asking about him. _____

(*or* false; Joseph showed his concern for his father *by bringing him to Egypt.*)

_____true_____ 16. The LORD used the brothers' evil deeds for a good purpose. _____

_____

_____true_____ 17. Joseph showed his love for his brothers by kissing them and weeping. _____

_____

_____false_____ 18. Jacob sent wagons to carry Joseph and his family back to Canaan. _____

Joseph sent wagons to carry *Jacob* and his family *down to Egypt.* _____

Where Is It Found?

19. Which chapter of Genesis tells about Joseph making himself known to his brothers?

_____Genesis 45_____

B. BIBLE WORD STUDY

★ *Write a word from the verse given to fit each definition. All references are from Genesis.*

_____peradventure_____ 1. Perhaps; maybe (42:4)

_____verified_____ 2. Proven true; confirmed (42:20)

_____sore_____ 3. Severe; intense (43:1)

_____ill_____ 4. Badly; unkindly (43:6)

_____surety_____ 5. A guarantee against loss or damage (43:9)

_____bereaved_____ 6. Made sorrowful by the loss of a loved one (43:14)

C. THINKING ABOUT BIBLE TRUTHS

Joseph is a good example for us in many ways. In the last lesson, you saw that he was faithful when things went against him. In this lesson, you learned that he was also faithful when he could have taken revenge on those who had wronged him.

Ephesians 4:32
Joseph lived long before this verse was written, yet he did what it tells us to do.

- People who have done wrong should not be surprised if others no longer trust them. They need to prove themselves first. Even children sometimes need to learn this.

1. When his brothers learned that the governor of Egypt was Joseph, they had good reason to be afraid. Selling their brother had been a terrible crime. Now he had the power and the right to punish them severely, or even kill them. What did Joseph do instead? _____

    Joseph was kind to his brothers. He forgave them instead of punishing them as they deserved.

Matthew 6:14, 15

2. These verses follow the Lord's Prayer. What did Jesus say that His disciples should do to those who mistreat them? _____

    Jesus told His disciples to forgive those who mistreated them.

When you read the verses in the first part of this lesson, it might have seemed that Joseph was returning evil for evil to his brothers. However, if you have thought carefully about what he did, you know that Joseph was testing his brothers and helping them to see what a great wrong they had done. He was willing to forgive them long before they asked for forgiveness.

Proverbs 20:11

This verse gives a clue to another reason why Joseph tested his brothers before he told them who he was. When his brothers were younger, they had earned a bad reputation. Now Joseph wanted to see if they had changed. They needed to prove themselves before he could trust them again.

3. Joseph could not trust his brothers when they first came to Egypt. What lesson can we learn from this?
    a. We should always trust everyone, even those who have been unfaithful in the past. We can be sure that they will not want to do wrong again.
    b. As we grow older, people no longer think about what we did when we were young.
    c. If we become known for doing wrong, people will stop trusting us. We will need to prove that we have changed before they will have confidence in us again.

Many people feel that Joseph was a type of Jesus. This means they believe that Joseph was like Jesus in many ways.

★ *For each pair of verses, write one way that Joseph was like Jesus.*

4. Genesis 37:28; Matthew 26:14–16   Joseph was sold for silver.

5. Genesis 41:41–43; Philippians 2:9, 10   Joseph was given a high place of authority, and men were commanded to bow before him.

6. Genesis 50:17–21; Luke 23:34 _____

    Joseph forgave those who had treated him cruelly.

D. LEARNING MORE ABOUT THE BIBLE

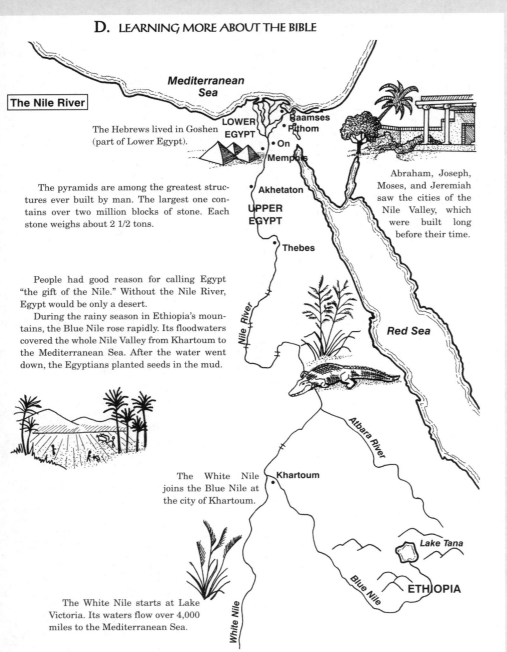

The Nile River

The Hebrews lived in Goshen (part of Lower Egypt).

The pyramids are among the greatest structures ever built by man. The largest one contains over two million blocks of stone. Each stone weighs about 2 1/2 tons.

People had good reason for calling Egypt "the gift of the Nile." Without the Nile River, Egypt would be only a desert.

During the rainy season in Ethiopia's mountains, the Blue Nile rose rapidly. Its floodwaters covered the whole Nile Valley from Khartoum to the Mediterranean Sea. After the water went down, the Egyptians planted seeds in the mud.

Abraham, Joseph, Moses, and Jeremiah saw the cities of the Nile Valley, which were built long before their time.

The White Nile joins the Blue Nile at the city of Khartoum.

The White Nile starts at Lake Victoria. Its waters flow over 4,000 miles to the Mediterranean Sea.

Mediterranean Sea

LOWER EGYPT

Raamses
Pithom
On
Memphis
Akhetaton

UPPER EGYPT

Thebes

Nile River

Red Sea

Atbara River

Khartoum

Lake Tana

Blue Nile

ETHIOPIA

White Nile

1. Year after year, the Egyptians depended on the Nile to flood their lands and provide a bountiful harvest. But for seven years, the Nile failed to rise. When was this? (See Genesis 41:53, 54.) __during the seven years of famine (dearth)__

2. Some Egyptians pumped water out of the Nile with pumps driven by their feet. In this way they watered their crops on the flat land near the Nile River. According to Deuteronomy 11:10, 11, the Israelites would not do this in the land of Canaan. Give at least one reason why. __The LORD would send "water of the rain of heaven." (Also, Canaan was a land of hills and valleys that would be difficult to irrigate.)__

3. A water plant called papyrus grew along the Nile.

   a. What is this plant called in Isaiah 19:7? __paper reed__

   b. Look up papyrus in a Bible dictionary to see why it was also known by the name used in Isaiah 19:7. __Papyrus was used to make paper.__

   c. Moses' mother hid him in an ark made of papyrus or a similar plant. What is this plant called in Exodus 2:3? __bulrushes (flags)__

The Corn and Bread of Egypt

The "corn" of Egypt was not the same grain that North Americans call corn. Most likely it was wheat, but it could have been barley, oats, rye, or some other grain.

As far as we know, the Egyptians were the first people to use yeast to make light, fluffy bread. They may have also been the first ones to bake bread in ovens. Bread, made in different ways from a variety of grains, has been an important food for man since the world began (Genesis 3:19).

Discuss this with the students.

98

Lesson 14. God's Chosen People Suffer Bondage

Jacob was very happy that he would see Joseph again before he died, but he was troubled about moving to Egypt. During a previous famine, God had told his father, Isaac, not to go there. However, this time God told Jacob not to fear going. He promised to be with him and to bring his family back to Canaan after they had become a great nation.

Jacob and his family settled in the land of Goshen. There, on the fertile delta of the Nile River, they lived safely and comfortably for many years.

Goshen was a pleasant land, but God did not want the Israelites to always live there. He allowed a new pharaoh to make slaves of the Israelites and oppress them severely.

This pharaoh forced them to work in his fields, to make bricks in the hot sun, and to build cities for him. He even gave orders that their baby boys must be destroyed. But God spoiled Pharaoh's plan, and the Israelites greatly increased in number.

The Israelites no longer enjoyed living in Goshen. They cried to God for deliverance from their hard bondage. God heard their cries and prepared a man named Moses to lead them back to the Promised Land.

God allowed hard times to come to the Israelites so that they would be ready to move to Canaan. Sometimes God allows things to happen that men cannot understand until many years later. But these things are always for His children's good.

A. ANSWERS FROM THE BIBLE

A New Pharaoh

Genesis 47:27, 28

Jacob's family were called the *Israelites*, or simply *Israel*, after the new name that God had given Jacob.

1. Where in Egypt did the Israelites live? __in the country of Goshen__

_____

Exodus 1:7–14, 22

No one knows for sure how long it was until the Egyptians forgot Joseph, or what else happened between Joseph's death and Moses' birth. Rulers from many different families governed Egypt during ancient times. Sometimes Egypt was divided and several pharaohs reigned at once. Foreign invaders even ruled part of Egypt for a while. With so much turmoil in their nation, it is no wonder that the Egyptians forgot Joseph.

2. Why did the new pharaoh of Egypt fear the Israelites? _____
   __The Israelites were increasing greatly, and Pharaoh was afraid they would rise up__
   __against the Egyptians.__

3. At first, how did he plan to weaken and control the Israelites? _____
   __Pharaoh made the Israelites work very hard.__

4. Instead of being weakened, the Israelites _____multiplied_____ and _____grew_____.

Lesson 14

Oral Review

1. What did God compare Abraham's descendants to? [7, 8] **the dust of the earth, the stars of the heaven, the sand of the seashore**
2. Why did Sarah want to send Hagar and Ishmael away? [9] **Sarah saw Ishmael mocking Isaac.**
3. What large sea lies west of Canaan? [11] **the Mediterranean Sea**
4. Why did Joseph's brothers hate him? [12] **They were jealous because their father loved Joseph better than the rest of them. (They also hated him because of his dreams, his**

special coat, and the evil report of them that he gave to their father.)
5. How did Joseph become a blessing to many people? [12] **He stored up food that people could buy during the seven years of famine.**
6. Why did Jacob refuse to let Benjamin go to Egypt until his family needed food very badly? [13] **He was afraid that something bad would happen to Benjamin.**
7. How could Joseph tell that his brothers' hearts had changed? [13] **by their love and concern for Benjamin**
8. How did Joseph show that he had forgiven his brothers? [13] **He treated them kindly and took care of them.**

Next Pharaoh told the nurses to kill all the baby boys born to Israelite mothers. But the nurses feared God and disobeyed Pharaoh's evil command.

5. What wicked command did Pharaoh give to all his people? _____

   <u>Pharaoh told his people to cast every Israelite son into the river.</u>
   _____

Moses in Egypt

Exodus 2:1–4

This man and woman of the family of Levi were Amram and Jochebed. Their baby boy was Moses.

6. Moses' mother placed him in an _____<u>ark</u>_____ near the edge of the _____<u>river</u>_____.

7. Moses' _____<u>sister</u>_____ watched to see what would happen to him.

Exodus 2:5–10

8. Who found Moses? ____<u>Pharaoh's daughter</u>____

9. What was this lady's father trying to do to the Israelite baby boys? _____

   <u>He was trying to kill them.</u>_____

10. This lady had compassion on Moses (felt sorry for him) because
    a. his mother was one of her close friends.
    b. he was smaller than most babies.
    (c.) he was crying when she found him.

11. Whom did she ask to take care of Moses? _____<u>Moses' mother</u>_____

Exodus 2:11–15

12. Moses loved his own people, even though he was raised as an Egyptian by Pharaoh's daughter. When he was a man, he visited his _____<u>brethren</u>_____ and looked on their _____<u>burdens</u>_____.

13. Why did Moses have to flee from Egypt? _____

    <u>He was afraid because he had killed an Egyptian, and now Pharaoh wanted to kill him.</u>

God Calls Moses

Exodus 3:1–7

Moses fled to the land of Midian and worked as a shepherd there for forty years. During that time, the pharaoh died, but the new pharaoh was no better than the old one. Finally the Israelites started to call on the God of their fathers for deliverance.

14. One day while Moses was in the desert, he saw a bush on fire. What was strange about this fire? ____<u>The fire did not burn up the bush.</u>_____
    _____
    _____.

In This Lesson

Scope: Genesis 47–Exodus 4

Main Events

- The Israelites are mistreated in Egypt by a new pharaoh.
- Moses is rescued by Pharaoh's daughter.
- Moses tries to help his people, but he has to flee to Midian instead.
- God calls Moses and identifies Himself as "I AM THAT I AM."

Objectives

- Students should know
  —where the Israelites settled in Egypt. (in the country of Goshen)
  —why the Israelites became slaves. (A new Pharaoh, who did not know Joseph, came to power. He was afraid the rapidly increasing Israelites would rise up against the Egyptians, so he made them slaves.)
  —how it came about that Moses was saved by Pharaoh's daughter. (See Part A, numbers 6–11.)

100   Chapter Three   God's Chosen Family in Egypt

15. a. Who spoke to Moses from the bush? ___God___

   b. What did He tell Moses to do? ___He told Moses to take off his shoes.___

   _____

   c. Why did He tell Moses to do this? ___Moses was standing on holy ground.___

   _____

- The ground was holy because of God's presence.

Exodus 3:11–14

16. Moses had changed during the forty years he spent in Midian. In Egypt he had tried to deliver the Israelites by himself. What three words in his answer to God show that now he realized how small he actually was? ___Who am I?___

17. Many of the Israelites had forgotten the God of their fathers. Moses knew that these people would want to know who the God was that had sent him. God told Moses to tell the Israelites that _____I_____ _____AM_____ had sent him.

   Moses did not want to go to Egypt. He was happy where he was. He no longer wanted to be a great person. Furthermore, he was afraid that no one would believe him and that Pharaoh would not listen to him. But God did not accept his excuses. He showed Moses some miracles that would prove to the Israelites and to Pharaoh that God had sent him. He also told Moses that his brother Aaron would go with him and speak for him.

Where Is It Found?

18. Which chapter of Exodus tells

   a. why Moses had to flee from Egypt? ___Exodus 2___

   b. how God spoke to Moses from a burning bush? ___Exodus 3___

B. BIBLE WORD STUDY

★ *Match these definitions with the Bible words on the right. Read the verses given or use a dictionary if you need help.*

___f___ 1. To become; grow to be (Exodus 1:7)   a. flag

___e___ 2. Strictness; harshness (Exodus 1:13)   b. recompence (recompense)

___g___ 3. Fine; of pleasing appearance (Exodus 2:2)   c. memorial

___a___ 4. A plant that grows in marshes (Exodus 2:3)   d. reproach

___c___ 5. Something that helps people remember (Exodus 3:15) e. rigour (rigor)

___h___ 6. To punish or get back at someone who has done   f. wax
        wrong (Acts 7:24)   g. goodly

___d___ 7. Shame; disgrace (Hebrews 11:26)   h. avenge

___b___ 8. A payment in return for something (Hebrews 11:26)

—why Moses fled from Egypt. (He was afraid because he had killed an Egyptian, and now Pharaoh wanted to kill him.)

—how God spoke to Moses, and what He called Himself. (from a burning bush that did not burn up; I AM)

—who Moses' spokesman was. (Aaron)

Truths to Instill

- God allowed hard times to come to the Israelites so that they would be ready to move to Canaan. Moses was raised as the son of Pharaoh's daughter because of a cruel law Pharaoh had made. We often do not understand why God allows difficult experiences such as these, but we know He uses them to accomplish His purposes.

- Moses could have found many reasons to reject his people. He was "the son of Pharaoh's daughter," trained in Egyptian knowledge, with the treasures of Egypt at his disposal. But he chose rather "to suffer affliction with the people of God, than to enjoy the pleasures of sin for a season; esteeming the reproach of Christ greater riches than the treasures in Egypt" (Hebrews 11:25, 26).

Lesson 14. God's Chosen People Suffer Bondage   **101**

C. THINKING ABOUT BIBLE TRUTHS

Acts 7:22–34

Sometimes people run ahead of God. They do not have the patience to wait on Him. Moses had learned many helpful things from the Egyptians, but God had other things He wanted to teach him before Moses was ready to lead God's people.

1. Moses was learned in ___all the wisdom of the Egyptians___, and was mighty __in words and in deeds__.

2. What did Moses think his brethren would understand, even before he left Egypt? _____ __that God would use him to deliver them from Egypt__

3. Moses was _____forty_____ years old when he went out to see his brethren. Then he lived in the land of Midian (or Madian) for _____forty_____ years. According to these figures, how old was Moses when God called him to deliver the Israelites? _____eighty_____

4. a. What was Moses' occupation while he lived in the land of Midian? (Exodus 3:1) _____ __He was a shepherd.__

   b. How might this have helped to prepare him for leading the Israelites through the wilderness? ___(Sample answers) Moses learned how to live in the desert and where to find water and pasture for the flocks. He learned to care about the needs of others. He also learned to be humble, even though he had been raised as a prince in Egypt.__

Hebrews 11:24–27

When Moses was old enough to make his own decisions, he decided to follow the God of the Israelites rather than the Egyptian gods. He probably remembered what his parents had taught him about the true God before he went to live with Pharaoh's daughter.

5. What did Moses refuse to be called after he was grown? _____ __the son of Pharaoh's daughter__

6. Moses did not fear the wrath of the king, because _____ __he could see Him who is invisible__.

D. LEARNING MORE ABOUT THE BIBLE

Brave Women

Pharaoh thought he was a powerful man. He thought no one could do anything against him. But God used women to bring his plans to nothing.

1. Two women refused to kill the Israelites' baby boys. They were _____Shiphrah_____ and _____Puah_____. (See Exodus 1:15.)

2. A woman hid Moses from Pharaoh's men. She was _Moses' mother (Jochebed)_.

3. A girl helped to save Moses from Pharaoh's law to have the baby boys killed. She was ___>>___.

4. A woman rescued Moses and raised him. She was ___Pharaoh's daughter___.

- Moses had faith that God would be with him, even though he could not see God.

3. Moses' sister (probably Miriam; see Numbers 26:59)

The Name God Gave Himself

When God spoke to Moses from the burning bush, He spoke in the Hebrew language. God said His name is *'EHYEH* (EH yeh), which means "I AM." But the Hebrews never called Him *'EHYEH*. They called Him *YAHWEH* (YAH weh), which means "HE IS" or "HE CAUSES TO BE." In the Old Testament we use today, the name *YAHWEH* is usually translated *Lord* (with all capital letters). A few times in our Old Testament, the name *YAHWEH* is translated *JEHOVAH*.

Jehovah is the way we say the name that God gave Himself.

**'EHYEH = YAHWEH =
JEHOVAH**

Discuss this with the students.

1. How many times is *YAHWEH* translated *Lord* in Exodus 3:15–18? _____ four _____

2. Find *Jehovah* in a concordance. Copy one verse and reference that uses this form of God's

   name. __(Any one of the four verses given below)__

   _____

   _____

In our Old Testament, the term *Lord* (with only the first letter capitalized) also refers to God. Usually *Lord* is translated from the Hebrew word *Adonai*, which means "lord, master, or owner." *Jehovah (Lord)* is one of God's proper names, and *Adonai (Lord)* is a title of respect and honor.

3. Notice that both *Lord* and *Lord* are used in Exodus 4:10. When Moses spoke to God in this

   verse, what did he call God: *Jehovah* or *Adonai*? _____ Adonai _____

Exodus 6:3. "And I appeared unto Abraham, unto Isaac, and unto Jacob, by the name of God Almighty, but by my name JEHOVAH was I not known to them."

Psalm 83:18. "That men may know that thou, whose name alone is JEHOVAH, art the most high over all the earth."

Isaiah 12:2. "Behold, God is my salvation; I will trust, and not be afraid: for the Lord JEHOVAH is my strength and my song; he also is become my salvation."

Isaiah 26:4. "Trust ye in the Lord for ever: for in the Lord JEHOVAH is everlasting strength."

- The term *Lord* (with small capitals) is generally not used in modern text. However, this course uses it as a proper name of God to remind students of its significance in the Old Testament.

- The distinction between *Lord* and *Lord* in our English Old Testament is significant. *Lord* always refers to *Jehovah (Yahweh)*, one of God's proper names. *Lord* is usually translated from *Adonai*, a title meaning "lord, master, or owner." Note the use of both *Lord* and *Lord* in Exodus 4:10.

  The practice of substituting *Lord* for *Jehovah* stems from the late Jewish practice of not pronouncing *Jehovah*. The Jews of that time used *Adonai* for *Jehovah* when reading the Scriptures aloud.

Because of this custom, the Greek translators of the Old Testament used *Kurios (Lord)* for both *Jehovah* and *Adonai*. The New Testament writers followed this practice when quoting from the Old Testament. For an example, compare Matthew 4:7 with Deuteronomy 6:16. Because a direct translation of *Jehovah* was not used in the Greek New Testament, *Lord* (with small capitals) is not used in our English New Testament.

103

Lesson 15. God Delivers His Chosen People

How do you think Moses felt as he entered Egypt for the first time in forty years? Perhaps he feared that the Egyptians would again try to kill him. He wondered what Pharaoh would say, and whether the Israelites would believe his message from God. But in spite of how he felt, Moses obeyed God and went. He had faith that God was with him and would deliver the Israelites out of Egypt.

Moses and Aaron said to Pharaoh, "Thus saith the LORD God of Israel, Let my people go." Pharaoh replied, "Who is the LORD, that I should obey his voice?" Pharaoh thought he was greater than the God of his slaves. So God

sent ten terrible plagues to show him who He was, and why even Pharaoh must obey Him.

First God turned the waters of the Nile River into blood. Then He sent swarms of frogs, lice, and flies over the land. For three days and three nights, He sent a fearful darkness upon Egypt, so thick that it could be felt. Yet Pharaoh still would not listen to God!

Pharaoh continued to rebel until the night when all the oldest sons in Egypt died, including the oldest son of Pharaoh himself. God spared only the sons of the Israelites, who had put the blood of the Passover lamb on their doorposts and lintel. At last Pharaoh was ready to let Israel go.

A. ANSWERS FROM THE BIBLE

God had heard the cries of His people. He was ready to deliver them from their bondage, and it was time to punish the Egyptians. God sent Moses to Pharaoh with a command that He knew Pharaoh would not obey.

Moses and Aaron Meet Pharaoh

Exodus 5:1–3, 10–14

1. When God sent Moses and Aaron to Pharaoh, what did He command Pharaoh to do? _____

   "Let my people go, that they may hold a feast unto me in the wilderness."

2. What was Pharaoh's answer? _____

   "Who is the LORD, that I should obey his voice to let Israel go? I know not the LORD, neither will I let Israel go."

3. How did Pharaoh make the Israelites' bondage worse because of Moses and Aaron's request?

   Pharaoh commanded that the Israelites gather their own straw and still keep making as many bricks as before.

The Israelites were discouraged. Moses had promised to help them, but now Pharaoh was making them work harder than ever.

Lesson 15

Oral Review

1. What do the abbreviations *A.M.*, *B.C.*, and *A.D.* mean when they are used with dates? [6] **A.M.—in the year of the world; B.C.—before Christ; A.D.—in the year of our Lord**
2. What is the meaning of the names *Jacob* and *Israel*? [10] **Jacob—heel catcher, supplanter; Israel—having power with God**
3. Which of these two countries received more rain: Canaan or Egypt? [11] **Canaan**
4. Why did Pharaoh choose Joseph to gather food during the seven good years? [12] **Pharaoh saw that**

the Spirit of God was in Joseph and that no one else was as discreet and wise as he.
5. When did Joseph's dreams come true? [13] **when his brothers bowed before him**
6. Where in Egypt did the Israelites live? [14] **in the land of Goshen**
7. What did the new pharaoh of Egypt force the Israelites to do? [14] **to work hard as slaves**
8. Why did Moses have to flee from Egypt? [14] **He had killed an Egyptian, and now Pharaoh wanted to kill him.**

Exodus 7:8–13

4. What sign did Moses show to Pharaoh? _____

   Aaron's rod became a serpent.

5. Why did Pharaoh refuse to believe that this sign came from God? _____

   Pharaoh's magicians could also make their rods turn into serpents.

   _____

6. Aaron's rod swallowed up the magicians' rods. This shows that
   a. God's power was greater than the magicians' power.
   b. Aaron's rod was bigger than the magicians' rods.
   c. Aaron was a better magician than the Egyptian magicians were.

God Sends the Ten Plagues

Pharaoh had no respect for God. He refused to do what God told him to do. He felt certain that the gods of powerful Egypt could protect him from the God of the lowly, enslaved Israelites.

7. For each reference, write the plague that the LORD brought upon Egypt.

   a. Exodus 7:19–22   Water turned to blood.

   b. Exodus 8:6   frogs

   c. Exodus 8:16, 17   lice

   d. Exodus 8:24   flies

   e. Exodus 9:6, 7   Cattle died.

   f. Exodus 9:10   boils

   g. Exodus 9:22–26   hail

   h. Exodus 10:13–15   locusts

   i. Exodus 10:21–23   darkness

   j. Exodus 12:29, 30   death of the first-born

8. Could the magicians imitate all the miracles that God did? (Exodus 8:18)   no

> • The Hebrew word *ken*, translated *lice* in the King James Version (Exodus 8:16–18), is of uncertain meaning. Some believe it means "gnats," "sand flies," or "fleas." The traditional rendering, "lice," is used in this lesson.

The First Passover

Exodus 12:3–13

9. God told Moses to tell all the Israelites to take a (a) _____ lamb _____ for each house.

   It was to be without (b) _____ blemish _____, a (c) _____ male _____ of the first

   (d) _____ year _____. It could be either from the (e) _____ sheep _____ or from

   the (f) _____ goats _____.

In This Lesson

Scope: Exodus 5–12

Main Events
- God sends Moses and Aaron to tell Pharaoh to let the Israelites leave Egypt.
- Pharaoh refuses and hardens his heart.
- God sends ten plagues upon Egypt.
- After their first-born sons die, the Egyptians urge the Israelites to leave.

Objectives
- Students should know
  —what God commanded Pharaoh to do, and what Pharaoh replied. (See Part A, numbers 1, 2.)
  —the number of plagues, and which one caused Pharaoh to let the Israelites go. (ten; the tenth one, the death of the first-born)
  —what the Israelites needed to do to keep the Passover. (See Part A, number 9.)

Lesson 15. God Delivers His Chosen People   **105**

The Israelites were to kill it in the evening, and strike the (g) _____blood_____ on the doorposts and lintels of their houses. They were to eat the flesh with (h) ____unleavened____ bread and with (i) _____bitter_____ _____herbs_____. That which was left over was to be (j) _____burned_____.

They were to call the meal the LORD's Passover because the LORD promised to (k) _____pass_____ _____over_____ the houses that had blood on the doorposts when He killed the first-born of the Egyptians.

Israel Is Sent Out

The Israelites ate the Passover quickly, with their shoes on and with their clothes ready for travel. Meanwhile, the Egyptians went to bed, but they did not get much sleep. Both the Israelites and the Egyptians would remember that night for a long time.

Exodus 12:29–36

10. That night at _____midnight_____, the _____LORD_____ smote all the _____first-born_____ of Egypt.

11. a. When did Pharaoh call for Moses and Aaron? ____during the night____

    b. What did he tell them to do? _____
    He told them to leave Egypt and serve the LORD as they had asked.

12. The Egyptians urged the Israelites to leave their land right away because they were afraid
    _that the Egyptians would all be killed_____.

13. After being slaves for many years, the Israelites were probably poor. Moses told them to ask the Egyptians for the things that they needed. What did the Egyptians give them? _____
    _jewels of silver, jewels of gold, and raiment (and such things as they required)_____
    _____

14. Why were the Egyptians so ready to give the Israelites the things that they needed? _____
    The LORD gave the Israelites favor in the eyes of the Egyptians. (Also, the Egyptians wanted the Israelites to leave.)

Where Is It Found?

15. In which chapter of Exodus is the story of the Passover found? _____Exodus 12_____

- The Hebrew word translated *borrow* in Exodus 12:35 is often translated *ask* (as in Zechariah 10:1, where God told the Israelites to ask Him for rain). The Israelites had no intention of returning these items. It was God's way of taking wages from the Egyptians for Israel's years of labor.

Truths to Instill

- God's purposes are always fulfilled. Even Pharaoh's determined opposition only served to accomplish those purposes. God used the Egyptians' hardened hearts to enrich His people. They hardened themselves against God's judgments, until they became so desperate to get rid of the Israelites that they showered their riches upon them.

B. BIBLE WORD STUDY

★ *Match these definitions with the Bible words on the right. Read the verses given or use a dictionary if you need help. All references are from Exodus.*

__f__   1. A magician (7:11)

__d__   2. An act of magic (7:11)

__a__   3. To dislike greatly (7:18)

__e__   4. A disease of animals (9:3)

__b__   5. A skin disease (9:9)

__i__   6. The inside parts of an animal (12:9)

__g__   7. A bushy, sweet-smelling plant (12:22)

__h__   8. A beam or stone over a doorway (12:22)

__c__   9. To rob; take things from (12:36)

a. lothe (loathe)

b. blains

c. spoil

d. enchantment

e. murrain

f. sorcerer

g. hyssop

h. lintel

i. purtenance

C. THINKING ABOUT BIBLE TRUTHS

1. The Egyptians worshiped many gods, but none of their gods could protect them from Jehovah, the God of Israel. By bringing judgment on the Egyptians, God was also bringing judgment on their _____gods_____. (See Numbers 33:4.)

2. The Israelites did not leave Egypt by themselves. According to Exodus 12:38, a "mixed multitude" went with them. This mixed multitude might have included
   a. Egyptians who were so impressed by God's power that they decided to go with the Israelites.
   b. Families that were part Egyptian and part Israelite because they or their parents had intermarried.
   c. Slaves or captives from other nations who thought this was a good chance to escape from Egypt.
   (d.) All the choices above.

3. The Passover lamb was like Jesus because
   (a.) it died so that someone else would not need to die.
   b. it ate bitter herbs before it was killed.
   c. only one lamb was needed for the whole nation.

God sometimes lets wicked men rule over His people to remind them that they need Him. Often such rulers are proud and stubborn until God shows them that He rules over all men. The following verses tell how God used Pharaoh, and how He feels about rulers who stand up against Him.

Exodus 9:16

4. Who raised up Pharaoh and made him a ruler? _____God_____

5. Why did He raise up Pharaoh? (Give two reasons.)

　a. to show in him His great power (to show His great power to or through Pharaoh)

　b. so that His name would be declared throughout all the earth

Psalm 2:1–4

6. What did God say He will do when rulers stand up against Him? _____

　God says that He will laugh.

- Verse 5 says that He will speak to them in wrath, and vex them.

D. LEARNING MORE ABOUT THE BIBLE

The Plagues of Egypt

The Egyptians did not believe in the LORD. They were proud, rebellious, and self-confident. They worshiped false gods. Then the LORD began to show them the truth about their gods. He showed them that their gods could not save them or help them.

★ *On the following page is a table with the plagues on the left and Egyptian gods and beliefs on the right. Match each plague with the Egyptian god or belief that the plague affected.*

LETTUCE

Crunchy but sometimes bitter lettuce grew along the Nile River thousands of years ago. Egyptians ate lettuce leaves before the plant went to seed, just as we do today. They thought lettuce was a good tonic.

Lettuce seeds, if eaten in large amounts, are mildly narcotic. Some people used them instead of opium.

When God told the Israelites to eat the Passover lamb, He said: "And they shall eat the flesh in that night, roast with fire, and unleavened bread; and with bitter herbs they shall eat it" (Exodus 12:8). Lettuce may have been one of the "bitter herbs" that the Israelites ate with the Passover.

What would have happened to the Israelites if they would not have obeyed these instructions about the Passover? (Exodus 12:12, 13).

	_h_ 1. God changed the Nile's water to blood.	a. The Egyptians believed their gods controlled everything, even insects such as lice.
	_d_ 2. God plagued the Egyptians with millions of frogs.	b. The Egyptians believed their gods controlled insects such as flies.
	_a_ 3. God sent lice upon the Egyptians and their animals.	c. The Egyptians lived by working the land. They believed their gods protected their crops.
	_b_ 4. God sent swarms of flies upon the Egyptians.	d. The Egyptians worshiped frogs. The goddess Hekt was pictured with a frog's head.
	_i_ 5. God struck the Egyptians' livestock with a deadly disease.	e. The Egyptians believed that their gods decided when people were born and when they died.
	_j_ 6. God afflicted the Egyptians with boils.	f. The Egyptians trusted in their gods to control the weather.
	_f_ 7. God sent a great hailstorm with thunder and lightning upon the Egyptians.	g. The Egyptians worshiped the sun and the light it gives to the earth.
	_c_ 8. God sent locusts upon the Egyptians' crops to destroy them.	h. The Egyptians depended on the Nile and worshiped it as a God. They also worshiped some of its fish.
	_g_ 9. God caused thick darkness to come upon Egypt for three days.	i. The Egyptians worshiped bulls, cows, and rams. They thought these "cattle gods" brought prosperity.
	_e_ 10. God killed the first-born of every Egyptian family.	j. The Egyptians trusted in their gods to protect them from sickness.

109

Chapter Three Review

A. ORAL REVIEW

★ *Be sure you know the answers to these questions. Give as many answers as you can without looking back in your book. If you need help, you may check the Bible reference or the lesson given in brackets.*

Who

1. Who saved Joseph's life by suggesting that his brothers throw him into a pit? [Genesis 37:21, 22]   Reuben
2. Who told Pharaoh the meaning of his dreams? [Genesis 41:25]   Joseph (with God's help)
3. Who was with Joseph all the time he was in Egypt? [Genesis 39:23]   the LORD
4. Who promised his father that he would bring Benjamin back from Egypt? [Genesis 43:8, 9]
   Judah

Where

★ *Match the descriptions on the left with the rivers and seas on the right. (To study for the test, cover the list on the right and answer from memory.) [Lesson 11]*

5. Lowest spot on earth   Dead Sea
6. Called Chinnereth in the Old Testament   Sea of Galilee
7. Large sea west of Canaan   Mediterranean Sea
8. Flowed through Canaan   Jordan River
9. Flowed through Egypt   Nile River
10. East of the Euphrates River   Tigris River

Sea of Galilee
Mediterranean Sea
Dead Sea
Nile River
Jordan River
Tigris River

What   >>

11. What work did Moses do while he lived in Midian? [Exodus 3:1]
12. What did God name Himself? [Exodus 3:14; Lesson 14]
13. What did God command Pharaoh to do to the Israelites? [Exodus 5:1]
14. What did the Israelites get from the Egyptians before they left Egypt? [Exodus 12:35]

When   >>

15. When did Joseph's life become a blessing to people of many countries? [Genesis 41:56, 57]
16. When did Joseph's dreams come true? [Genesis 42:9]
17. When did Jacob change his mind about letting Benjamin go to Egypt? [Genesis 43:2]
18. When did Pharaoh let the Israelites go? [Exodus 12:29–32]

Why   >>

19. Why did Jacob think Joseph was dead? [Genesis 37:31–33]
20. Why did Joseph's brothers come to Egypt? [Genesis 42:3]
21. Why did Moses flee to the land of Midian? [Exodus 2:11–15]

11. He kept the flock of Jethro. (He was a shepherd.)
12. I AM [THAT I AM] (Jehovah)
13. God commanded Pharaoh to let His people leave Egypt.
14. silver, gold, and clothes
15. when he sold them corn (grain) during the famine
16. when his brothers came to buy corn (grain)
17. when their food ran out
18. Pharaoh and the Egyptians urged the Israelites to leave after the death of their first-born sons.
19. Joseph's brothers dipped his coat in blood and showed it to Jacob.
20. They needed to buy corn (grain, food).
21. Pharaoh tried to kill Moses after Moses had killed an Egyptian.

110   Chapter Three   God's Chosen Family in Egypt

How

22. How did Joseph prepare for the famine? [Genesis 41:48, 49] He gathered grain for seven years.
23. How did Jacob travel to Egypt? [Genesis 45:27] He traveled in the wagons Joseph had sent.
24. How did Moses' parents save his life? [Exodus 2:2, 3]
They hid him and then put him in a small ark on the Nile.

B. WRITTEN REVIEW

★ *Write answers to these questions. If you need help, use the Bible reference or the lesson given in brackets.*

Where

1. Where in Egypt did the Israelites live? [Genesis 47:27]   in Goshen

2. Where did the Israelites apply the blood of the Passover lamb? [Exodus 12:7]
on the lintel and the two side posts of their doors

3. Where did the Israelites receive more rain: in Canaan or in Egypt? [Lesson 11]
in Canaan

What

4. What does the Bible mean when it says Joseph was *discreet*? [Lesson 12]
He was careful in his speech and actions.

5. What did the new pharaoh of Egypt force the Israelites to do? [Exodus 1:11, 14]
He forced them to build cities and work in his fields.

6. What did Pharaoh tell his people to do to all the Israelite baby boys? [Exodus 1:22]
He told his people to throw all the baby boys into the river.

7. What did Moses refuse to be called after he became a man? [Hebrews 11:24]
He refused to be called the son of Pharaoh's daughter.

8. What did Pharaoh say when God commanded him to let the Israelites go? [Exodus 5:2]
"Who is the LORD, that I should obey his voice?"

9. What is hyssop? [Lesson 15]
a bushy, sweet-smelling plant

When

10. When could a slave be set free under Hebrew law? (Give three answers.) [Lesson 12]
    a.   after six years of service
    b.   if his master injured or mistreated him
    c.   if someone bought him out of slavery

Why

11. Why did Joseph's brothers hate him? [Genesis 37:4] <u>They saw that their father loved Joseph</u>
    <u>the best. (They also hated him because of his dreams, his coat, and his reports of their evil deeds.)</u>

12. Why did the new pharaoh of Egypt fear the Israelites? [Exodus 1:9, 10] _____
    <u>He was afraid they would rise up against the Egyptians.</u>

13. Why did God send ten plagues upon Egypt? [Lesson 15] <u>Pharaoh refused to let the</u>
    <u>Israelites go. (God also brought judgment upon the Egyptian gods.)</u>

How

14. How could Joseph see that his brothers' hearts had changed? [Genesis 44:33, 34; Lesson 13]
    <u>He saw that they had love and concern for Benjamin.</u>

    _____

    _____

15. How did Joseph treat his brothers after he told them who he was? [Genesis 45:4–15] _____
    <u>He treated them kindly and took care of them.</u>

16. How did God appear to Moses in the land of Midian? [Exodus 3:2–4] _____
    <u>in a burning bush</u>

Bible Outline

★ *Match these chapters with the events they record. The headings in your Bible may give you*
   help if you need it.

<u>f</u>   17. Genesis 37–39

<u>d</u>   18. Genesis 40, 41

<u>a</u>   19. Genesis 42–47

<u>c</u>   20. Genesis 48–50

<u>g</u>   21. Exodus 1, 2

<u>e</u>   22. Exodus 3–6

<u>b</u>   23. Exodus 7–12

a. Jacob's sons buy food in Egypt; Joseph makes himself known; Jacob moves to Egypt.

b. God sends the ten plagues on Egypt; the Israelites keep the Passover.

c. Jacob blesses his descendants; Jacob and Joseph die.

d. Joseph interprets dreams and is made ruler of Egypt.

e. God appears to Moses and sends him to Pharaoh; Pharaoh refuses to listen.

f. Joseph is sold into Egypt and later put into prison, but the LORD is with him.

g. The Israelites become slaves; Moses is born; Moses flees to Midian.

CHAPTER FOUR

Israel in the Wilderness

Give unto the LORD the glory due unto his name: bring an offering, and come before him: worship the LORD in the beauty of holiness.

O give thanks unto the LORD; for he is good; for his mercy endureth for ever. (I Chronicles 16:29, 34)

TIME LINE—Chapter Four

Forty Years Wandering in the Wilderness

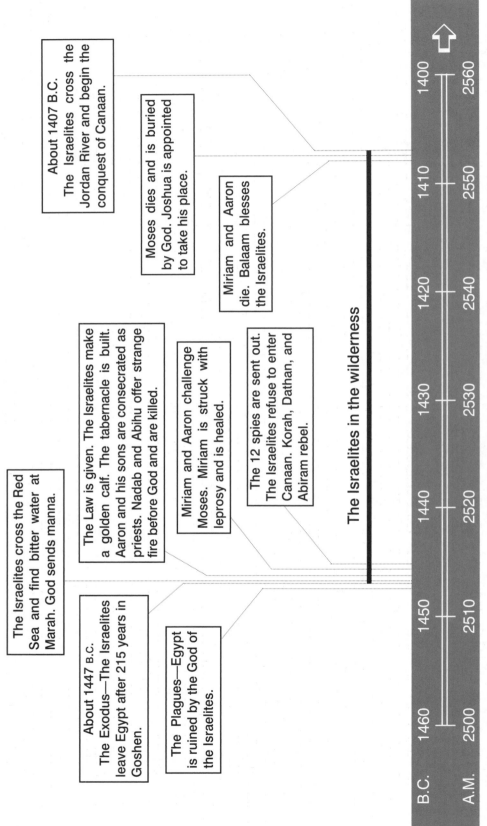

The Israelites cross the Red Sea and find bitter water at Marah. God sends manna.

The Law is given. The Israelites make a golden calf. The tabernacle is built. Aaron and his sons are consecrated as priests. Nadab and Abihu offer strange fire before God and are killed.

About 1447 B.C. The Exodus—The Israelites leave Egypt after 215 years in Goshen.

The Plagues—Egypt is ruined by the God of the Israelites.

Miriam and Aaron challenge Moses. Miriam is struck with leprosy and is healed.

The 12 spies are sent out. The Israelites refuse to enter Canaan. Korah, Dathan, and Abiram rebel.

Miriam and Aaron die. Balaam blesses the Israelites.

Moses dies and is buried by God. Joshua is appointed to take his place.

About 1407 B.C. The Israelites cross the Jordan River and begin the conquest of Canaan.

The Israelites in the wilderness

B.C.	1460	1450	1440	1430	1420	1410	1400
A.M.	2500	2510	2520	2530	2540	2550	2560

NOTE: The Law was given in the third month after the Exodus (Exodus 19:1). The Israelites stayed in the Sinai wilderness almost one year (Numbers 10:11), so the twelve spies were sent into Canaan during the second year after the Exodus. We have very little history about Israel from then until they neared Canaan again, about 38 years later.

115

Lesson 16. God Gives His Word to Man

God has always wanted man to know Him. Before Adam and Eve sinned, God walked with them and visited with them in the Garden of Eden. Even after man sinned, God talked with man on special occasions. In your studies so far this year, you have seen how God talked personally with Cain, Noah, Abraham, Isaac, Jacob, and Moses. However, God wanted to give His message to everyone. He therefore inspired some men to write His message in a book so that many others could read it.

In the last chapter, you saw how the children of Israel multiplied and grew while they lived in Egypt. In this chapter, you will see how God taught them His ways. He gave them laws that showed them how to serve Him. God also gave laws to show them how to treat other people. Moses wrote all these laws in a set of books called the Law of Moses. In this lesson you will learn more about how God gave us His Word and how it has been passed down from generation to generation.

A. ANSWERS FROM THE BIBLE

★ *Study the Bible passages given. Fill in the short blanks with words, using exact words from the Bible whenever possible. Write complete answers for the questions with long blanks. For multiple choice questions, circle the letter of the correct answer or underline the correct word in parentheses.*

Why Does God Speak to Man?

Deuteronomy 6:1–7
The Israelites had almost forgotten God while they lived in Egypt. After God brought the Israelites out of Egypt, He told Moses many things that he was to teach them about Him. Moses wrote God's teachings in books so that the Israelites would not forget them.

1. God wanted His people to know His words so that they would ____fear____ Him and keep all His commandments (verse 2).

2. God promised the Israelites that if they observed His commandments, it would be ____well____ with them, and they would increase mightily (verse 3).

3. God wanted the Israelites to ____love____ Him with all their heart, soul, and might.

4. The Israelites were to remember the words of God and to ____teach____ them diligently to their children.

How Does God Speak to Man?

God has spoken to man in many ways. The following references show you some of them.

• We believe that the Scripture autographs (the original manuscripts of the writers) were inspired by God. They were perfect and inerrant in every detail. We believe that copies of the Scriptures in the original languages, and translations of those copies, are inerrant to the extent that they are true to the original manuscripts. None of the autographs are known to exist today, but the manuscripts that have been preserved are for the most part in agreement. Variants caused by scribal errors are minor and affect no major Bible doctrine.

An example of a variant is found in 2 Chronicles 36:9. Most Hebrew manuscripts read "Jehoiachin was eight years old when he began to reign." But other old manuscripts read "eighteen years old," which agrees with 2 Kings 24:8. (In this case, both ages might be correct, since some kings began reigning before their fathers died. If so, Jehoiachin was eight when he began reigning with his father, and eighteen when he began reigning alone.)

Lesson 16

Oral Review

(The numbers in brackets tell which lessons are being reviewed.)

1. What are five ways (from Lesson 1) that God wants us to use the Bible? [1] **read, hear, study, believe, obey**

2. Where can we find the meanings of difficult Bible words? [1] **in a Bible dictionary**

3. How did Noah prove that he had faith in God? [4] **He obeyed all of God's commandments.**

4. Why did Abraham not want his servant to take Isaac back to Haran? [9] **Isaac was to receive the promise of the land of Canaan, and Abraham's relatives at Haran worshiped idols.**

5. What did Jacob see in his vision at Bethel? [10] **Jacob saw angels on a ladder and the LORD standing above it.**

6. How did Joseph show that he had forgiven his brothers? [13] **He treated them kindly and took care of them.**

7. How did Moses' parents save his life? [14] **They hid him and then put him in a small ark on the Nile.**

8. When God sent Moses to Pharaoh, what did He command Pharaoh to do? [15] **"Let my people go."**

116   Chapter Four   Israel in the Wilderness

Exodus 33:11

5. God spoke to Moses _____face_____ to _____face_____, as a man speaks to a friend.

    We do not know exactly what this verse means, since God did not allow Moses to see the full glory of His face (Exodus 33:20). However, it is clear that Moses received God's words directly from God himself.

Zechariah 1:9

6. God spoke to the prophet Zechariah by an _____angel_____.

Genesis 28:12

7. God spoke to Jacob in a _____dream_____.

Hebrews 1:1, 2

8. In Old Testament times, God often spoke through _____prophets_____; but in New Testament times, He spoke to man through His _____Son_____.

Acts 10:19

9. The _____Spirit_____ of God spoke to Peter.

2 Timothy 3:15

10. God spoke to Timothy through the Holy _____Scriptures_____.

    God usually speaks to Christians today through the church and through the ways that He spoke to Peter and Timothy (numbers 9 and 10).

Remembering God's Words

    It is easy to forget spoken words. God told men to write His words in a book so that we can read them again and again.

Exodus 34:1

11. God wrote the Ten Commandments on _____tables_____ of _____stone_____. The Israelites kept these in the ark of the covenant.

Deuteronomy 17:18, 19

12. Every new king in Israel was to make a copy of God's Law to keep for himself. He was to _____read_____ from this book all the days of his life so that he would learn to _____fear_____ God and _____keep_____ all His words.

Jeremiah 36:4

13. Sometimes a man would write down the words that God had given to another man. Baruch wrote down the words of God in a _____roll_____ (scroll) of a book as God gave them to Jeremiah.

Revelation 1:11

14. What the apostle John saw, he was to write in a _____book_____.

In This Lesson

Main Points
- God's written Word is a record of His will that can be preserved and read by each new generation.
- The Holy Spirit moved men to write God's perfect, inerrant Word.
- Scribes throughout history have faced the challenge of copying God's Word correctly.
- The discovery of the Dead Sea Scrolls helps to show the accuracy of our Old Testament.

Objectives
- Students should know
  —the advantages of the written Word of God over the spoken words of God. (See Part A, number 15.)
  —the original language of the Old Testament. (Hebrew)
  —how scribes preserved the Old Testament from generation to generation. (They copied it onto scrolls.)
  —how the Dead Sea Scrolls show the accuracy of the Old Testament. (See Part B, Extra assignment.)

15. You might think that hearing God's voice would be better than reading His Word. Hearing God speak directly to us *would* be awesome. However, in many ways, God's written Word is better for us. From the list below, choose *three* advantages of God's written Word.

   (a.) People can reread God's written Word and remember it much longer than they can remember His spoken words.

   (b.) Men can make copies of God's written Word and give them to many other people.

   c. People who cannot read can understand God's written Word better than spoken words.

   (d.) God's written Word can be read by people who live many years after it was given.

Preserving God's Word

The early copies of the Old Testament did not look like the Bibles we have today. They were written on parchment (scraped animal hides) or papyrus (coarse paper). The sheets of parchment or papyrus were sewn together to make scrolls sometimes 30 feet or more in length. The words were written in the Hebrew language, using no vowels or punctuation marks. The scribes started at the right edge of the page and wrote to the left. They did not divide their writings into chapters and verses or paragraphs and sentences.

16. Read Psalm 113:1, 2 on the scroll below, arranged as Old Testament writers would have written it. Then rewrite it in ordinary English sentences. First try to write the verses without turning to your Bible; then use your Bible to see if you wrote them correctly.

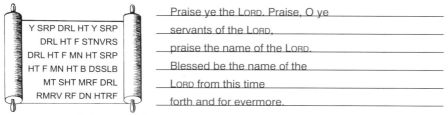

```
Y SRP DRL HT Y SRP
 DRL HT F STNVRS
DRL HT F MN HT SRP
HT F MN HT B DSSLB
 MT SHT MRF DRL
 RMRV RF DN HTRF
```

Praise ye the LORD. Praise, O ye

servants of the LORD,

praise the name of the LORD.

Blessed be the name of the

LORD from this time

forth and for evermore.

Do you see why it was difficult to read and recopy these very old Bibles?

God helped the writers of the Old Testament know exactly what He wanted the Scriptures to say. Every word and letter on the original scrolls was perfect. However, the Israelites needed more than just the original scrolls, so men called scribes neatly copied the original writings onto other scrolls.

Most scribes who copied the Old Testament books worked very carefully. But making a perfect copy of the Scriptures was difficult. Could you write the entire Old Testament without making one mistake?

Even though scribes sometimes made small mistakes, God made sure that some good copies of the Scriptures were preserved. For many years the Jews kept the oldest and best copies of the Old Testament books in the temple at Jerusalem. The priests read from them on Sabbath days and special holidays. People became used to hearing the same Scriptures, year after year, and came to treasure them.

17. Read Nehemiah 8:1–3.

   a. Which scribe is mentioned in these verses? ___Ezra___

   b. What did he do with the book of the Law? _____

      He read the book of the Law to the people.

18. Read Acts 15:21. How often was the Law of Moses read in the synagogues? _____

      It was read every Sabbath Day.

Truths to Instill

- God will always preserve the message of His Word. "The grass withereth, the flower fadeth: but the word of our God shall stand for ever" (Isaiah 40:8). The Bible text has passed through many hands and many translations, yet God's message stands intact and unchanged.

- God expects man to use great care in preserving and translating His Word.

Your students may need help understanding this exercise. As an example, you could write "DRHPHS M S DRL HT" on the chalkboard and show them how to decipher "The LORD is my shepherd." Remind your students that the Old Testament writers used Hebrew words and letters.

- Most of the material in this lesson that was not taken from the Bible itself comes from the article "Biblical Literature" in the Encyclopedia Britannica. Many other sources were consulted, including the ones listed below.

The New Unger's Bible Dictionary entries "Scripture Manuscripts, OT"; "Dead Sea Scrolls"; "Scroll"

Between the Testaments, by Charles F. Pfeiffer, Baker Book House, Grand Rapids, MI, 1959

Cities of the Biblical World: QUMRAN, by Philip R. Davies, William B. Eerdmans Publishing Co., Grand Rapids, MI, 1982

My People: The Story of the Jews, by Abba Eban, Random House, 1968

B. BIBLE STUDY BOOKS

Bible Dictionaries

Several Hebrew words are found in our English Bibles. You can find their English meanings in a Bible dictionary (sometimes in parentheses at the beginning of the explanation). You will read some of these words in Scripture references later in this chapter.

★   *Use a Bible dictionary and the Bible to answer these questions.*

1. a. What does the word *manna* mean?   <u>"What?" ("What is it?")</u>

   b. Read Exodus 16:15, 31. Why do you think this food was called *manna*? <u>   </u>
   <u>The people did not know what it was.</u>

2. a. The high priest wore an ephod. What is the meaning of *ephod*?   <u>"a covering"</u>

   b. According to Exodus 28:6, what colors were used in the ephod? <u>   </u>
   <u>gold, blue, purple, scarlet</u>

3. a. *Hallelujah* is a Hebrew expression of praise we still use today. What does it mean? <u>   </u>
   <u>"praise ye Jah"</u>

   b. This Hebrew expression was used many times in the Psalms, but our Bibles always give
   its English translation. Find its English translation in Psalm 117, and write it here. <u>   </u>
   <u>"Praise the LORD." ("Praise ye the LORD.")</u>

4. a. *Abib* was the first month of the Hebrew year. It was the month barley harvest began.
   What does the word *Abib* mean?   <u>"an ear of corn"</u>

   b. The Israelites left Egypt in the month Abib. What celebration were the Israelites to keep
   in this month? (Deuteronomy 16:1).   <u>the Passover</u>

The Dead Sea Scrolls (Extra assignment)

For many words, a large Bible dictionary gives much more than just the meaning or a short explanation. Large Bible dictionaries have longer articles, like those in encyclopedias. If you look in a Bible dictionary under the heading *Dead Sea Scrolls*, you will find this interesting story.

About one hundred years before Jesus' birth, a group of scribes lived near the Dead Sea at a place called Qumran (koom RAHN). These scribes spent much of their time copying the Hebrew Old Testament Scriptures. They wrote the Scriptures on leather scrolls and sealed them in tall clay jars with lids. Then they hid these jars in nearby caves.

In 1947, Arab shepherd boys discovered some of these old scrolls in one of the caves. During the next several years, other caves in the area were searched. Among the thousands of pieces of old scrolls discovered in eleven caves, parts of every Old Testament book except Esther were found. One scroll contained the complete Book of Isaiah.

The Scriptures of Qumran, called the Dead Sea Scrolls, are the oldest known copies of the Old Testament. They are almost a thousand years older than the manuscripts used to translate the Old Testament in the King James Version of the Bible. But when scholars compared the old copies with the newer ones, they found very little difference. God had kept the copies accurate through all those years so that man could know His Word!

★ *Look up* Dead Sea Scrolls *in your Bible dictionary to find more information about them. You probably will not understand everything that your Bible dictionary says about them, but try to find answers to the following questions. Then, using another paper, write a short report, giving your answers in paragraph form. (The paragraphs above answer some of these questions.)*

—What did the people at Qumran do with the Scriptures?
—When was their work discovered?
—Who discovered it?
—How many caves had scrolls in them?
—What scrolls did they find?
—How many scrolls did they find?
—How old are these scrolls?
—How did the researchers figure out how old the scrolls were?
—How do the Dead Sea Scrolls show to unbelievers that the Old Testament was carefully preserved?

(Individual work. Students' reports should include the points listed below.)
—The people at Qumran copied the Scriptures (and hid them in caves).
—The Dead Sea Scrolls were discovered in 1947.
—The first scrolls were discovered by Arab shepherd boys.
—Scrolls were found in eleven caves.
—Parts of every Old Testament book except Esther were found.
—Thousands of scroll pieces have been found. [However, most of them are small fragments.]
—The Dead Sea Scrolls are about two thousand years old.
—Researchers could tell about how old the scrolls were by studying the coins and pottery found with them. (Unger's Bible Dictionary also mentions the use of Carbon 14 tests, comparisons of handwriting, and linguistics. Fifth grade students will probably understand coins and pottery better.)
—The Dead Sea Scrolls are very similar to Hebrew manuscripts that were copied about a thousand years later. (Note: As Bible believers, we have faith that God has kept His Word pure. We do not need additional evidence. However, the Dead Sea Scrolls can strengthen our faith, and they provide tangible evidence to unbelievers that our copies of the Old Testament are reliable.)

120

Lesson 17. God Leads His Chosen People

Soon after the Israelites left Egypt, they set up camp by the Red Sea. They were happy to be free from their Egyptian masters. But suddenly their happiness changed to fear. Pharaoh and his army were coming after them!

How the Israelites cried to the LORD, and how they wished they had never come with Moses! The Red Sea lay before them. The enemy was rapidly coming up behind them. There was no escape! Then the calm, powerful voice of God spoke to Moses: "Wherefore criest thou unto me? . . . Lift thou up thy rod, and stretch out thine hand over the sea, and divide it: and the children of Israel shall go on dry ground through the midst of the sea."

God came to the rescue of His chosen family, just as He had done before. He had planned one more judgment on the proud Egyptians. He parted the Red Sea to save the Israelites, but He used the same water to destroy the army of the once-mighty Egyptians.

Even though God's people saw His mighty acts, they often failed to believe in Him. Not long after crossing the Red Sea, they complained for lack of food and water. God knew their needs, and in spite of their lack of faith, He provided for them in wonderful ways. How much happier they could have been if they had always trusted and obeyed Him!

A. ANSWERS FROM THE BIBLE

Freedom From Egypt!

It was like a dream come true for the Israelites! After a lifetime of cruel slavery, they were finally free and leaving Egypt.

Exodus 13:17–22

1. God did not lead the Israelites through the land of the _____Philistines_____, because He was afraid they would return to Egypt if they saw _____war_____ .

2. The Israelites took the bones of ___Joseph___ along with them.

3. The LORD led the Israelites with a _____pillar of a cloud_____ by day and a _____pillar of fire_____ by night.

Trouble at the Red Sea

God was not yet finished with the Egyptians. He was preparing to strike a final blow against them. At the same time, He would teach the Israelites another lesson about His power. But first He led the Israelites to the shores of the Red Sea, where it seemed impossible for them to escape the Egyptians.

Exodus 14:5–9

4. After the Israelites left, Pharaoh was (happy, <u>sorry</u>, relieved) that he had let them go.

5. Pharaoh pursued the Israelites because the LORD had (told him to do so, promised to help him, <u>hardened his heart</u>).

Lesson 17

Oral Review

1. What did God ask Abraham to do to show his love for God? [8] **to offer his son as a burnt offering**

2. What two things did God tell Rebekah about her sons before they were born? [9] **They would become two manner of people, and the elder would serve the younger.**

3. Why did Joseph's brothers hate him? [12] **They were jealous that their father loved him better than the rest of them. (They also hated him because of his dreams, his special coat, and the evil report of them that he gave to their father.)**

4. Why did Jacob think Joseph was dead? [12] **His sons showed him Joseph's bloodstained coat.**

5. When did Pharaoh let the Israelites go? [15] **after God destroyed the first-born in every Egyptian family**

6. What did the ten plagues prove about the gods of Egypt? [15] **The LORD was more powerful than any of Egypt's gods.**

7. What are several ways that God has spoken to man? [16] **face to face, by prophets, by angels, through dreams, by Jesus, by His Spirit, through His Word**

8. How do the Dead Sea Scrolls show that the Old Testament was carefully preserved? [16] **The Dead Sea Scrolls are very similar to Hebrew**

Exodus 14:10–18

6. When the Israelites saw the Egyptian army coming after them, they cried out to (Moses, <u>God</u>, Pharaoh).

7. The Israelites felt that Moses had brought them out into the desert to (mistreat them, <u>let them die</u>, help them).

8. Moses told the Israelites not to be afraid, but to stand still and see _____
   <u>the salvation of the LORD</u>   .

9. God told Moses that when He was finished dealing with Pharaoh and his army, the Egyptians would know that He was the LORD. Why did He say this?
   a. The Egyptians had never heard about the God of the Israelites while the Israelites were in Egypt.
   (b.) The Egyptians would finally realize that the God of the Israelites was greater than the gods of Egypt or any other gods.
   c. The Egyptians had already forgotten the plagues that God had just sent on Egypt.

Exodus 14:19–22

10. (Moses, <u>The angel of God,</u> The sea) moved from the front of the camp of Israel to the back and stood between the Israelites and the Egyptians.

11. The pillar of cloud was a light to the Israelites and (shade, fire, <u>darkness</u>) to the Egyptians.

12. The LORD parted the waters of the sea with (His powerful voice, <u>a strong east wind</u>, heat from the pillar of fire).

A Miraculous Deliverance

God made a path for the Israelites through the Red Sea. On each side of the path was a wall of water! The Israelites passed safely through the Red Sea, and the Egyptians decided to follow them.

Exodus 14:23–31

13. Why did the Egyptians decide to flee from the Israelites before they caught up with them?
    <u>God troubled them and took off their chariot wheels.</u>

14. What did God tell Moses to do after the Israelites had crossed safely through the sea? ____
    <u>God told Moses to stretch out his hand over the sea.</u>

15. What did the waters cover? _____
    <u>the chariots, the horsemen, and all of Pharaoh's host</u>

manuscripts that were copied about a thousand years later.

In This Lesson

Scope: Exodus 13–18

Main Events
- God leads His people out of Egypt.
- God parts the Red Sea and destroys the Egyptian army.
- God tests His people and provides for them when they cry to Him.

Objectives
- Students should know
  —how God led the Israelites. (with a pillar of a cloud by day and a pillar of fire by night)
  —what Pharaoh did after the Israelites left Egypt. (He pursued after them.)
  —how the Israelites escaped from Pharaoh. (See Part A, numbers 10–12.)
  —what happened to Pharaoh and his army. (See Part A, numbers 13–15.)
  —how God provided food and water. (See Part A, numbers 17–19.)

16. What three things did the Israelites do when they saw what had happened to the Egyptians?

   a. They feared the LORD.

   b. They believed the LORD.

   c. They believed Moses.

Grumbling in the Desert

After crossing the Red Sea, the Israelites praised God for delivering them from Egypt. But soon they were complaining about their difficult life in the desert. They had trouble finding good water, they ran out of food, and the Amalekites attacked them.

God was testing the Israelites. He wanted to show them that He could supply all their needs. The Israelites often failed to trust God, but God never failed to help them when they cried to Him.

17. a. Read Exodus 15:22–25. The Israelites came to ____Marah____ , where the water was bitter. They complained and said, " ___"What shall we drink?"___

   _____?"

   b. God showed them a certain _____tree_____. They cast it into the water, and the water became sweet.

18. a. Read Exodus 16:1–4, 13–15. The Israelites complained and said, "Would to God we had died by the hand of the LORD in the land of Egypt, when_____

   _we sat by the flesh pots, and when we did eat bread to the full;_____;

   for ye have brought us forth into this wilderness, to kill this whole assembly with

   _____hunger_____."

   b. God provided _____quails_____ and _____manna_____.

19. a. Read Exodus 17:1–7. The Israelites complained and said, "*Give*___us water that we may

   _drink_____."

   b. God provided ___water from a rock._____.

Where Is It Found?

20. The account of the Israelites crossing the Red Sea is found in
   a. Exodus 12.   (b.) Exodus 14.   c. Exodus 15.   d. Exodus 16.

21. The story of God giving the Israelites manna is found in
   a. Exodus 12.   b. Exodus 14.   c. Exodus 15.   (d.) Exodus 16.

• In some cases, the mixed multitude that left Egypt with the Israelites was responsible for stirring up rebellion in the camp (Exodus 12:38; Numbers 11:4). However, the negative response of the entire multitude when the twelve spies returned shows that many Israelites had the same problem.

Truths to Instill

• God's sovereignty. With the Red Sea ahead and the Egyptians behind, defeat and slavery looked certain to the Israelites. But the pursuing Egyptian army was part of God's plan for complete victory. We need to believe that God's sovereign hand is at work in all that takes place.

• God's providence. God provided water and manna in the wilderness. This example is to strengthen our faith (1 Corinthians 10:6). We must avoid complaining, and commit our problems to God. Complaining shows a lack of trust.

• Respect for a day of rest. Even before God gave the commandment on Mount Sinai to "remember the sabbath day, to keep it holy," He taught respect for the day by not sending manna on the Sabbath.

G
A
R
L
I
C

From the lunch remains that the workers who built the great pyramids left behind, archaeologists can tell that they liked to eat garlic.

Garlic cloves, which grow in onionlike bulbs wrapped in papery skin, are more than just tasty. They are also healthy. People in ancient times believed garlic was a good medicine. Modern scientists have proved that they were right. We now know that garlic helps to prevent or cure intestinal infection, high blood pressure, pneumonia, and other diseases.

What group of people were hungry for garlic after not having it for a while? (Numbers 11:4, 5).

B. BIBLE WORD STUDY

★ *Write a word or phrase from the verses given to fit these definitions. All references are from Exodus.*

harnessed	1. Armed; arranged in orderly ranks (13:18)
host	2. An army (14:17)
morning watch	3. The last part of the night (14:24)
prove	4. To test (16:4)
omer	5. A measure containing about five pints (16:16)
seethe	6. To boil; cook (16:23)
discomfited	7. Defeated in battle (17:13)
obeisance	8. The act of bowing before someone to show honor and respect (18:7)

C. THINKING ABOUT BIBLE TRUTHS

God had many lessons to teach the Israelites. Many of the Israelites knew little about God and what He expected of them. God started to teach them these lessons soon after they left Egypt. We too can benefit from these lessons.

Philippians 4:19

1. The Israelites were constantly afraid that God would let them starve or die of thirst in the barren wilderness through which they were traveling. They were used to living in the land of Egypt, where there had always been plenty of food and water.

    a. In the wilderness, God was trying to teach the Israelites that He would supply ___all___ their needs.

    b. This does not mean that God will give us everything we might *want* to have. A real *need* is something that we cannot live without. List four real needs that you have.(Examples)

food	water
clothing	shelter

1 Thessalonians 5:18

2. The Israelites were constantly grumbling about something. Even when they had enough water to drink and food to eat, they grumbled. They forgot that God had rescued them from slavery in Egypt. They forgot the times that He had given them water when they could find none. They even forgot how glad they were when God started to send them manna to eat.

    a. The Israelites needed to learn to give ___thanks___ to God for everything that happened to them.

    b. List two things that you sometimes forget to be grateful for.

    (Individual answers) _____

    _____

Some of the Israelites left Egypt for the wrong reason. They did not leave to worship and obey God. Instead, they left because they thought life would be easier if they went with Moses. Every time these people faced trouble in the wilderness, they grumbled. They needed to learn to follow God because He is a great God, and everything that He asked of them was for their good. When people learn this lesson, they stop grumbling and start thanking God for what He does for them.

Exodus 20:8

3. When God created the earth, He rested on the seventh day as an example of what He expected man to do.

    a. God did not want the Israelites to gather manna on the ___Sabbath___ Day, because it was to be a ___holy___ day.

    b. We keep ___Sunday___ as our day of rest because that is the day that Jesus rose from the dead.

D. LEARNING MORE ABOUT THE BIBLE

The Escape From Egypt

★ *Use the clues at the bottom of the map to label the numbered places.*

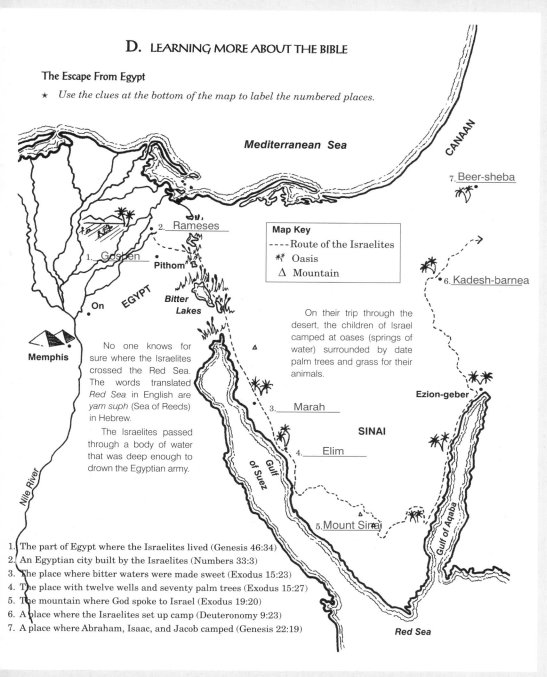

Mediterranean Sea

CANAAN

7. Beer-sheba

2. Rameses

Map Key
- - - Route of the Israelites
✳ Oasis
△ Mountain

1. Goshen

Pithom

6. Kadesh-barnea

On

EGYPT

Bitter Lakes

On their trip through the desert, the children of Israel camped at oases (springs of water) surrounded by date palm trees and grass for their animals.

Memphis

No one knows for sure where the Israelites crossed the Red Sea. The words translated *Red Sea* in English are *yam suph* (Sea of Reeds) in Hebrew.

The Israelites passed through a body of water that was deep enough to drown the Egyptian army.

Ezion-geber

3. Marah

SINAI

4. Elim

Gulf of Suez

5. Mount Sinai

Gulf of Aqaba

Nile River

1. The part of Egypt where the Israelites lived (Genesis 46:34)
2. An Egyptian city built by the Israelites (Numbers 33:3)
3. The place where bitter waters were made sweet (Exodus 15:23)
4. The place with twelve wells and seventy palm trees (Exodus 15:27)
5. The mountain where God spoke to Israel (Exodus 19:20)
6. A place where the Israelites set up camp (Deuteronomy 9:23)
7. A place where Abraham, Isaac, and Jacob camped (Genesis 22:19)

Red Sea

- The exact route that the Israelites took out of Egypt is uncertain. The Bible makes it clear, however, that they crossed the sea at a place wide and deep enough to drown the Egyptian army when the water returned.

126

Lesson 18. God Tells Man How to Live

So far in this chapter, you have learned how God delivered the Israelites from Egypt. You have seen how God marvelously destroyed their enemies in the Red Sea and how He cared for them in the wilderness. In this lesson, you will study the laws that God gave to the Israelites. This will help you learn more about how God wants His people to live.

God is always good. Everything He makes and does is good. God wants people to be good too so that they can walk with Him and be His children.

But how can people be good if they do not know what is right and what is wrong? God spoke to His people from the mountain at Sinai. He told them what they should do and what they should not do.

When God spoke, the ground shook and lightning flashed. Thunder rolled through the sky. A thick cloud of God's glory covered Mount Sinai, and the mountain burned with fire. The Israelites trembled and drew back while trumpet sounds grew louder and louder. God spoke to them from the smoking mountain and gave them instructions about what was right and what was wrong.

Later, God wrote these laws on stone tablets, which He gave to Moses. Moses gave them to the Israelites, and the Israelites passed them on to their children. God wanted the Israelites to read His laws often so that they would remember them.

These laws of God were good because they told the people how to live good lives.

A. ANSWERS FROM THE BIBLE

After they left Egypt, God showed His power to the Israelites in many ways. He turned the bad water of a desert oasis into good water when they were thirsty. He gave them quails and manna to eat when they were hungry. God helped Israel to overcome the Amalekites in battle, and He gave them water to drink out of a rock. Now God was ready to give His laws to the people.

God Meets With His People

Exodus 19:1, 2

1. Where did the Israelites set up camp?   __in the desert of Sinai__

2. They arrived at this place in the _____third_____ month after they had left Egypt.

Exodus 19:10–12, 16–19

God wanted to show the Israelites some of His power and His glory so that they would believe what Moses told them about Him. It took the Israelites several days to get ready to meet God.

3. The LORD told Moses to sanctify the people, and to have them wash their ___clothes___.

4. Moses set ___bounds___ to keep the Israelites away from Mount _____Sinai_____.

This would be a good time to review the travels of the Israelites after they left Egypt. Use a Bible map to show the route that they took.

Impress on your students how awesome it would be to meet the almighty God. Spend some time discussing the Israelites' reactions to their encounter with God.

Lesson 18

Oral Review

1. Name the things God made on each day of Creation. [2] *First day*: **light (also heaven and earth);** *Second*: **firmament;** *Third*: **dry land, seas, and plants;** *Fourth*: **sun, moon, and stars;** *Fifth*: **sea animals and birds;** *Sixth*: **land animals and man**

2. What river flows through Egypt? [11] **the Nile River**

3. What did God call Himself at the burning bush? [14] **I AM [THAT I AM] (Jehovah)**

4. What did Pharaoh say when the LORD commanded him to let His people go? [15] **"Who is the LORD, that I should obey his voice?"**

5. In what ways is God's written Word better than God's spoken words? [16] **We can remember it better, since we can reread it often. We can make copies of it to give to others. We can read it, even though we live many years after God gave it.**

6. Why did God not lead the Israelites through the land of the Philistines? [17] **He was afraid that they would return to Egypt if they saw war.**

5. When the LORD descended on the mountain, the Israelites saw lightning, a thick ___cloud___, fire, and ___smoke___.

6. They heard thunder and the voice of a loud ___trumpet___, and they felt the mountain ___quake___ greatly.

God Gives the Ten Commandments

These commandments show us what God expects of people who want to follow Him. To this day, God's people still obey the principles on which these laws are based.

7. Write the Ten Commandments. For some of them, you will not need to copy the complete verse. Copy only the part that gives the basic command. Memorize the Ten Commandments.

(1) Thou shalt have no other gods before me.

_____ Exodus 20:3

(2) Thou shalt not make unto thee any graven image.

_____ Exodus 20:4

(3) Thou shalt not take the Name of the LORD thy God in vain.

_____ Exodus 20:7

(4) Remember the Sabbath Day, to keep it holy.

_____ Exodus 20:8

(5) Honour thy father and thy mother. Exodus 20:12

(6) Thou shalt not kill. Exodus 20:13

(7) Thou shalt not commit adultery. Exodus 20:14

(8) Thou shalt not steal. Exodus 20:15

(9) Thou shalt not bear false witness. Exodus 20:16

(10) Thou shalt not covet. Exodus 20:17

Exodus 20:18–21

When the Israelites saw God's power on the mountain, they asked Moses to speak the words of God to them, rather than having God speak to them directly.

8. Which of these statements tells why the people did not want to hear God speaking?
   a. They did not love God.
   b. They had heard all His words before.
   (c.) They were afraid of God.

9. Which of these statements tells why God spoke to the people in this way?
   (a.) God wanted them to fear Him and stop sinning.
   b. God wanted them to listen to Him instead of to Moses.
   c. God knew they would enjoy hearing Him speak.

7. What did Moses tell the people when they saw the Egyptians coming? [17] **"Fear ye not, stand still, and see the salvation of the LORD."**

8. What did God tell Moses to do after the Israelites had safely crossed the Red Sea? [17] **God told him to stretch out his hand over the sea so that the waters would come back.**

In This Lesson

Scope: Exodus 19–24

Main Events
- God reveals His power as He descends on Mount Sinai.
- God gives the Ten Commandments from Mount Sinai.
- God leads the Israelites in an orderly way.

Objectives
- Students should be able to
  —describe the scene on Mount Sinai when God gave the Law. (See Part A, numbers 5, 6.)
  —recite the Ten Commandments in simple form. (See Part A, number 7.)
  —tell who ate and drank with Moses in God's presence. (the Israelite leaders)
  —tell how long Moses stayed on Mount Sinai. (forty days and forty nights)

God Meets With the Leaders of Israel

The Israelites promised to obey all the words of the LORD (Exodus 24:3, 7). However, they did not want God to speak to them directly anymore. So God asked Moses to come up into the mountain.

Exodus 24:9–18

10. Who went up with Moses to meet God?
    a. the leaders of the Israelites
    b. all the men of Israel
    c. only those men of Israel who obeyed God

These men must have seen God only in part because any man seeing the full glory of God would have died (Exodus 33:20).

11. What did these men do in God's presence?
    a. They read the Bible.
    b. They ate and drank.
    c. They prayed to God.

12. Why did God want Moses to come up into the mountain? ____
    God wanted to give Moses His Law on tables of stone.

13. What was Moses to do with what God gave him in the mountain? ____
    Moses was to teach the Israelites God's Law.

14. How long was Moses on the mountain with God? forty days and forty nights

This was the first time that God gave His commands to man in writing. Before this, God had spoken to one family at a time, but now He spoke to His people as a nation. A written law would be easier for His people to remember and follow. Moses also wrote the other words that God spoke to him in books that we can still read today. The books that Moses wrote are Genesis, Exodus, Leviticus, Numbers, and Deuteronomy.

Where Is It Found?

15. The Ten Commandments are found in chapter __20__ of Exodus.

GOD'S WORD

God's Word is a light on the pathway ahead,
To show me the way that my footsteps should tread.

God's Word is a fountain whose waters so pure
Give life to my soul and salvation assure.

God's Word is the food which my Saviour supplies;
It's sweeter than honey, my soul satisfies.

It's God's final message, our guidebook, the key,
That we may be ready for eternity.

—Ada Wine

—tell which two Old Testament commandments Jesus said are the greatest. (See Part C, number 3.)

Truths to Instill

- The Israelites promised God, "All that the LORD hath said will we do, and be obedient" (Exodus 24:7), but they broke their promise before Moses came down from the mountain. This shows that it is impossible for man to live up to God's laws without the help of the Holy Spirit.
- God gave the Law to Israel from an untouchable mountain that burned with fire, in "blackness, and darkness, and tempest"—a sight so terrible that Moses said, "I exceedingly fear and quake." Today, under a better covenant, we have the Spirit of the living God writing His law upon our hearts. See Hebrews 12:18–24 and 2 Corinthians 3.
- Because we live under the New Covenant, we no longer keep the letter of the Old Testament Law (2 Corinthians 3:7). However, the principles of the Ten Commandments and other laws God gave from Mount Sinai have been carried over to New Testament applications. For this reason, it is profitable to study the Law and its applications in Israel's time.

B. BIBLE WORD STUDY

★ *Match these definitions with the Bible words on the right. Read the verses given or use a dictionary if you need help. All references are from Exodus.*

c   1. Lower; bottom (19:17)

e   2. An idol carved from wood or stone (20:4)

f   3. To set apart for holy purposes (20:11)

a   4. To wish greatly for something that belongs to another person (20:17)

d   5. An important person (24:11)

b   6. A thin slab (24:12)

a. covet

b. table

c. nether

d. noble

e. graven image

f. hallow

C. THINKING ABOUT BIBLE TRUTHS

Exodus 20:1–17

1. The Ten Commandments can be divided into two groups. One group of commandments tells us how to honor God, and the other group tells us how to treat other people.
   a. Which of the Ten Commandments tell us how to honor God? (the first four, the last six)
   b. Which of the Ten Commandments tell us how to treat other people? (the first four, the last six)

2. Which one of the Ten Commandments includes a promise? "Honour thy father and thy mother."

Mark 12:28–31

The Ten Commandments were a foundation for the laws that God gave the Israelites. Later, He gave them more laws to guide them as a nation.

3. In these verses, a scribe asked Jesus which commandment was the most important. Jesus told him what the two most important commandments are. These two commandments are not among the Ten Commandments, but anyone who obeys them is obeying all the Ten Commandments.
   a. Copy the most important Old Testament command as Jesus gave it in Mark 12. The first few words are given for you. *Thou shalt* love the Lord thy God with all thy heart, and with all thy soul, and with all thy mind, and with all thy strength."
   b. Copy the second most important command. *Thou shalt* love thy neighbour as thyself."

- This commandment is given in Deuteronomy 6:4, 5.

- This commandment is given in Leviticus 19:18.

EXTRA ASSIGNMENT

What the New Testament Says About the Ten Commandments

God gave the Old Testament Law to the children of Israel. Later, He gave a new covenant to the church. That is why we follow the New Testament instead of the Old Testament.

However, God still wants His people to obey the principles, or general truths, taught by the Ten Commandments. The New Testament repeats some of the Ten Commandments almost exactly as God gave them to Moses. For others, the New Testament gives better ways to do what God wants. For example, the sixth commandment says, "Thou shalt not kill," but the New Testament adds, "Whosoever hateth his brother is a murderer." The New Testament does not mention the Sabbath (Saturday) as a day of rest. Instead, it shows how Jesus' disciples honored Him by worshiping on the Lord's Day (Sunday), the day He rose from the dead.

★ *Each reference on the right shows how we should keep one of the Ten Commandments today. Match each reference with the commandment to which it refers.*

<u> h </u> 1. Thou shalt have no other gods before me. a. 1 John 3:15

<u> j </u> 2. Thou shalt not make unto thee any graven image. b. Acts 20:7

<u> i </u> 3. Thou shalt not take the Name of the LORD thy God in vain. c. Ephesians 4:28

<u> b </u> 4. Remember the Sabbath Day, to keep it holy. d. Ephesians 6:1–3

<u> d </u> 5. Honour thy father and thy mother. e. James 4:11

<u> a </u> 6. Thou shalt not kill. f. Luke 12:15

<u> g </u> 7. Thou shalt not commit adultery. g. Mark 10:11, 12

<u> c </u> 8. Thou shalt not steal. h. Matthew 4:10

<u> e </u> 9. Thou shalt not bear false witness. i. Matthew 5:34–37

<u> f </u> 10. Thou shalt not covet. j. Acts 17:29, 30

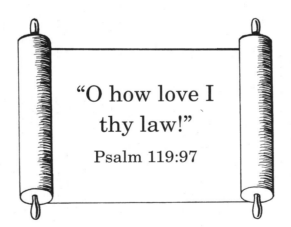

"O how love I thy law!"
Psalm 119:97

This section can be done in class or assigned to fast students who need a challenge. It is important to make clear to the students that we no longer keep the Old Testament Law. However, as this exercise shows, most of the Ten Commandments have been reinstated in the New Testament. The ones that have not, such as the fourth commandment, are still carried over in principle.

The Sermon on the Mount enlarges on many principles from the Ten Commandments. You might want to plan a series of devotionals on this theme to help the students see how we should apply these principles under the New Covenant.

D. LEARNING MORE ABOUT THE BIBLE

The Laws Given at Mount Sinai

God gave many laws at Mount Sinai besides the Ten Commandments. You have already seen that the Ten Commandments can be divided into two groups, those that tell us how to love God and those that tell us how to love our neighbors. All the other laws of God can also be divided between these two groups.

The following exercise lists a few of the additional laws that God gave to Israel through Moses. Some of these laws told the Israelites how to treat their neighbors, families, and servants. Other laws told them how to serve the LORD and keep themselves from ungodly things.

★ *Look up each reference, and write it under the law to which it refers.*

Exodus 22:22	Leviticus 11:4–8	Leviticus 19:32	Deuteronomy 6:6, 7
Exodus 23:1	Leviticus 19:9, 10	Leviticus 20:7	Deuteronomy 10:19
Exodus 23:2	Leviticus 19:11	Leviticus 22:21	Deuteronomy 20:19
Leviticus 7:26	Leviticus 19:14	Leviticus 27:32	Deuteronomy 22:5

Laws Relating to God

1. Live holy lives.
   Leviticus 20:7

2. Give a tithe (tenth) to the Lord.
   Leviticus 27:32

3. Offer only perfect offerings to the Lord.   Leviticus 22:21

4. Teach your children God's laws.
   Deuteronomy 6:6, 7

5. Men and women must not wear the same clothing. Deuteronomy 22:5

6. Do not eat the blood of animals.
   Leviticus 7:26

7. Do not eat unclean animals.
   Leviticus 11:4–8

8. Do not follow a multitude to do evil.   Exodus 23:2

Laws Relating to Our Neighbors

1. Be kind to widows and orphans.
   Exodus 22:22

2. Be kind to the handicapped (deaf and blind).   Leviticus 19:14

3. Have love for strangers.
   Deuteronomy 10:19

4. Share your crops with others.
   Leviticus 19:9, 10

5. Respect and honor older persons.
   Leviticus 19:32

6. Do not start a false report.
   Exodus 23:1

7. Do not tell lies.
   Leviticus 19:11

8. Do not destroy your enemy's trees.
   Deuteronomy 20:19

132

Lesson 19. The Israelites Learn to Worship God

In the last lesson, you saw how God spoke to the Israelites from Mount Sinai. The Israelites promised to obey all His words. But they were so frightened by His power that they begged Moses to speak to God for them. They were afraid that they would die if God spoke directly to them again. Soon after this, God told Moses to come up the mountain to talk with Him.

Moses stayed on Mount Sinai for forty days. God told Moses how He wanted His people to worship Him. He also gave him tables of stone on which He had written His laws. But after Moses had been on the mountain for a while, the Israelites grew tired of waiting for him. They did not know what had happened to Moses, so they begged Aaron to make them some gods to lead them.

The Israelites had just seen God's mighty power when He spoke to them from Mount Sinai. They had eaten the manna He sent them every day. They had drunk the water He gave them from a rock. Yet they wanted to worship other gods! Aaron should have rebuked the people for asking for such dreadful things. But Aaron was afraid to stand against them. He melted their golden earrings and made a calf for them to worship.

God was grieved and greatly displeased. He threatened to destroy the Israelites completely. But Moses fell down before God and pleaded with Him to give the people another opportunity. God had mercy on them and forgave them.

After this rebellion, God showed the Israelites the right way to worship Him. God did not want them to worship Him in the same way that they worshiped idols. They could not worship Him by eating, drinking, and rising up to play. Worshiping God was a holy and beautiful experience. God also showed the Israelites how to build a tabernacle in which to worship Him.

A. ANSWERS FROM THE BIBLE

Instructions on the Mountain

Up on the mountain, God told Moses how to make a tabernacle (a tent) in which to worship Him. He also explained what furniture the tabernacle was to have, and how to make clothing for the priests. You can read these instructions in Exodus, chapters 25–31.

Exodus 25:1–9

1. What did God ask the Israelites to bring as an offering to Him?

   a. __gold__ , __silver__ , and __brass__ (verse 3)

   b. __blue__ , __purple__ , and __scarlet__ yarn; __fine__ __linen__ ; and __goats'__ __hair__ (verse 4)

   c. __rams'__ __skins__ dyed red, __badgers'__ __skins__ , and __shittim__ __wood__ (verse 5)

   d. __oil__ and __spices__ (verse 6)

   e. __onyx__ __stones__ and __stones__ for the ephod and breastplate (verse 7)

- Number 1-c. The original word translated *badger* (badgers' skins) does not appear to be a native Hebrew word, and scholars are uncertain of its meaning. Some believe that it refers to porpoises or sea cows. Others think it must refer to a "clean" animal, since the skins were used to cover the tabernacle, and that badgers' skins were simply cured skins (leather).
- Number 1-c. Shittim wood is the beautiful, close-grained wood of the acacia tree, which grows in the deserts of Sinai and southern Palestine. The wood is orange when first cut, but it darkens with age until it is almost black.

Lesson 19

Oral Review

1. What did God compare Abraham's descendants to? [7, 8] **the dust of the earth, the stars of the heaven, the sand of the seashore**
2. How did Joseph know that his brothers had changed? [13] **He could see that they loved Benjamin.**
3. What does the word *manna* mean? [16] **"What is it?"**
4. Say the Ten Commandments. [18]
   (1) Thou shalt have no other gods before me.
   (2) Thou shalt not make unto thee any graven image.
   (3) Thou shalt not take the Name of the LORD thy God in vain.
   (4) Remember the Sabbath Day, to keep it holy.
   (5) Honour thy father and thy mother.
   (6) Thou shalt not kill.
   (7) Thou shalt not commit adultery.
   (8) Thou shalt not steal.
   (9) Thou shalt not bear false witness.
   (10) Thou shalt not covet.
5. Which two Old Testament commandments did Jesus say are the greatest? [18] **"Thou shalt love the Lord thy God with all thy heart, and with all thy soul, and with all thy mind, and with all thy strength." "Thou shalt love thy neighbour as thyself."**

Lesson 19. The Israelites Learn to Worship God   **133**

2. According to verse 2, Moses was to accept only the offering of every man who gave it "___willingly___ with his ___heart___."

3. The Israelites had been slaves in Egypt. Where did they get all these expensive things? (Read Exodus 12:35, 36 again, if you do not remember.) _____
___The Egyptians had given these things to the Israelites.___

Sin in Israel's Camp

While Moses was talking with God on the mountain, the Israelites grew tired of waiting for him. They decided that they needed a god like the gods of Egypt.

Exodus 32:1–6

4. The Israelites asked for other gods
   a. before God spoke to them from Mount Sinai.
   (b.) while Moses was still on Mount Sinai.
   c. because they wanted to go back to Egypt.

5. The golden calf was made by
   (a.) Aaron, the brother of Moses.
   b. the idol worshipers.
   c. Moses' enemies.

6. According to verse 5, Aaron proclaimed a feast
   (a.) to the LORD.
   b. to the golden calf.
   c. to the gods of Egypt.

God told Moses to go down and see what the Israelites were doing. God knew about their rebellion. He could see into their hearts because God sees everything. God told Moses that He would destroy the Israelites at once. But Moses begged Him to have patience and to remember His promises to Abraham, Isaac, and Jacob. Because of Moses' plea, God showed mercy to His people again.

Exodus 32:15–20

7. At first, Joshua thought the noise of the people was
   a. dancing and singing.
   (b.) fighting and shouting.
   c. praying and praising God.

8. The noise was really the sound of
   (a.) dancing and singing.
   b. fighting and shouting.
   c. praying and praising God.

9. The tables of stone on which God had written His laws
   a. were broken by the people.
   b. were broken by God.
   (c.) were broken by Moses.

- The Israelites could not have forgotten what they had experienced in their encounter with God just weeks before they worshiped the golden calf. However, it seems they still did not understand that the God of their fathers is the *only* God. Evidently they felt it was possible to choose between gods, and the gods of Egypt had not been as fearful as this "new" God appeared to be. So they washed their hands of God and went back to the ways that they were more comfortable with. The mixed multitude that left Egypt with the Israelites may have had much to do with this decision.

- Number 6. This exercise brings out an intriguing point. Did Aaron actually think that they could worship God with this idolatrous feast? Or was he trying to salve his conscience by proclaiming the feast as one to the LORD? Perhaps the Israelites were trying to use heathen ways to worship the true God. Whichever is true, their actions were inexcusable in God's eyes. He would have destroyed the entire group had it not been for Moses' intercession.

In This Lesson

Scope: Exodus 25–40

Main Events

- Moses receives instructions from God while he is on Mount Sinai for forty days.
- While Moses is on the mountain, the Israelites persuade Aaron to make a golden calf.
- Moses breaks the stone tablets, destroys the golden calf, and commands the Levites to slay their brethren.
- Moses pleads with God to spare the Israelites.
- The Israelites build the tabernacle and worship God.

Objectives

- Students should know
  —how the Israelites were able to build the costly tabernacle in a desert. (The Egyptians had given them many things when they left Egypt.)
  —who made the golden calf, and what Moses did about it. (See Part A, numbers 4–13.)
  —how God showed His approval of the tabernacle when it stood complete. (His glory filled the tabernacle.)
  —what four pieces of furniture were in the tabernacle. (the altar of incense, the table of shewbread, the candlestick, the ark and mercy seat)

10. Moses had the golden calf *(choose three)*

a. thrown down.
(b.) burned.
c. buried.
(d.) ground to powder.

(e.) scattered on the drinking water.
f. broken to pieces.
g. melted so that they could use the gold in the tabernacle.

Sin Is Punished

The Bible says that "the wages of sin is death" (Romans 6:23). God will not let sin go unpunished. Even though He had promised Moses that He would not destroy the Israelites entirely, God still needed to deal with the sin among them.

Exodus 32:26–28

11. When Moses asked, "Who is on the LORD's side?" those who stood with him were
a. the older, more mature men.
b. those who had not helped to make the calf.
(c.) the men of the tribe of Levi.

12. Because of the Israelites' disobedience,
a. three hundred men died.
(b.) three thousand men died.
c. ten thousand men died.

After Moses had put an end to the idol worship, he climbed Mount Sinai again to plead for his people. He realized now why God had been so angry with them.

Exodus 32:30–35

13. Which statement best tells how Moses showed his great love for his people?
a. He told the Israelites that he would try to make atonement for their sin.
b. He told God that the Israelites had sinned.
(c.) He offered to have his name blotted out of God's book to save his people.

The Tabernacle Is Built

Many of the Israelites were ready to help with the tabernacle. This was one way for them to show God and Moses that they were sorry for making the golden calf and worshiping it.

Exodus 35:20–35

14. The Israelites showed they wanted to worship God by
a. weeping and bringing beautiful presents to Moses.
(b.) giving willingly for the building of the tabernacle.
c. promising never to disobey Moses again.

15. One thing that the men brought was
(a.) red skins of rams.
b. vessels of gold.
c. spice and oil for the light.

Truths to Instill

- The meekness of Moses. When God offered to destroy the people and make of Moses a great nation, Moses took the lowest position, asking God to blot his name out of His book rather than to destroy Israel. Ask your students how they can display meekness at school, "in honour preferring one another" (Romans 12:10).

- God's omnipresence. God allowed the Israelites to build a tabernacle for His dwelling place, but even in this, His omnipresence was symbolized. The tabernacle was to be movable, showing that God is not limited to one place. The Israelites were to follow the moving cloud, rather than establish a certain place of worship. Later, Stephen testified before the Sanhedrin, "The most High dwelleth not in temples made with hands; as saith the prophet, Heaven is my throne, and earth is my footstool: what house will ye build me? saith the Lord: or what is the place of my rest? Hath not my hand made all these things?" (Acts 7:48–50).

16. The women brought
   a. onyx stones and stones to be set.
   b. food and drink for the workmen.
   c. colored yarn, fine linen, and goats' hair.

17. The rulers brought
   a. precious stones and spices.
   b. money and jewels.
   c. bracelets and earrings.

The people gave so willingly that they brought much more than enough to build the tabernacle. Moses had to tell them to stop bringing more. Bezaleel and Aholiab built the tabernacle, with the help of every man "whose heart stirred him up." For many hours they worked carefully, cutting trees and carving the wood, melting and shaping metal, and weaving and sewing material. Finally the tabernacle was finished.

Exodus 40:34–38

18. The Israelites knew that the LORD was pleased with the work they had done because
   a. He blessed them with much to eat and to wear.
   b. He promised He would always give them what they wanted.
   c. His glory filled the tabernacle.

19. The cloud of the LORD stayed with the Israelites
   a. until they left Mount Sinai.
   b. throughout all their journeys.
   c. for forty days.

Where Is It Found?

20. The story of the Israelites making the golden calf is found in
   a. Exodus 22.   b. Exodus 30.   c. Exodus 32.   d. Exodus 35.

21. The story of God's presence filling the tabernacle is found in
   a. Exodus 25.   b. Exodus 32.   c. Exodus 35.   d. Exodus 40.

Spend some time discussing the building of the tabernacle. God had given special abilities to the men who did this work. It is very difficult, even with modern technology, to overlay wood with metal as they did.

The Traditional
Mount Sinai

Library of Congress

B. BIBLE WORD STUDY

The High Priest's Clothing

★ *God told Moses how to make the clothes worn by Aaron and other high priests after him. Read the verses given to find the names for the different parts of the high priest's clothing.*

On the front of the (1) __mitre__ (turban) was a gold plate engraved with the words "HOLINESS TO THE LORD" (Exodus 28:36–38).

The (2) __breastplate__ was a folded piece of material, like a pocket. On it were set twelve precious stones (Exodus 28:15, 17).

The (3) __girdle__ (belt) was made with gold thread, with blue, purple, and scarlet yarn, and with finely twisted linen (Exodus 28:8).

The (4) __ephod__ was an apron-like coat. It was also made with gold thread, with blue, purple, and scarlet yarn, and with finely twisted linen. On its shoulders lay two onyx stones set in gold, with the names of the twelve tribes engraved on them (Exodus 28:6, 9–12).

Within the breastplate lay the (5) __Urim__ and __Thummim__. The high priest used these to ask counsel of God. We do not know what they looked like or exactly how they were used (Exodus 28:30; Numbers 27:21).

The (6) __robe__ of the ephod was made of blue cloth. It had a special border around the neck to keep it from tearing (Exodus 28:31, 32).

Around the bottom of the high priest's clothes hung a string of golden (7) __bells__ and pomegranates. As long as they were making a noise, the people knew that the priest was still alive and was ministering to the LORD (Exodus 28:33–35).

- Number 1. The modern spelling is *miter*.

C. THINKING ABOUT BIBLE TRUTHS

Exodus 40:36–38

1. Most places of worship are buildings that stay in one place. Why was the tabernacle made of movable boards and tent materials? _____

   The tabernacle was taken down each time the Israelites moved.

   _____

2 Chronicles 2:4–6

Many years later, King Solomon built a temple to take the place of the tabernacle. These verses record what Solomon said about God when he started to build the temple.

2. Can man build a temple or a tabernacle large enough to contain God? ___no___

3. Why did Solomon build a temple for the LORD? _____

  as a place of worship where people could offer sacrifices to God

4. Which of the following statements is the best reason why the Israelites built a tabernacle for God?

    a. All the nations around them had temples for their gods. If the Israelites did not have one, the other nations might think they did not have a god.

    (b) It was a place where they could worship God and offer sacrifices to Him. It would also remind them of who God is and what He expected of them.

    c. A tabernacle was cheaper to build than a temple.

D. LEARNING MORE ABOUT THE BIBLE

The Tabernacle

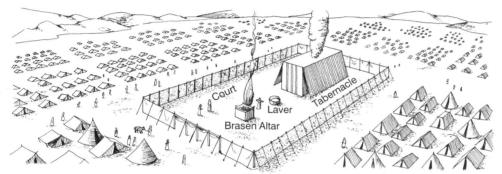

The entrance to the tabernacle was 20 cubits (30 feet) wide. It always faced east.

The court of the tabernacle was 100 cubits (150 feet) long and 50 cubits (75 feet) wide.

Three layers of material covered the tabernacle.

The first layer was made of (1) ____goats' hair____ (Exodus 26:7).
The second layer was made of (2) __rams' skins dyed red__ (Exodus 26:14).
The top layer was made of (3) ____badgers' skins____ (Exodus 26:14).

1. 2. 3.

Make sure students realize that worship at the tabernacle was quite different from our worship services today. Old Testament worship centered around the offering of animal sacrifices. Regular offerings included daily sacrifices, Sabbath sacrifices, monthly sacrifices, and sacrifices for special days such as the Passover, Pentecost, and the Day of Atonement. In addition to these public sacrifices, individuals brought sacrifices when they had sinned, needed ceremonial cleansing, or wanted to give a special gift to God. These many sacrifices illustrated that sin requires the shedding of blood, for "without shedding of blood is no remission" (Hebrews 9:22).

Most of the furniture in the tabernacle was made of shittim (acacia) wood and was covered with thin sheets of gold. Acacia trees, common on the Sinai Peninsula, produce lumber that wood-eating insects do not destroy. The candlestick in the holy place and the mercy seat on top of the ark were made of pure gold.

Inside the holy place of the tabernacle stood:

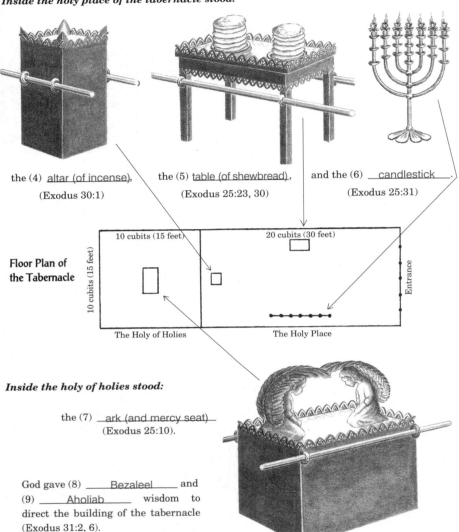

the (4) altar (of incense),   the (5) table (of shewbread),   and the (6) candlestick .

(Exodus 30:1)   (Exodus 25:23, 30)   (Exodus 25:31)

Floor Plan of the Tabernacle

10 cubits (15 feet)

20 cubits (30 feet)

10 cubits (15 feet)

Entrance

The Holy of Holies   The Holy Place

Inside the holy of holies stood:

the (7) ark (and mercy seat) (Exodus 25:10).

God gave (8) Bezaleel and (9) Aholiab wisdom to direct the building of the tabernacle (Exodus 31:2, 6).

139

Lesson 20. The Israelites' Faith Is Challenged

In this chapter, you have studied about some things that the Israelites learned from God while traveling through the desert. They learned to depend on God for their food and water. They learned how to live godly lives and how to worship God. But had they really learned to trust God and to follow wherever He would lead them?

Before He allowed the Israelites to enter Canaan, God tested their faith one more time. He told Moses to send twelve spies into the Promised Land. What kind of report would they bring back? Would the Israelites be ready to enter the Promised Land?

The spies all agreed that Canaan was a good land. But only Joshua and Caleb believed that God was able to give it to them. The other ten felt that they were not strong enough to conquer it. Because of their report, the Israelites rebelled against God. They even talked about electing a new captain to lead them back to Egypt.

God does not tolerate rebellion. What would He do now? You will find out what happened to the Israelites as you study this lesson.

A. ANSWERS FROM THE BIBLE

The Twelve Spies Report on Canaan

When it was time for Israel to enter Canaan, the LORD told Moses to send twelve men to look over the Promised Land and bring back a report.

Numbers 13:17–20

1. Moses sent twelve men to _____spy_____ out the land of Canaan.

2. They were to bring back some of the _____fruit_____ of the land.

Numbers 13:26–33

3. The spies showed the fruit of the land "unto _____all_____ the _congregation_."

4. Ten of the spies said, "The people are ___strong___, and the cities are _____walled_____ and very ___great___."

5. But Caleb said, "Let us _____go up at once_____, and possess it; for we are _____well able to overcome it_____."

6. The ten spies were afraid of the sons of ____Anak____, who were ____giants____.

The People Fear to Enter the Promised Land

The report of the ten spies was a bitter disappointment to the Israelites.

Lesson 20

Oral Review

1. About how many years have passed since the Creation? [6] **about 6,000**
2. How did God guide the Israelites through the wilderness? [17] **with a pillar of cloud by day and a pillar of fire by night**
3. What did the Israelites see and hear when God descended upon Mount Sinai? [18] **(The students should know at least several of these.) They saw lightning, a thick cloud, fire, and smoke. They heard thunder and a loud trumpet sound.**

4. Say the Ten Commandments. [18]
   (1) Thou shalt have no other gods before me.
   (2) Thou shalt not make unto thee any graven image.
   (3) Thou shalt not take the Name of the LORD thy God in vain.
   (4) Remember the Sabbath Day, to keep it holy.
   (5) Honour thy father and thy mother.
   (6) Thou shalt not kill.
   (7) Thou shalt not commit adultery.
   (8) Thou shalt not steal.
   (9) Thou shalt not bear false witness.
   (10) Thou shalt not covet.
5. Who made the golden calf? [19] **Aaron**

140 Chapter Four Israel in the Wilderness

Numbers 14:1–5

7. The Israelites wept all night and said, "Would God _____
   that we had died in the land of Egypt _____!
   or would God __we had died in this wilderness_____!"

8. They said one to another, "Let us _____make a captain_____, and let us
   _____return into Egypt_____."

Numbers 14:26–32

9. How did God give the Israelites exactly what they had asked for? __The Israelites had said,__
   "Would God we had died in this wilderness," so God told them that they would die there.

10. Who would not enter the land of Canaan? _____
    all those twenty years old and upward who had murmured

11. Who would enter the land of Canaan? _____
    Caleb, Joshua, and the children of the murmurers

The Israelites Rebel Against God

After God told the Israelites that they would die in the wilderness, they changed their minds and decided to try to conquer Canaan. But God was not with them, and their efforts failed, as all rebellion against God does. The Israelites rebelled a number of other times during their years in the wilderness. Each time, God punished them for their sin.

★ *Look up the references given, and match the punishment with the rebellion.*

Rebellion	Punishment
__c__ 12. Miriam and Aaron speak against Moses (Numbers 12:1–3, 9, 10).	a. The earth opens and swallows the rebellious men and their families. Fire consumes the rebellious princes.
__d__ 13. The Israelites try to enter the Promised Land, even though Moses warns them not to go (Numbers 14:39–45).	b. Fiery serpents bite the people.
__a__ 14. Korah, Dathan, and Abiram rise up against Moses (Numbers 16:1–4, 30–35).	c. God sends leprosy on one of the rebellious persons.
__b__ 15. The Israelites speak against God and against Moses (Numbers 21:4–6).	d. The rebellious people are defeated and driven back.

6. What three pieces of furniture were in the Holy Place of the tabernacle? [19] **the golden candlestick, the altar of incense, and the table of shewbread**

In This Lesson

Scope: Numbers and Deuteronomy

Main Events

- Twelve spies see that Canaan is a good land, but ten of them discourage the Israelites.
- Caleb and Joshua encourage the people to trust God, but they refuse.
- The Israelites wander in the wilderness forty years because of their unbelief.
- Moses and Aaron die in the wilderness because of their sin.

Objectives

- Students should know
  - how Caleb and Joshua's report differed from the ten spies' report. (See Part A, numbers 4–6.)
  - how the Israelites responded to these reports, and the result of their lack of faith. (See Part A, numbers 7–11.)
  - why Moses and Aaron could not enter the Promised Land. (Moses disobeyed God when he brought water out of a rock by hitting it twice instead of by speaking to it.)

G
R
A
P
E
S

Grapes have been cultivated since ancient times. Noah planted grapes after he left the ark on Mount Ararat (Genesis 9:20). Juicy clusters of grapes hanging among dark green leaves became the symbol of peace and prosperity for the Israelites. They raised grapes on wooden arbors outside their homes, where the grapevines made shady places to sit during the midday heat (1 Kings 4:25).

The Israelites ate grapes fresh or dried them as raisins. Grape juice was pressed directly into the cup (Genesis 40:11) or fermented in goatskins to become wine. The Bible warns against using intoxicating wine (Proverbs 23:29–35).

Grape juice in Bible times was sometimes preserved by boiling it until it thickened into a sweet syrup called *dibs*. This syrup was used like honey as a sweetener. Sometimes when the Bible speaks of honey, it may be referring to this grape honey.

What proves that the Canaanites raised grapes before the Israelites conquered Canaan? (Numbers 13:23, 24).

Moses Strikes the Rock

For almost forty years, Moses meekly obeyed God and led the Israelites through the wilderness. However, Moses disobeyed God's command one time. The Israelites needed water, so God told Moses to speak to a rock, and water would come forth. Instead, Moses hit the rock twice.

Numbers 20:10–12, 28

16. Because Moses and Aaron sinned, God said that
    a. He would not sanctify them in the eyes of the people.
    b. they would not lead the Israelites into the land of Canaan.
    c. they would need to wander in the wilderness for another forty years.

17. Aaron died soon after this, and ____Eleazar____, his son, became the next high priest.

Deuteronomy 34:1–6

God refused to let Moses enter the Promised Land. Joshua would lead the Israelites into Canaan. However, before Moses died, God showed him the land of Canaan from the top of Mount Nebo.

18. Why does no man know where Moses' sepulcher (grave) is? _____

    The LORD buried Moses without anyone knowing where. _____

Where Is It Found?

19. Most of the Bible stories you have studied so far are in the first two Books of Moses. Write the names of those two books here.
    a. _____Genesis_____
    b. _____Exodus_____

—where Moses died and who buried him. (on Mount Nebo; God)

Truths to Instill

- Discouragement. The children of Israel suffered from a lack of faith and an unwillingness to obey God. Because they lacked faith, the task God gave them looked impossible. This made them unwilling, and they became discouraged. Students sometimes become discouraged for the same reason.

- Caleb and Joshua show us how to overcome discouragement. They were willing to do what was right, and they believed that God would help them do it.

- Appreciation for God's laws. God had set before His people wise and holy laws—laws far superior to those of any other nation. He told the Israelites that if they kept His laws, other nations would say, "Surely this great nation is a wise and understanding people." After giving His laws, God cried out, "O that there were such an heart in them, that they would fear me, and keep all my commandments always, that it might be well with them, and with their children for ever!" (Deuteronomy 5:29).

20. There are three more Books of Moses. Leviticus is a book of laws. Numbers tells how Moses numbered the Israelites. Deuteronomy gives Moses' last instructions and warnings to the Israelites.

a. In which book can you find the number of people in the tribe of Judah?

_____ Numbers _____

b. In which book can you find warnings about what would happen to the Israelites if they disobeyed God? _____ Deuteronomy _____

c. In which book can you find laws telling the Israelites how to offer sacrifices?

_____ Leviticus _____

B. BIBLE WORD STUDY

★ *Read the verses in which the following words appear. Then circle the letter of the meaning that matches the word as it is used in that verse. This may be different from the meaning given in your dictionary.*

1. Meek (Numbers 12:3)
   a. happy; rejoicing in God
   (b.) humble; willing to endure patiently
   c. helpless; lacking determination

2. Pomegranates (Numbers 13:23. Also read 1 Samuel 14:2.)
   a. small, juicy watermelon raised in Egypt
   (b.) round, seedy fruit of a semitropical tree
   c. grapes that grow in very large clusters

3. Stature (Numbers 13:32)
   (a.) the height of a man or an animal
   b. a monument, image, or idol
   c. the position or condition of a person

4. Prey (Numbers 14:3)
   a. an animal hunted by another for food
   (b.) people or goods captured by an enemy
   c. to ask God for help

5. Carcases (Numbers 14:29)
   (a.) dead bodies
   b. knitted woolen jackets
   c. tents made of camels' hair

6. Censers (Numbers 16:6, 7)
   a. papers containing lists of names
   b. wooden blocks burned on the altar of incense
   (c.) metal pans in which incense was burned

The students should not use their dictionaries for this exercise, because some of the meanings have changed substantially since the translation of the KJV. Insist that they deduct the meanings from context. A fifth grade student should be able to do this.

• Number 5. The modern spelling is *carcasses*.

C. THINKING ABOUT BIBLE TRUTHS

Moses led the Israelites for forty years. By the end of that time, all the people who had rebelled were dead, just as God had said. Those who had left Egypt as children were now grown men and women.

Near the end of his life, Moses called the people together and reminded them of what had happened in the wilderness. He repeated God's laws, and he warned the Israelites not to be rebellious as their parents had been. He wrote these words in the book we call Deuteronomy.

1. Read Deuteronomy 4:5–8. How could the Israelites be wise in the sight of other nations? __
   by keeping God's commandments

2. Read Deuteronomy 5:29. Why did God want the Israelites to keep all His commandments always? ____ "That it might be well with them, and with their children for ever."

3. Read Deuteronomy 8:2, 3.
   a. Why did God lead the Israelites in the wilderness for forty years? _____
      "To humble thee, and to prove thee, to know what was in thine heart, whether thou wouldest keep his commandments, or no."
   b. Why did God feed them with manna in the wilderness? _____
      "That he might make thee know that man doth not live by bread only, but by every word that proceedeth out of the mouth of the LORD."

4. Read Deuteronomy 31:24–26. To whom did Moses give the book of the Law after he had finished writing it? _____ to the Levites

D. LEARNING MORE ABOUT THE BIBLE

A Bad Keepsake

Once when the Israelites sinned in the wilderness, God sent poisonous serpents among them. Many people were bitten and died. When the people cried out for help, God told (1) ____ Moses ____ (Numbers 21:8) to make a serpent of brass and put it on a pole. Anyone who looked at the brass serpent was healed.

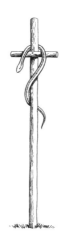

The Israelites kept this serpent even after they no longer needed it. Years later, they began to burn incense to it and worship it as an idol.

When (2) ____ Hezekiah ____ (2 Kings 18:1–4) was king of the Israelites, he destroyed this snake by breaking it in pieces. He called it Nehushtan (only a piece of brass).

Many years later, (3) ____ Jesus ____ (John 3:14–16) explained that He was like the brazen serpent. Everyone who looks to Him in faith can be saved from sin and can live forever.

The Israelites' Camp

God is orderly. He did not free the Israelites from slavery in Egypt only to have them rush like a mob through the desert, with everyone doing as he pleased. Rather, God showed them how to travel in an orderly way. The following diagrams show the orderly arrangement of the Israelite camp and the way they traveled. The tribes numbered 1–6 are the families of the sons of Jacob's wife Leah. Tribes 7–9 descend from Rachel, tribes 10 and 11 from Bilhah, and tribes 12 and 13 from Zilpah. (Compare the names of the tribes with the exercise "Jacob's Family" in Lesson 10. Notice that Joseph's two sons, Ephraim and Manasseh, were each founders of a separate tribe.)

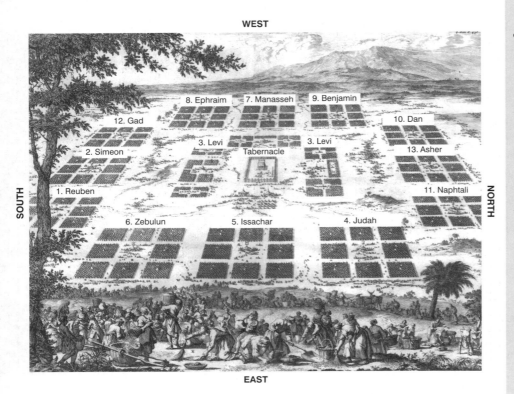

- This diagram is based on Numbers 2, but the exact arrangement of the three tribes on each side is not certain.

• The Israelites' traveling order is based on Numbers 10:14–28.

The Israelites' Traveling Order

★ When the Israelites moved to a new camp, they traveled in the order God had established. The blanks below show this order. Write the name of each tribe in the box with its number. (The numbers are taken from the drawing on Page 144.) The tribe of Levi, which traveled in two groups, has been filled in for you.

Tribes on the north side

10. ____ Dan

13. ____ Asher

11. ____ Naphtali

Tribes on the west side

8. ____ Ephraim

Levites carrying the tabernacle furniture

7. ____ Manasseh

9. ____ Benjamin

Tribes on the south side

1. ____ Reuben

2. ____ Simeon

12. ____ Gad

Levites transporting the tabernacle

Tribes on the east side

4. ____ Judah

5. ____ Issachar

6. ____ Zebulun

Tribes to be colored blue (Leah): Judah, Issachar, Zebulun, Reuben, Simeon, Levi
Tribes to be colored purple (Rachel): Ephraim, Manasseh, Benjamin
Tribes to be colored yellow (Bilhah): Dan, Naphtali
Tribes to be colored green (Zilpah): Gad, Asher

★ After filling in the blanks, lightly color each tribe according to these directions.
1. Color the six tribes from Leah blue. (This includes the tribe of Levi.)
2. Color the three tribes from Rachel purple. (Joseph's two sons and Benjamin.)
3. Color the two tribes from Bilhah yellow.
4. Color the two tribes from Zilpah green.

146

Chapter Four Review

A. ORAL REVIEW

★ *Be sure you know the answers to these questions. Give as many answers as you can without looking back in your book.*

★ *In the first two sections, give an answer for each description. If you need help, match with the lists on the right. To study for the test, cover the lists on the right.*

Who

1. Made the golden calf   Aaron
2. Stood with Moses on the LORD's side and killed three thousand men   Levites
3. Pleaded with God to spare the Israelites   Moses
4. Gave a good report of Canaan   Caleb and Joshua
5. Buried Moses   the LORD
6. Copied the Dead Sea Scrolls   Qumran scribes
7. Found the Dead Sea Scrolls   Arab shepherd boys

The LORD
Caleb and Joshua
Qumran scribes
Moses
Levites
Arab shepherd boys
Aaron

Where

8. The area of Israel's camp where the tabernacle was pitched   The center
9. The part of the tabernacle where the golden table, the candlestick, and the altar of incense stood   The holy place
10. The part of the tabernacle where the ark was kept   The holy of holies

The holy place
The center
The holy of holies

★ *If you need help with the sections below, turn to the Bible reference or the lesson given in brackets.*

What >>

11. What did Moses do after the Israelites were all safely through the Red Sea? [Exodus 14:27]
12. What happened to the first tables of stone? [Exodus 32:19]
13. What Hebrew measure is equal to about five pints? [Lesson 17]
14. What did God ask the Israelites to offer for the building of the tabernacle? (Name at least four things.) [Exodus 25:3–7; Lesson 19]
15. What is an ephod? [Lesson 19]
16. What is a pomegranate? [Lesson 20]

Why >>

17. Why did God not lead the Israelites through the land of the Philistines? [Exodus 13:17]
18. Why did the Israelites call the food God sent them *manna*? [Exodus 16:15; Lesson 16]
19. Why did the people not want to hear God's voice? [Exodus 20:18, 19; Lesson 18]
20. Why were the ten spies afraid to enter Canaan? [Numbers 13:28, 33]

11. Moses stretched out his hand over the sea.
12. Moses broke them.
13. an omer
14. (Any four) gold; silver; brass; blue, purple, and scarlet yarn; fine linen; goats' hair; rams' skins dyed red; badgers' skins; shittim wood; oil; spices; onyx stones; stones
15. an apronlike coat worn by the priests
16. round, seedy fruit of a semi-tropical tree
17. He was afraid they would want to return to Egypt if they saw war.
18. They did not know what the food was, so they called it manna, which means "What is it?"
19. They were afraid of God. (They were afraid they would die.)
20. They were afraid of the strong people, walled cities, and giants that they saw in Canaan.

How   >>

21. How did God guide the Israelites through the wilderness? [Exodus 13:21]
22. How long was Moses on the mountain with God? [Exodus 24:18]
23. How had the Israelites gotten the gold they had with them? [Exodus 12:35, 36; Lesson 19]
24. How did the Israelites know that God was pleased with the tabernacle? [Exodus 40:34]

B. WRITTEN REVIEW

★ *Write the answers to the following questions. If you need help, turn to the Bible reference or the lesson given in brackets.*

What

1. What are several ways that God spoke to men in Old Testament times? Give at least four ways. [Lesson 16] (At least four of these) face to face, by prophets, by angels, in dreams, through His written Word

2. What did the Jews read in their synagogues every Sabbath Day? [Acts 13:14, 15; 15:21] the Law and the Prophets (*or* the Scriptures)

3. What did Moses say when the people saw the Egyptians coming? [Exodus 14:13] "Fear ye not, stand still, and see the salvation of the LORD."

4. What did the spies bring back with them? [Numbers 13:23, 27] fruit from Canaan

5. What did the Israelites wish for after the spies returned? [Numbers 14:2] They wished they had died in Egypt or in the wilderness.

6. What two commandments from the Old Testament did Jesus say are the greatest? [Mark 12:30, 31] "Thou shalt love the Lord thy God with all thy heart, and with all thy soul, and with all thy mind, and with all thy strength." "Thou shalt love thy neighbour as thyself."

Why

7. Why did God give His Word in written form rather than just speaking directly to men? Give three reasons. [Lesson 16] We can remember it better, since we can reread His Word often. We can make copies of His Word to give to others. We can read it, even though we live many years after God gave His Word.

8. Why did most of the Israelites have to die in the desert? [Numbers 14:22, 23; Lesson 20] When God wanted them to enter Canaan, they rebelled and wished they were back in Egypt.

21. with a pillar of cloud by day and a pillar of fire by night
22. forty days and forty nights
23. The Egyptians had given these things to the Israelites.
24. God's glory filled the tabernacle.

9. Why did Moses make a serpent of brass? [Numbers 21:7–9] _____
   so that those who looked at it could be saved from the serpent bites

How

10. How do the Dead Sea Scrolls show that the Old Testament was carefully preserved? [Lesson 16]   The Dead Sea Scrolls are very similar to Hebrew copies that were made about a thousand years later.

The Ten Commandments

11. Write the Ten Commandments from memory. After you finish, use Exodus 20:1–17 to check them. Be sure you know them by memory for the test.
   (1)   Thou shalt have no other gods before me.
   (2)   Thou shalt not make unto thee any graven image.
   (3)   Thou shalt not take the Name of the LORD thy God in vain.
   (4)   Remember the Sabbath Day, to keep it holy.
   (5)   Honour thy father and thy mother.
   (6)   Thou shalt not kill.
   (7)   Thou shalt not commit adultery.
   (8)   Thou shalt not steal.
   (9)   Thou shalt not bear false witness.
   (10)   Thou shalt not covet.

Bible Outline

★ *Match these chapters or books with their descriptions or the events they tell about.*

  b   12. Exodus 13–18
  d   13. Exodus 19–31
  c   14. Exodus 32–34
  a   15. Exodus 35–40
  e   16. Leviticus
  g   17. Numbers
  f   18. Deuteronomy

a. The Israelites build the tabernacle.
b. The Israelites cross the Red Sea and travel toward Mount Sinai.
c. The Israelites worship a golden calf, and Moses pleads to God for them.
d. God gives the Ten Commandments and other laws from Mount Sinai.
e. This book records many of God's laws about sacrifices.
f. This book records Moses' last words.
g. This book tells the number of Israelites and describes their journey through the wilderness.

Map Exercise

★ *Fill in the blanks with these names: Egypt, Canaan, Mount Sinai, Red Sea, Mediterranean Sea, Nile River.*

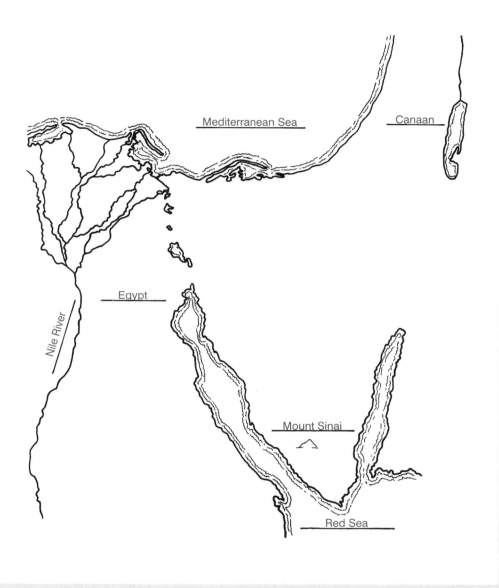

CHAPTER FIVE

Israel Conquers Canaan

They that trust in the LORD shall be as mount Zion, which cannot be removed, but abideth for ever.

As the mountains are round about Jerusalem, so the LORD is round about his people from henceforth even for ever.

(Psalm 125:1, 2)

TIME LINE—Chapter Five
The Conquest of Canaan

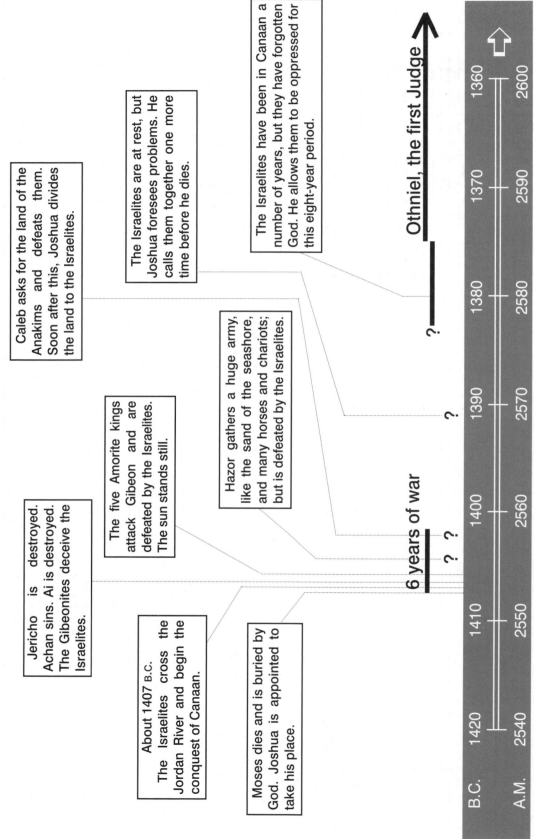

Caleb asks for the land of the Anakims and defeats them. Soon after this, Joshua divides the land to the Israelites.

The Israelites are at rest, but Joshua foresees problems. He calls them together one more time before he dies.

The Israelites have been in Canaan a number of years, but they have forgotten God. He allows them to be oppressed for this eight-year period.

Jericho is destroyed. Achan sins. Ai is destroyed. The Gibeonites deceive the Israelites.

The five Amorite kings attack Gibeon and are defeated by the Israelites. The sun stands still.

Hazor gathers a huge army, like the sand of the seashore, and many horses and chariots; but is defeated by the Israelites.

About 1407 B.C. The Israelites cross the Jordan River and begin the conquest of Canaan.

Moses dies and is buried by God. Joshua is appointed to take his place.

Othniel, the first Judge

6 years of war

? ?

?

?

?

| B.C. | 1420 | 1410 | 1400 | 1390 | 1380 | 1370 | 1360 |
| A.M. | 2540 | 2550 | 2560 | 2570 | 2580 | 2590 | 2600 |

NOTE: The dates on this time line are approximate because of a number of unanswered questions about Bible dates for this period.

153

Lesson 21. Geography of Canaan

In chapter 2, you studied how God called Abraham to move to Canaan from Ur of the Chaldees. In this chapter you will study how God brought Abraham's descendants back into Canaan many years after Jacob took his family to Egypt.

Why did God decide that Canaan would be the homeland of His chosen family? Canaan was an ideal land for the kind of people that God wanted the Israelites to be. It was well suited for pasturing sheep and goats. It had enough good farmland to meet their needs. God described it as a land *flowing* with milk and honey, which shows that it could supply their needs and more besides.

There were other reasons Canaan was the ideal place for God's people. The Egyptians could usually rely on the Nile River for plenty of irrigation water. In Canaan, however, the Israelites needed to depend on the Lord for rain. The Lord promised to send rain as long as His people obeyed Him. But when they turned away from Him, He sometimes sent drought to remind them of their disobedience and that they needed His blessing to live from day to day.

We do not know all the reasons God had for placing His people in Canaan, but in this lesson you will learn some good reasons for His choice.

A. ANSWERS FROM THE BIBLE

★ *Study the Bible passages given. Fill in the short blanks with words, using exact words from the Bible whenever possible. Write complete answers for the questions with long blanks. For multiple choice questions, circle the letter of the correct answer or underline the correct word in parentheses.*

You are going to take a "journey" across Canaan in the next sections of this lesson, starting at the west of Canaan (left) and traveling east (right). The main regions of Canaan are arranged in "rows" running north and south, so you will see each of them as you cross Canaan from west to east. These regions are also marked on Map 1.

Cross Section of Canaan

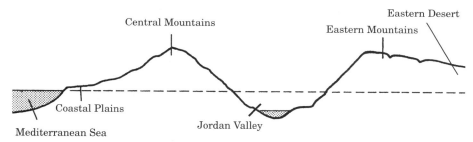

Lesson 21

Oral Review

(The numbers in brackets tell which lessons are being reviewed.)

1. When did Timothy first learn about the Scriptures? [1] **when he was a child**
2. How did God create light and many other things? [2] **He said, "Let there be . . ."**
3. How did Abraham show that he had faith in God? [8] **Abraham left his home without knowing where God would lead him. Abraham believed God's promise even before he had a son. Abraham was willing to sacrifice his promised son.**
4. What do the names *Jacob* and *Israel* mean? [10] **Jacob—heel catcher, supplanter; Israel—having power with God**
5. How is God's written Word better than God's spoken words? [16] **We can remember it better, since we can reread it often. We can make copies of it to give to others. We can read it, even though we live many years after God gave it.**
6. Who stood with Moses on the LORD's side after Israel worshiped the golden calf? [19] **the Levites**
7. Why did the Israelites have to wander in the desert for forty years? [20] **When God wanted them to enter Canaan, they rebelled and wished they were back in Egypt.**

Mountains and Plains of Canaan

8. What did the Israelites wish for after the ten spies gave their report? [20] **They wished they had died in Egypt or in the wilderness.**

In This Lesson

Main Points
- God chose Canaan as the ideal place for His people.
- Canaan can be divided into four main land regions: the coastal plain, the central mountains, the Jordan Valley, and the eastern mountains. East of Canaan lies the eastern desert.
- This lesson teaches how to use a map index.

Objectives
- Students should know
  —where most of the Israelites lived. (in the hill country, which God watered with rainfall)
  —where the Philistines lived. (along the southern coastal plain)
  —that Tyre and Sidon were seaports just north of Israel.
  —that Canaan was the meeting ground of various nations.
  —that the Israelites found it easier to defend the hills than the plains.
  —how to use a map index.

To the west of Canaan lies the Mediterranean Sea. Along the sea is a strip of flat land called a **coastal plain**. Some parts of these lowlands are only a few miles wide. Other parts, especially in the north, were swampy in Bible times. But in the southern part of the coastal plain, a good climate and good soils made the Philistines rich.

Except for small ports at Joppa and Accho, Israel's part of the Mediterranean coast had no deep or sheltered bays to serve as natural harbors. Years later, around the time of Christ, King Herod built a large artificial harbor at Caesarea. Just north of Israel, in the land of the Phoenicians, were the excellent harbors of Tyre and Sidon.

The main route between Egypt and Mesopotamia crossed the coastal plain of Canaan. Travelers from Africa, Asia, and Europe used this route. So did the armies of powerful kings. Because of this, the cities of the coastal plain faced many dangers from invaders passing through to other lands.

1. Who lived in the southern and most fertile part of the coastal plain? ___the Philistines___

_____

2. From what harbor did Jonah leave Israel (Jonah 1:3)? ___Joppa___

3. Name at least six things brought to market in the great harbor city of Tyre (Ezekiel 27:12–24). (Any six) The examples given here are from verses 12–14. Many other items are mentioned in the rest of the passage.

   a. ___silver, iron___   d. ___vessels of brass___

   b. ___tin, lead___   e. ___horses, horsemen___

   c. ___persons of men (slaves)___   f. ___mules___

- Note the exports from Israel (verse 17). Apparently the Israelites raised more wheat than they needed. Wheat was a staple crop, in contrast to the many luxury items at Tyre's markets.

The Central Mountains

Not many miles inland from the Mediterranean Sea, the **central mountains** of Canaan rose up sharply from the coastal plains. The highlands, in contrast to the plains, were not very suitable for roads. Travelers bypassed the highlands if they could. Armies did not like to be caught in them.

The central mountains were not well suited for farming either. Scrub forests, pasturelands, and small, stony fields sloped steeply down to creeks that often lay dry. During winter rains, the thin soil on highland farms washed away and became cut through with deep gullies. In some valleys and level areas, small fields of grain could be raised. Vineyards and olive trees grew on some slopes. But much of the highlands was better suited for grazing flocks of sheep and goats.

The highlands also had advantages. The mountains made good hiding places for the people who lived there. Cities like Hebron, Jerusalem, and Shechem sat securely on protected heights. These cities could be defended more easily than the cities on the plains.

4. Why did the main roads through Canaan follow the Mediterranean Sea? _____

   ___It was easier to travel on the level plain along the sea.___

5. The Israelites held out much longer against the Egyptian, Assyrian, and Babylonian armies than did the Philistines. Why were the Israelite cities easier to defend than the Philistine cities? ___Some of the main Israelite cities were in the mountains.___

   _____

   _____

6. Which occupation was most suitable for the people of the highlands: raising grain, herding sheep, or trading? ___herding sheep___

- Students should know where the following items are on a map of Bible lands:
  —the Jordan Valley
  —the central and eastern mountains
  —the coastal plain
  —Hebron
  —Jerusalem
  —Jericho

Truths to Instill
- God provided the Israelites with an ideal place to live and an abundance of material blessings (Deuteronomy 11:9–12). But the Israelites revealed their human nature by quickly forgetting to be thankful.

156   Chapter Five   Israel Conquers Canaan

7. The Syrians thought it would be easier to fight the Israelites in the valleys than on the hills (1 Kings 20:23). In the valleys they could make better use of their chariots. What did a prophet say the Lord would do to the Syrians (1 Kings 20:28)? _____

The LORD would deliver them into Israel's hand.

The Jordan River Valley

East of the central mountains, the land drops steeply into the **Jordan River Valley**. This valley is part of a long crack in the earth that begins north of Israel. The crack includes the Jordan Valley and the Red Sea, and it continues southward into Africa.

The Sea of Galilee, at 700 feet below sea level, is the lowest body of fresh water on the earth. From it the Jordan River flows into the Dead Sea, which is the lowest spot on earth—1,300 feet below sea level. The city of Jericho, located near the northern end of the Dead Sea, is about 800 feet below sea level.

The Sea of Galilee and the Dead Sea lie only 65 miles apart, but the section of the Jordan River that connects the two is over 200 miles long. Its twisting course winds through dense thickets of tamarisk, willow, cane, and oleander.

- The "long crack" to which this valley belongs is known by geographers as the Great Rift Valley. It begins in Syria and extends to Mozambique, in southeastern Africa.

8. When going from Jerusalem to Jericho, would a person travel uphill or downhill? (Read Luke 10:30 if you are not sure.) ___downhill___

9. Which Bible character lived in Sodom, an old city near the Dead Sea? _____Lot_____

10. Between which two bodies of water does the Jordan River flow? _____

between the Sea of Galilee and the Dead Sea

The Eastern Mountains

Along the eastern edge of the Jordan Valley, the **eastern mountains** stand like a wall that separates the valley from the eastern desert. On the side of these mountains facing the Jordan River, enough rain falls for sheep pasture.

11. Read Numbers 32:1–5. Why did the tribes of Gad and Reuben want to settle in the mountains east of the Jordan River? _____

It was a good land for their cattle.

12. From what great mountain east of the Jordan River did Moses view the Promised Land? (Read Deuteronomy 34:1 if you are not sure.) ___Mount Nebo (Pisgah)___

★ *Study Map 1 and memorize the location of the coastal plain, the central mountains, the Jordan Valley, and the eastern mountains.*

- The highlands east of Jordan include plateaus. These highlands have a higher average elevation than the central mountains. They are known by various names, including the Transjordan Plateau and the Eastern Range. At this grade level we call them the eastern mountains.

Canaan—the Crossroads of the Middle East

God put His people in one of the busiest meeting places on earth. In the area of Canaan, the continent of Asia meets two other continents, Africa and Europe. Ships from the Indian Ocean and the Atlantic Ocean can sail to Canaan through the Red Sea and the Mediterranean Sea. For thousands of years, people from the east, the west, the north, and the south have met in Canaan.

Acts 2:5–12

These verses tell who heard the apostles speak after the Holy Spirit came on the day of Pentecost. As you read, notice the many different places from which people had come to Jerusalem at this time.

13. The people in Jerusalem heard that something strange was taking place, and soon a large crowd had gathered around the apostles.

   a. According to verse 5, Jews from how many different countries heard the apostles speak?

   Jews "out of every nation under heaven"

   b. What miracle took place at this meeting? _____

   Every man heard the message in his own language.

14. Why was a meeting point like Canaan a good place for Bible events to happen and for Jesus to live on the earth? _____

   Many people would hear about the true God as they passed through Canaan.

B. BIBLE STUDY BOOKS

Bible Atlases—Maps for Bible Study

A map is a diagram of an area. This area may be a country, a continent, a city, or any part of one of these. You could even draw a map of your house.

Maps give information about an area. They show the locations of things like cities, lakes, and rivers. Your father probably has some road maps that show where the roads of certain states or provinces go. These maps help him to find places where he has never been.

The maps in a Bible atlas also show how countries and cities have changed. For instance, one map of Canaan may show how things were when Abraham lived. Another map of Canaan may show the land as it was when David was king. Still another map may show what the land of Canaan is like today. The three maps would be different because they show what Canaan was like at three different times.

Using a Map Index

Most atlases have an index at the back. This index lists the names of the places, rivers, lakes, mountains, and other things that are shown on the maps in the atlas. The names are in alphabetical order, the same as in your dictionary.

A map index will tell you which map to use to find the place you are looking for. Some places may be found on several different maps in the atlas. If the map index lists more than one map for the place you want to find, you may need to look at each map to see which is the most useful for you.

A map index may be called by different names, but if you look in the back of the atlas, you will find it. The proper name for a map index is a gazetteer (gaz ih TIHR).

Some gazetteers include letters and numbers from the map grid to help you find the place you are looking for. In Baker's Bible Atlas, for instance, you would see directions like "F6—7." This means that the place you want to find is at F6 on Map 7. Look at the illustration on the following page.

• Map 85 in *The Moody Atlas of Bible Lands* shows the regions mentioned in these verses.

The use of a map index and grid system might be new for your students. Take time to work through at least part of this section together in class. Number 3 provides practice with using a map index to locate places. If your atlases use the grid system, you might want to require students to tell which map and grid block the index gives for each city.

Not every Bible atlas uses the grid system. The Moody Atlas of Bible Lands gives map numbers only, and its index is called a map citation index rather than a gazetteer.

158   Chapter Five   Israel Conquers Canaan

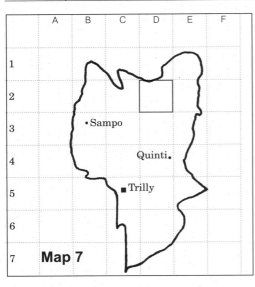

Map 7

This is a map of an imaginary island. Do you see the letters across the top of the map and the numbers down the side? These numbers and letters help us to find places.

Place your finger on the block marked B. Follow the column of blocks down to the town called Sampo. Place another finger on the block marked 3, and follow the row of blocks across to Sampo. Do you see how the row and the column of blocks come together at the block where Sampo is? Sampo is located in the block called B3.

Since this map is labeled Map 7, the gazetteer would tell you to look at B3—7 to find Sampo. Now try to determine the location of the town Quinti. Do you see that it is in column D and row 4 of Map 7? Quinti is found at D4—7.

1. What is the location of Trilly?
   <u> C5—7 </u>

2. The people on this island would like to build another town at the location D2—7. Use a colored pencil to outline the block on the map where they are planning to build their town.

Using a Bible Atlas

In Chapter 6 of this Bible study course, you will be studying the Book of Judges. Map 2 is a map of Canaan as it was when the Israelites conquered it.

3. Use the index of a Bible atlas to find the following places. Carefully notice where each place is located on the map, and then write its name on the correct blank on Map 2.

   Jericho. This was the first city captured by the Israelites after they entered Canaan. They destroyed it completely, and it was not rebuilt until many years later.

   Hebron. This is the area that Caleb asked for as his inheritance. It is also where Abraham, Isaac, and Jacob were buried.

   Jerusalem. Joshua defeated the king of this city at the battle during which the sun stood still, but the Jebusites continued to live here until David's reign. David made this city the capital of Israel.

   Hazor. This city was ruled by Jabin. It was one of the largest cities in Canaan and may have had a population of about 40,000 people when Joshua conquered and burned it. Later the Canaanites rebuilt it, and another king named Jabin oppressed Israel until Barak defeated him.

   Shiloh. The Israelites pitched the tabernacle here after entering Canaan. Here the ark of the covenant remained until Eli's sons took it to a battle. Samuel grew up here while serving in the tabernacle.

4. On Map 2, label the Coastal Plain, the Central Mountains, the Jordan Valley, and the Eastern Mountains. No blanks are supplied for these names.

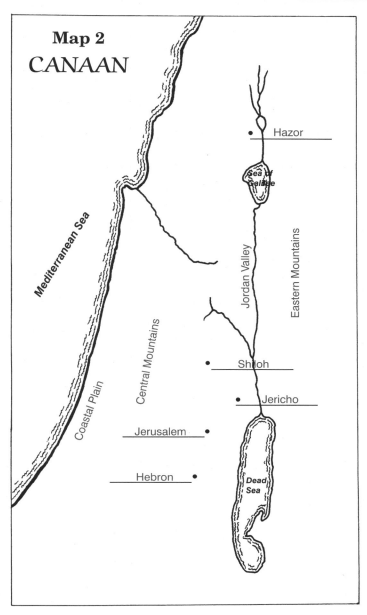

Map 2

CANAAN

Mediterranean Sea

Hazor

Sea of Galilee

Jordan Valley

Eastern Mountains

Central Mountains

Coastal Plain

Shiloh

Jericho

Jerusalem

Hebron

Dead Sea

160

Lesson 22. Israel Enters Canaan

Forty years after leaving Egypt, the Israelites finally crossed the Jordan River and entered Canaan. By then, all the people who had left Egypt as adults had died in the wilderness, except for Joshua and Caleb. Even Moses had died, because he had become angry and had struck the rock when God had told him to speak to it.

Can you imagine how disappointed Moses must have been? For nearly forty years he had looked forward to entering Canaan. For forty years he had put up with the Israelites' grumbling. Now he could not enter the Promised Land himself!

God took Moses to the top of a mountain that overlooked Canaan and showed him the Promised Land. Then Moses died, and God buried him. None of the Israelites were present at his burial. God had been his best friend on earth, and God took care of him when he died. Back in the camp, Moses' place

as leader was taken by Joshua, who had been Moses' servant.

Almost all the Israelites had grown up in the desert. Only the oldest ones remembered leaving Egypt when they were children. The younger mothers and fathers had eaten manna all their lives. Every boy and girl had seen the pillar of cloud and the pillar of fire resting above the tabernacle. They had watched the pillar of cloud move ahead when it was time to leave a campsite.

How strange the land of Canaan must have looked to the Israelite children! Busy cities with high walls, roads and fields and vineyards—everything was so different from the desert.

Even though the land of Canaan seemed strange and hard to conquer, the Israelites did not rebel against God. Instead, they trusted Him completely, and He led them through the Jordan River.

A. ANSWERS FROM THE BIBLE

A New Leader

The Israelites were almost ready to enter the Promised Land for which they had waited so long. But Moses was dead, and they needed someone to lead them before they could go any farther.

★ *Write* true *or* false. *If a statement is false, rewrite it to make it true.*
In the rewritten sentences for numbers 1–6, the corrections are in italics. The pupil's sentences
Joshua 1:1–3   may vary somewhat.

_____false_____ 1. After Moses died, God told Joshua to lead the Israelites across the Red Sea. _

   After Moses died, God told Joshua to lead the Israelites across the *Jordan River*.

_____true_____ 2. God promised Joshua that every place he would walk upon would be given to

   the children of Israel. _____

   _____

Lesson 22

Oral Review

1. What lie did Satan tell Eve? [3] **He said that she would not die if she ate the forbidden fruit.**
2. Why did Abraham not want his servant to take Isaac back to Haran? [9] **Isaac was to receive the promise of the land of Canaan, and Abraham's relatives at Haran worshiped idols.**
3. What did Rebekah do for Abraham's servant? [9] **She drew water for him and his camels.**
4. What happened to Pharaoh's army? [17] **They were drowned in the Red Sea.**
5. What is an ephod? [19] **an apronlike coat worn by the Israelite priests**
6. Which two of the twelve spies gave a good report of Canaan? [20] **Joshua and Caleb**
7. Why was Canaan a good place for Jesus to live and teach? [21] **Many people passed through Canaan and heard His teaching.**
8. Why did the main roads through Canaan follow the Mediterranean Sea? [21] **It was easier to travel on the level plain along the sea than through the mountains.**

Lesson 22. Israel Enters Canaan   **161**

Joshua 2:1–4, 8–11

____false____ 3. Joshua sent twelve spies to search out the country. _____

Joshua sent *two* spies to search out the country. _____

____true____ 4. Rahab believed that the LORD would give the land to the Israelites. _____

_____

Joshua 2:15–24

____false____ 5. The men helped Rahab and her family to escape through a window in the wall. *Rahab* helped *the men* to escape through a window in the wall. ____

_____

____true____ 6. The spies believed that the LORD was able to give them the land. _____

_____

Crossing the Jordan River

When the Israelites left Egypt and entered the wilderness, God dried up the Red Sea so that they could cross over safely. Now they needed to cross the Jordan River to enter Canaan. But the Jordan was in full flood, overflowing its banks. Would God open the way for them again, as He had forty years before?

Joshua 3:14–17

7. Who went before the rest of the Israelites as they prepared to cross the Jordan River? ____
   the priests bearing the ark of the covenant _____

8. Where did these men stand while the people crossed the Jordan River? _____
   in the middle of the Jordan River _____

Joshua 4:19–24

9. At Gilgal, Joshua set up ___twelve___ stones from the ___Jordan___ River.

10. Who would ask about these stones? __the children of those who crossed the Jordan River__

Conquering Jericho

Jericho was a large and important city in Joshua's time. It was surrounded by thick walls wide enough to build a house on. How would the Israelites be able to defeat this city?

Joshua 6:1–5

11. Why did the people of Jericho shut up their city? _____
    They were afraid of the children of Israel. _____

12. God told Joshua to march the Israelite army around the city ___one___ time(s) each day for ___six___ days.

13. On the ___seventh___ day, they were to go around the city ___seven___ times.

In This Lesson

Scope: Joshua 1–6

Main Events
- God tells Joshua how to lead the Israelites into Canaan.
- Rahab helps the spies that Joshua sent to view the land.
- The Israelites cross the Jordan River.
- Joshua sets up twelve stones as a memorial.
- The Israelites conquer Jericho.

Objectives
- Students should know
  —how Rahab helped the spies, and how she and her family were saved later. (She helped the men escape through a window; the two spies brought them out of the city.)
  —how the Israelites crossed the Jordan River. (God stopped the waters of Jordan while they crossed over on dry ground.)
  —why Joshua set up twelve stones at Gilgal. (so that the Israelites' children would later ask what the stones mean, and they could be told how God had helped them pass over Jordan.)

Joshua 6:20–25

14. What happened when the priests blew the trumpets and the people shouted?

    a. The trumpet of God sounded from heaven.

    (b.) The walls of the city fell down.

    c. Fire fell from heaven and burned the city.

15. What happened to the people and animals in Jericho?

    a. The angel of the LORD killed them and burned them with fire.

    b. The Israelites captured them and kept them as prisoners.

    (c.) The Israelites utterly destroyed them.

16. What happened to Rahab and her family?

    a. The Israelites killed them.

    (b.) The two spies brought them out of the city.

    c. The Israelites gave them the valuable things they found in Jericho.

17. What did the Israelites do with the silver, gold, brass, and iron they found in Jericho? ____

    They put these things into the LORD's treasury.

Where Is It Found?

18. In which of the first six chapters of Joshua do you read about

    a. Rahab helping the spies?   Joshua 2

    b. the fall of Jericho?   Joshua 6

    c. God's promise to give Israel all the land Joshua walked upon?   Joshua 1

    d. the Israelites crossing the Jordan River?   Joshua 3

B. BIBLE WORD STUDY

★ *Match these definitions with the Bible words on the right. Some words or definitions may not be in your dictionary, since they are not used in modern English. If you need help, read the verses given. All references are from Joshua.*

_d_	1. An old English word meaning "knew" (2:4)	a. scarlet
_a_	2. A bright red color (2:18)	b. befall
_j_	3. To tell (2:20)	c. straitly
_f_	4. Freed; released (2:20)	d. wist
_b_	5. To come to pass; happen (2:23)	e. pitch
_h_	6. An edge (3:15)	f. quit
_e_	7. To set up (4:20)	g. compass
_c_	8. Tightly; securely (6:1)	h. brim
_i_	9. Courage; bravery (6:2)	i. valour (valor)
_g_	10. To go around (6:4)	j. utter

Some of these words have archaic meanings that will not be found in the average school dictionary. The students should use their Bibles rather than their dictionaries to complete this exercise. You may want to explain why they will not find these meanings in their dictionaries. The King James Version uses many more words like this.

—how the Israelites destroyed Jericho. (They marched around the city thirteen times. Then, when the priests blew the trumpets, the people shouted, and the walls of the city fell down.)

Truths to Instill

• This lesson abounds with examples of faith.

    —Rahab believed in God, even though the following factors would have made it difficult: she had been a wicked woman, Jehovah was the God of her enemies, she would be different from her people, and she had not been taught about God.

    —Joshua moved ahead with plans to conquer Canaan, in spite of apparently insurmountable obstacles.

    —The people obeyed Joshua's seemingly irrational orders: they carried the ark into a flooded river, they marched around a city without attacking it, and they shouted to make the walls fall down.

• It is interesting that Rahab did not fear the Israelites as much as she feared their God. She helped the enemy spies, and she told them, "I know that the LORD hath given you the land" and "The LORD your God, he is God in heaven above, and in earth beneath." She asked them to swear by the LORD, which she no doubt understood to be the most binding oath that she could request.

C. THINKING ABOUT BIBLE TRUTHS

The Israelites had changed during the forty years since they had first tried to enter Canaan. They still were not perfect, but they were different from their parents. As you do these exercises, try to decide how they had changed, and why.

Hebrews 3:15–19

These verses tell about the generation of people who could not enter Canaan.

1. The provocation (provoking) mentioned in verse 15 took place when the twelve spies returned from Canaan, and the Israelites refused to believe that God could help them to conquer Canaan.

    a. When the Israelites heard God's message through the words of Joshua and Caleb, they ___hardened___ their hearts (v. 15).

    b. Because of this, they said things that ___provoked___ God (v. 16).

2. The Israelites had looked forward to Canaan as a place where they could rest. But they could not enter this land of rest because of their ___unbelief___ (v. 19). They did not have enough faith in God to believe that He could give them the land He had promised.

Hebrews 11:30

This verse tells about the next generation of Israelites—the ones Joshua led into the Promised Land.

3. One of the first tests that the Israelites faced in Canaan was the city of Jericho. God told them to conquer and destroy the city.

    a. These Israelites did not have any weapons that were mighty enough to knock down the walls of Jericho. But they had ___faith___ that God would help them to conquer it anyway.

    b. What do you think would have happened at Jericho if the Israelites had doubted that God could help them? ___(Sample answer) God could not have blessed them, and they likely would have been defeated.___

    c. How did the Israelites prove that they believed God would give them the city? ___They walked around the city (compassed the walls) seven days.___

4. Think about your answers to numbers 1–3. How had the Israelites changed during the forty years they had spent in the desert? ___(Sample answers) The Israelites believed that God would give them the land of Canaan. They had learned to trust God enough to follow His instructions.___

D. LEARNING MORE ABOUT THE BIBLE

The City of Jericho

Jericho has been destroyed and rebuilt many times. One city, possibly the one destroyed by the Israelites, had two walls, as shown here. Because the city was crowded, people built houses between the walls. The house of (1) __Rahab__ was built on the wall (Joshua 2:15).

A thick layer of ash shows that this city was destroyed by fire. Many clay jars full of grain have been found in this layer of ash. The full jars of grain show that the conquerors did not keep the grain and that they conquered the city quickly, before the people inside used up all their food. Perhaps the grain had just been gathered. Israel crossed Jordan at the time of (2) __harvest__ (Joshua 3:15).

- The sketch of the walls of Jericho is based on Bryant's conclusions and on a photograph taken at the site in the early 1900s.

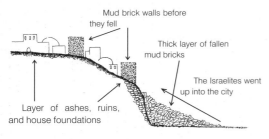

Mud brick walls before they fell

Thick layer of fallen mud bricks

The Israelites went up into the city

Layer of ashes, ruins, and house foundations

After the Israelites destroyed Jericho, Joshua gave it to the tribe of (3) __Benjamin__ (Joshua 18:21). But Joshua told the Israelites that the man who rebuilt the city would be (4) __cursed__ before the LORD (Joshua 6:26). The one who received this curse was (5) __Hiel__, a man from Bethel (1 Kings 16:34).

The water of Jericho was not good. A prophet named (6) __Elisha__ healed the water by throwing (7) __salt__ into it (2 Kings 2:19-22).

Jericho, lying far below sea level, near the Dead Sea, had a hot, dry climate. The Bible calls it the city of (8) __palm trees__ (Deuteronomy 34:3).

The winding road from Jericho to (9) __Jerusalem__ passed through lonely desert country. Robbers often attacked those who traveled on this road (Luke 10:30).

- The archaeological finds at Jericho illustrate the futility of trying to confirm every Bible detail with archaeology. Unbelievers tend to interpret their findings in light of their own theories, rather than in the light of God's revealed truth.

In the early 1900s, John Garstang claimed to have found evidence that the walls of Jericho fell down about 1400 B.C. Then, during the 1950s, Kathleen Kenyon conducted additional excavations. She discredited the Bible account, dating the walls that Garstang had found to a much earlier period and claiming that the city had had no walls during the time of Joshua.

Recently, Bryant G. Wood re-examined the question of Jericho ("Did the Israelites Conquer Jericho?—A New Look at Archaeological Evidence." *Biblical Archaeological Review*, March/April 1990). He believes that Kenyon's dating is faulty and that the Bible account is correct after all!

Other historians and archaeologists have recently argued that Egyptian chronology for this period should be shortened by several centuries (*Centuries of Darkness: A Challenge to the Conventional Chronology of Old World Archaeology*, Peter James and others). Since all ancient Middle Eastern sites are directly or indirectly dated by Egyptian pottery types, an error in Egyptian chronology would affect the dates assigned to Jericho and other early Palestinian

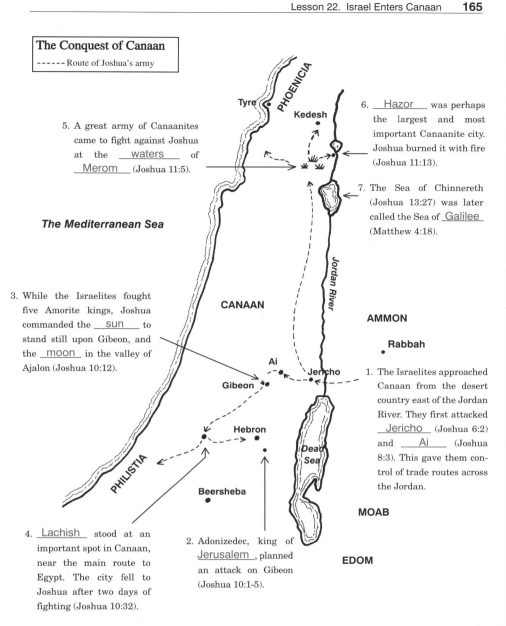

The Conquest of Canaan

------ Route of Joshua's army

5. A great army of Canaanites came to fight against Joshua at the ___waters___ of ___Merom___ (Joshua 11:5).

6. ___Hazor___ was perhaps the largest and most important Canaanite city. Joshua burned it with fire (Joshua 11:13).

7. The Sea of Chinnereth (Joshua 13:27) was later called the Sea of ___Galilee___ (Matthew 4:18).

The Mediterranean Sea

3. While the Israelites fought five Amorite kings, Joshua commanded the ___sun___ to stand still upon Gibeon, and the ___moon___ in the valley of Ajalon (Joshua 10:12).

1. The Israelites approached Canaan from the desert country east of the Jordan River. They first attacked ___Jericho___ (Joshua 6:2) and ___Ai___ (Joshua 8:3). This gave them control of trade routes across the Jordan.

4. ___Lachish___ stood at an important spot in Canaan, near the main route to Egypt. The city fell to Joshua after two days of fighting (Joshua 10:32).

2. Adonizedec, king of ___Jerusalem___, planned an attack on Gibeon (Joshua 10:1-5).

Map labels: PHOENICIA, Tyre, Kedesh, Jordan River, CANAAN, AMMON, Rabbah, Ai, Jericho, Gibeon, Hebron, Dead Sea, PHILISTIA, Beersheba, MOAB, EDOM

tells. Bible dates for the Flood support the need to shorten Egyptian chronology.

A correct interpretation of archaeological finds will always agree with Bible truth. But Bible believers do not need archaeological support for every Bible account. We have "a more sure word" from the almighty God, who crumbled the walls of Jericho.

166

Lesson 23. Israel and the Buried Treasure

When the Israelites entered the land of Canaan and started conquering its cities, they saw many tempting things. Lush pastures, vineyards, olive trees, and wheat fields lay before them. God had warned them not to let these things draw their hearts away from Him, but one Israelite did not listen. Achan wanted to get all he could of the things he saw in Canaan, as soon as possible.

God expected to have the first share of everything that He blessed the Israelites with. The first of every crop was to be offered to Him, and the first male born to an animal was His. The first son in every family was also God's. The parents had to buy him back from God by paying money to the priests. The Israelites knew all this. It should not have surprised them that God told them to give the spoils of Jericho to Him. Jericho was the first city of Canaan that they conquered.

Joshua told the Israelites to give all the treasures they found in Jericho to the LORD's treasury. But Achan did not obey God's orders. Instead, he kept some of the things that he found among the rubble. He took a beautiful garment, a stack of silver, and a wedge of gold. Achan had not learned how important it is to do exactly as God says.

A. ANSWERS FROM THE BIBLE

Defeat at Ai

God had told the Israelites not to keep any gold, silver, or other precious things from Jericho for themselves. All the valuable things were to be put into the LORD's treasury. God warned them that anyone who disobeyed would be cursed and would place the entire camp under a curse.

Joshua 7:1–5

1. Which statement tells why the spies did not think all the Israelites should go to fight against Ai?
   a. There would be fewer people to share the spoils that way.
   b. Ai was only a small city and did not have a large army.
   c. Many Israelites were needed to guard the prisoners from Jericho.

2. When three thousand men went up to fight against Ai, the men of Ai killed ___thirty-six___ of them, and they ___chased___ the rest away.

Joshua was dismayed because of the defeat at Ai. He fell on his face before the Lord and wished the Israelites had stayed on the other side of the Jordan.

Joshua 7:10–12

3. God gave Joshua six reasons the Israelites suffered defeat at Ai, but the first reason included the others. Israel had ___sinned___, and God could not be with them any more until they removed the sin from among them.

Joshua 6:17–20 records the clear instructions warning the Israelites to keep nothing from Jericho for themselves. Discuss with the students what might have caused Achan to deliberately disobey these orders (such as his lack of fear of God, his covetousness, and the thought that no one would ever know).

- The word *accursed* (Joshua 7:1, 11–15) is translated from the Hebrew word *cherem*. (See number 2764 in the Hebrew dictionary in *Strong's Exhaustive Concordance*.) This Hebrew word is sometimes translated *devoted* (Leviticus 27:21, 28, 29). Since Jericho had been devoted to the LORD (Joshua 6:17), everything in it was to be either destroyed or placed in the LORD's treasury. Achan placed himself under a curse by taking these goods.

  God did not place the same restriction on Ai. The Israelites killed all the people, but they took the spoil and the cattle for themselves (Joshua 8:2, 26, 27). Perhaps Jericho was considered the firstfruits of the land of Canaan.

Lesson 23

Oral Review

1. How did Adam and Eve feel after they had disobeyed God? Why? [3] **They felt afraid because they knew they had done wrong.**
2. Why did men start to build the Tower of Babel? [5] **to make a name for themselves, and to keep from being scattered**
3. How did God guide the Israelites through the wilderness? [17] **with a pillar of cloud by day and a pillar of fire by night**
4. What three pieces of furniture were in the holy place of the tabernacle? [19] **the golden candlestick, the altar of incense, and the table of shewbread**
5. What was in the holy of holies of the tabernacle? [19] **the ark of the covenant**
6. In a Bible atlas index, what does *A4—3* mean when it follows the name of a city? [21] **The city is found on Map 3, column A, row 4.**
7. How did Rahab help the spies? [22] **She hid them and helped them escape from the city. She gave them important information.**
8. Why did Joshua set up twelve stones at Gilgal? [22] **to serve as a memorial of how God had helped Israel to cross the Jordan**

Lesson 23. Israel and the Buried Treasure   167

Sin in the Camp

God's people cannot be successful while they have sin in their midst. God showed the Israelites what they needed to do to get rid of the sin in the camp.

Joshua 7:16–26

Joshua told the Israelites what God had told him. He warned them about what would happen the next day.

4. Joshua used the lot to find the guilty person, as God had instructed him. First, the tribe of (a) ___Judah___ was chosen. From them, the family of the (b) ___Zarhites___ was chosen. From them, the household of Zabdi was chosen. From the household of Zabdi, (c) ___Achan___ was chosen.

5. Achan waited to confess his sin until he was chosen by lot. What does this show about him?
   (a.) He confessed his sin only because he was caught, not because he was sorry for what he had done. If he had not been caught, he probably would never have confessed it.
   b. He had not realized before this that he had done something wrong. When he was chosen, he thought of the things he had taken and made a confession about them.
   c. He had forgotten about the things that he had taken, and he did not remember them until he was chosen.

6. Joshua did not hate Achan, but he hated Achan's sin. In verse 19 he called Achan his ___son___.

7. Where had Achan hidden his treasures? ___in the earth inside his tent___

8. Joshua and the Israelites took Achan and his family and ___all___ that he had, and brought them to the valley of ___Achor___.

9. The Israelites ___stoned___ them with ___stones___, and ___burned___ them with fire. Then they raised over him a great heap of ___stones___.

Victory at Ai

Joshua 8:1, 14–22

These verses show plainly that God was with the Israelites again. He gave Joshua specific instructions for conquering Ai, just as He had given instructions about Jericho.

10. After Achan was punished for his sin, God told Joshua to fight against ___Ai___ again.

11. How many of the Israelites were to go to Ai this time? ___all of the men of war___

12. How did the Israelites trick the men of Ai? ___First Joshua sent men to hide behind the city. When the battle began, the Israelite army started to flee, and all the men of Ai left the city to chase them. Then the men who were hiding entered the city and set it on fire.___

The students may wonder why God blamed all Israel for Achan's sin. Point out that the Israelites did not ask for God's direction before attacking Ai. Had they done so, He would surely have told them that there was sin in the camp and that they were not ready to go. Because they failed to ask for this direction, the sin became a problem for all the Israelites rather than just for Achan.

- Apparently Achan's children were involved in his sin, since the Law forbade killing children for the sins of their father (Deuteronomy 24:16). Korah's children were spared (Numbers 26:11). However, the innocent do suffer with the guilty at times. Young children died during the Flood (Genesis 7:23), and God commanded the Israelites to kill all the young boys when they conquered the Canaanite cities (Numbers 31:17).

In This Lesson

Scope: Joshua 7, 8

Main Events

- The Israelites are defeated at Ai.
- Achan is found guilty of sin, and he, his family, and all that he has are destroyed.
- The LORD grants Israel victory at Ai.
- Joshua builds an altar on Mount Ebal, and the Israelites review the blessings and curses of the Law.

Objectives

- Students should know
  —why the Israelites lost the first battle at Ai. (Achan had disobeyed God by taking some things from Jericho, and God could not bless Israel while they had sin in their midst.)
  —how Joshua found out who was the cause of their defeat. (He used the lot.)
  —why Achan's confession does not appear to be true repentance. (He waited to confess until he was chosen by lot. If he had not been caught, he probably would not have confessed.)
  —what happened to Achan. (He, his family, and all that he had were stoned and burned.)

13. What happened to the men of Ai when they saw their city burning? _____

   They had no power to flee, and they were defeated by the Israelites.

14. How many men from Ai escaped?   _none of them_ _____

A Meeting on Two Mountains

Before Moses died, he had instructed the Israelites to gather on Mount Ebal and Mount Gerizim after they entered Canaan. They were to build an altar on Mount Ebal and write the words of the Law upon it. Then six tribes were to stand on Mount Gerizim and bless those who would obey God's Law, and the other six tribes were to stand on Mount Ebal and curse those who would disobey.

Joshua 8:30–35

15. What did Joshua use to build the altar on Mount Ebal?   _whole stones_ _____

16. How much of the Law did Joshua read to the people?   _all the words of the Law_ _____

Where Is It Found?

17. In which chapter of Joshua do you read about

   a. the sin of Achan?   _Joshua 7_

   b. the victory at Ai?   _Joshua 8_

B. BIBLE WORD STUDY

★ *Write a word from the verse given to fit each definition. All references are from Joshua.*

trespass	1. A sin (7:1)
accursed	2. Under a curse (7:1)
dissembled	3. Acted deceitfully; hid the truth (7:11)
spoils	4. Goods taken during a battle (7:21)
dismayed	5. Greatly troubled or discouraged (8:1)
ambush	6. A surprise attack made from a hidden place (8:12)

C. THINKING ABOUT BIBLE TRUTHS

No one knows exactly why Achan dared to disobey God's command. He had seen God's power many times in the wilderness. He had seen other people punished severely for their sins. But he still thought that he could disobey God and not get caught.

Romans 6:23

God told man what the results of sin and disobedience were when He created him (see Genesis 2:17). But Adam and Eve did not listen to the warning and soon learned that God means what He says. In this lesson we see that Achan also learned this the hard way.

Be careful to avoid child evangelism in discussing this verse. It is important for children to realize that God judges sin, but you should not make personal applications that could burden innocent children with premature guilt.

—how the Israelites conquered Ai. (See Part A, numbers 10–14.)

—what Joshua did on Mount Ebal. (See Part A, "A Meeting on Two Mountains" and Joshua 8:30–35.)

Truths to Instill

• Achan said, "Indeed I have sinned"; but he waited to say it until God had revealed his guilt. His repentance was not the godly repentance of 2 Corinthians 7:11, but the forced confession of a man caught in wrongdoing. It is likely that Achan would never have acknowledged his sin if it had not been found out.

Challenge the children with this truth. Are they willing to acknowledge wrongdoing, or must they be prodded to do so?

• Satan is never able to deliver what he promises. What did he promise Achan for taking the silver, the gold, and the rich garment? Perhaps luxury, honor, and an easier life. Satan wants us to believe that things like these bring peace, happiness, and satisfaction. Even if Achan had gained the former, he would not have attained the latter.

1. The final result of unconfessed _____sin_____ is always ____death____.

2. Achan committed a sin (trespass) against God when he kept the Babylonish garment, the gold, and the silver that he saw in Jericho instead of giving them to the treasury as God had commanded.

3. Because of this, he needed to _____die_____.

1 Samuel 12:14, 15

In these verses, Samuel warned the Israelites about the results of disobeying God. Disobedience never brings happiness.

4. a. Do you think Achan would have been happy with his stolen treasures if he had not been caught? ____no____

   b. Why, or why not? ____(Sample answers) He would have worried about being discovered. He would have had a guilty conscience. He would have needed to keep the stolen things hidden.____

Joshua 7:26

5. How might the great heap of stones that was piled over Achan have helped the Israelites in the years to come? ____The stones could have reminded them of what had happened to Achan when he disobeyed God.____

E
T
R
O
G

Etrog trees are a variety of citron trees. These small trees have leathery leaves that stay green all year. Their yellow, thick-skinned fruit resembles lemons.

The Jews grew etrog trees in their gardens. They believed the etrog was the "goodly tree" mentioned in Leviticus 23:40. Therefore they carried a perfect etrog fruit, a palm branch, a willow wisp, and a myrtle sprig with them during the Feast of Tabernacles.

Candied etrog peel and a jam made from etrog, quince seeds, cloves, and lemon have long been enjoyed by Jewish families.

Why did God command the Israelites to keep the Feast of Tabernacles? (Leviticus 23:42, 43).

War in Bible Times

In very early battles, men threw stones. Later they learned to throw stones faster and harder with leather slings.

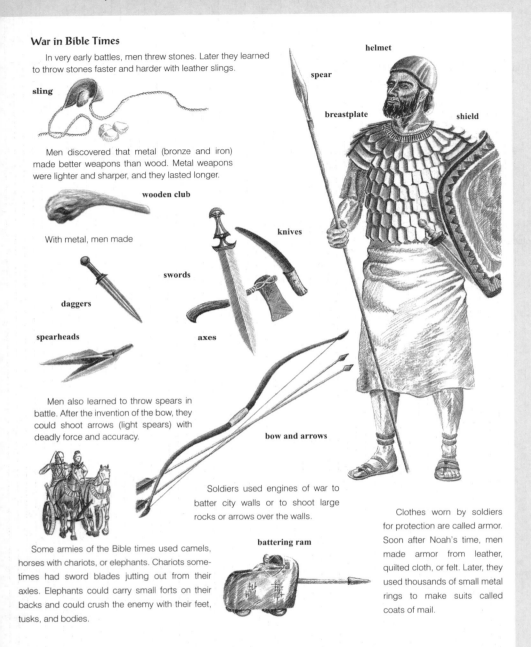

sling

Men discovered that metal (bronze and iron) made better weapons than wood. Metal weapons were lighter and sharper, and they lasted longer.

wooden club

With metal, men made

knives

daggers

swords

spearheads

axes

Men also learned to throw spears in battle. After the invention of the bow, they could shoot arrows (light spears) with deadly force and accuracy.

bow and arrows

Soldiers used engines of war to batter city walls or to shoot large rocks or arrows over the walls.

Some armies of the Bible times used camels, horses with chariots, or elephants. Chariots sometimes had sword blades jutting out from their axles. Elephants could carry small forts on their backs and could crush the enemy with their feet, tusks, and bodies.

battering ram

helmet

spear

breastplate

shield

Clothes worn by soldiers for protection are called armor. Soon after Noah's time, men made armor from leather, quilted cloth, or felt. Later, they used thousands of small metal rings to make suits called coats of mail.

Match each man to the weapon or armor that he used.

__j__	1. Abraham (Genesis 22:6)	a. javelin
__a__	2. Phinehas (Numbers 25:7)	b. sword
__i__	3. Joshua (Joshua 8:18)	c. helmet and coat of mail
__g__	4. Ehud (Judges 3:16)	d. engines of war
__c__	5. Goliath (1 Samuel 17:5)	e. sling
__e__	6. David (1 Samuel 17:50)	f. chariot
__h__	7. Jonathan (1 Samuel 20:35–38)	g. dagger
__f__	8. Ahab (1 Kings 22:35)	h. bow and arrows
__d__	9. Uzziah (2 Chronicles 26:15)	i. spear
__b__	10. Peter (John 18:10)	j. knife

In Old Testament times, God expected His people to fight against evil men with these weapons. But when Jesus came, He taught His followers to put away earthly weapons and to overcome evil with good.

11. Jesus said, "___Love___ your enemies, ___bless___ them that curse you, ___do___ ___good___ to them that hate you, and ___pray___ for them which despitefully use you, and persecute you" (Matthew 5:44).

12. Read Ephesians 6:14–18. A Christian's spiritual armor includes the "belt" of truth, the "breastplate" of _righteousness_, "shoes" that spread the Gospel, the "shield" of ___faith___, the "helmet" of _salvation_, the "sword" of the ___Spirit___ (God's Word), and prayer.

172

Lesson 24. Israel and the Gibeonites

The Canaanites had heard many stories about the Israelites. They knew about the plagues that had brought ruin to Egypt. They knew about the miraculous way that the Israelites had crossed the Red Sea and the Jordan River. They knew that God had destroyed the enemies of the Israelites in almost every battle they fought. They had also heard that God had commanded the Israelites to destroy the Canaanites. Now Jericho and Ai had fallen, and the rest of the Canaanites were greatly frightened.

Joshua led Israel through many battles. He was a brave and godly man who trusted in the Lord no matter how difficult things became. The Lord helped him, and Joshua usually asked the Lord to guide him. But one time Joshua forgot to ask the Lord for advice. Because of this, he made a very foolish mistake.

Because of Joshua's mistake, the Israelites made peace with the Gibeonites and could not destroy them. The Canaanites in other cities were angry with the Gibeonites when they heard about this. A band of enemy kings gathered their armies against Gibeon, and Joshua had to fight them to protect the Gibeonites.

God was kind to the Israelites in spite of their mistake, and He helped them to win this battle. He even made the sun stand still so that they would have more time to completely destroy the enemy!

God can do anything to help His people. Even stopping the sun and the moon is not too hard for Him. After all, He is the one who *made* the sun and the moon.

A. ANSWERS FROM THE BIBLE

The Gibeonites Deceive Israel

Joshua 9:3–7

The Gibeonites, also called Hivites in these verses, lived in a group of cities not far from Jericho and Ai. They were afraid after they heard what the God of the Israelites had done to those cities.

1. Why did the Gibeonites decide to make an agreement with Joshua and the Israelites, rather than fighting with them?   (Answers may vary slightly.) They knew what Joshua had done to Jericho and Ai, and they realized that they could not fight against Israel's God.

2. How did they deceive Joshua and the Israelites?   They took old food, clothes, and goods, and pretended to be ambassadors from a far country, who were seeking peace.

3. The men of Israel were afraid that
   a. the Gibeonites would attack them if they refused to make peace with them.
   b. the Gibeonites might be telling them lies about where they lived.
   c. the Gibeonites were Egyptians who were trying to trick them.

Lesson 24

Oral Review

1. What did Pharaoh say when the LORD commanded him to let His people go? [15] **"Who is the LORD, that I should obey his voice?"**

2. What did the ten plagues prove about the gods of Egypt? [15] **The LORD was more powerful than any of Egypt's gods.**

3. Say the Ten Commandments. [18]
   (1) Thou shalt have no other gods before me.
   (2) Thou shalt not make unto thee any graven image.
   (3) Thou shalt not take the Name of the LORD thy God in vain.
   (4) Remember the Sabbath Day, to keep it holy.
   (5) Honour thy father and thy mother.
   (6) Thou shalt not kill.
   (7) Thou shalt not commit adultery.
   (8) Thou shalt not steal.
   (9) Thou shalt not bear false witness.
   (10) Thou shalt not covet.

4. What happened to Rahab and her family when the walls of Jericho fell? [22] **The two spies brought them out of the city.**

Joshua 9:8–15

4. The Gibeonites were very careful about what they told the Israelites.

   a. The Gibeonites said that they had heard what God had done in ___Egypt___ and to the

     two kings of the __Amorites__ beyond the Jordan.

   b. Why did the Gibeonites not say anything about what had happened to Jericho and Ai? __

     The Israelites would not have expected men from a far country to know about their

     recent victories at Jericho and Ai.

5. The Israelites should have asked ___the LORD___ for counsel.

6. Joshua made ___peace___ and a ___league___ with the Gibeonites, and the princes of the

   congregation ___sware___ unto them.

It is never wise to listen to flattery. The Gibeonites made the Israelites feel good by their smooth words. They told them that they had heard of them and their God from very far away. They were so impressed, they said, that they had come a long way just to make friends with the Israelites. Flattery is a favorite trick of people who are trying to persuade someone to do what they want.

The Trick Is Discovered

The Israelites soon discovered their mistake. They had been tricked because they depended on their own wisdom instead of asking God for advice.

Joshua 9:16–21

7. After ___three___ days, the Israelites discovered that the Gibeonites had tricked them.

8. All the congregation murmured against the __princes__ of Israel.

9. Because of the ___oath___ that they had made, the Israelites let the Gibeonites live.

10. The Gibeonites were forced to be ___hewers___ of ___wood___ and ___drawers___ of

   ___water___.

An Unusual Battle

The other Canaanites soon heard that the Gibeonites had made peace with Israel. This disturbed them greatly because the Gibeonites were mighty men of war. If they started helping the Israelites, there was little hope indeed of withstanding the invaders!

Joshua 10:1–7

11. Adonizedec, king of Jerusalem, prepared for war after he heard how Joshua had destroyed

   ___Ai___ and ___Jericho___ and had made peace with ___Gibeon___.

5. Why were the Israelites defeated at Ai? [23] **because Achan had sinned in taking treasure from Jericho**

6. What did Jesus tell His followers to do to their enemies? [23] **to love them, bless them, do good to them, and pray for them**

In This Lesson

Scope: Joshua 9, 10

Main Events
* The Gibeonites deceive Joshua and the Israelites.
* The Israelites make the Gibeonites their servants.
* God helps the Israelites defeat five Amorite kings.

* The LORD fights for Israel by making the sun and moon stand still, and by sending a great hailstorm.

Objectives
* Students should know
  —how the Gibeonites deceived the Israelites. (See Part A, numbers 2–5.)
  —why the Israelites could not kill the Gibeonites, and what they required the Gibeonites to do. (The princes had made an oath with them. They made the Gibeonites hewers of wood and drawers of water.)
  —who Adonizedec was, and what he did. (He was king of Jerusalem. He and four other kings attacked Gibeon.)

12. Why did the five kings of the Amorites attack Gibeon instead of the Israelites? Circle the letters of the *two* best reasons.

   ⓐ They were angry with the Gibeonites and wanted to get even with them.

   ⓑ They were afraid to attack the Israelites because of what had happened to Jericho and Ai.

   c. They wanted to get rid of the Gibeonites so that the Israelites would be their friends.

13. When the five kings came to attack Gibeon, the Gibeonites quickly sent to ____Joshua____ for help.

14. ____Joshua____ came up from Gilgal with all the ____people____ of ____war____ and all the ____mighty____ ____men____ of ____valour____.

   You might think that the Israelites should have let the Amorites destroy the Gibeonites. However, the Israelites' league with the Gibeonites was so binding that it was their duty to help them out of trouble. God expects His people to keep their promises.

Joshua 10:8–14

   The call for help from the Gibeonites put the Israelites in the unusual position of protecting a Canaanite city against its enemies. However, the Lord used this as a way to destroy more of Israel's enemies.

15. God helped the Israelites to fight against the Amorites by causing great ____stones (hailstones)____ to fall upon them. More people were killed by these than by the Israelites.

16. Joshua told the ____sun____ and the ____moon____ to stand still, and they obeyed him.

17. How long did the sun stand still? ____until the people had avenged themselves upon their enemies (*or* about a whole day)____

18. This miracle took place because the ____LORD____ fought for Israel.

Where Is It Found?

19. Which chapter of Joshua tells how the Gibeonites deceived the Israelites? ____Joshua 9____

—what God did to help the Israelites win a battle. (He made the sun and the moon stand still and sent a hailstorm.)

Truths to Instill

- In a time of success, Joshua and the people of Israel let down their guard. The LORD had given them great victories at Jericho and Ai, and they were feeling quite confident. When the Gibeonites arrived, the Israelites "asked not counsel at the mouth of the LORD." Did they forget the command God had given Moses, "Thou shalt make no covenant with them, nor with their gods" (Exodus 23:32)?

- The Gibeonites would be a threat to Israel because of their proximity, which would increase their ungodly influence. God warned the Israelites that nearby heathen neighbors would be more dangerous to them than distant ones. (See Deuteronomy 20:10–16.) The lesson this has for us is that worldly influences close at hand are often a greater threat than serious sins that we would not even think of committing.

- This lesson shows how binding our word must be. God held the Israelites to their oath, even though He had told them to destroy all the heathen. When Saul broke the oath, God punished Israel with a famine for three years, until David righted the wrong (2 Samuel 21).

B. BIBLE WORD STUDY

★ *Match these definitions with the Bible words on the right. Read the verses given or use a dictionary if you need help. All references are from Joshua.*

  b   1. Cunningly, craftily (9:4)

  i   2. A person sent to represent his country (9:4)

  h   3. Torn (9:4)

  g   4. Patched; roughly mended (9:5)

  a   5. An agreement between two or more

        persons or countries (9:6)

  d   6. Supplies of food (9:11)

  c   7. Advice or guidance (9:14)

  e   8. Choppers; cutters (9:21)

  f   9. To listen; heed (10:14)

a. league

b. wilily

c. counsel

d. victuals

e. hewers

f. hearken

g. clouted

h. rent

i. ambassador

C. THINKING ABOUT BIBLE TRUTHS

Exodus 23:31–33

God had known that some Canaanites would want to make peace with the Israelites. He had made special mention of this already at Mount Sinai.

1. What command did Joshua and the princes of Israel disobey? _____
   "Thou shalt make no covenant with them."

2. Why did God give this command? _____
   God did not want the idol worshipers to lead His people into sin.

Joshua 11:18–20

3. Did Joshua make peace with any other cities? ____no____

2 Samuel 21:1–6

God expects His people to keep their promises. This is one reason we must be very careful not to make foolish promises that we will not want to keep later. The events in these verses took place almost five hundred years after the Israelites had made their promise to the Gibeonites.

4. Who killed some of the Gibeonites? ____Saul____

5. How did the LORD punish the Israelites for this? _____
   The LORD sent famine for three years.

6. How did David make peace again with the Gibeonites? _____
   David delivered seven men of Saul's sons to the Gibeonites to be put to death.

D. LEARNING MORE ABOUT THE BIBLE

Which City?

Write the names of these cities in the correct circles. Do as many as you can without reading the verses given.

Ai	Jerusalem
Gibeon	Jericho
Kadesh-barnea	Beersheba
Sodom	Pithom
Hazor	Lachish

Lesson 25. Joshua's Last Days

The wars of conquest continued for about six years after the Israelites entered Canaan. Then Joshua gave each tribe and family a portion of the land they had conquered. Most of the events of this lesson took place after Joshua divided the land.

Before Moses died, he had made a long speech to the children of Israel. Now Joshua did the same thing. Joshua was concerned for the Israelites. He had seen everything that had happened to them since they left Egypt. He had seen the Israelites' many rebellions. He had heard their murmurings. No doubt Joshua was concerned about what they might do after his death. Therefore he called everyone together and spoke earnestly to them.

All the Israelites listened carefully as Joshua spoke. He told them the story of how God had brought them out of Egypt into the Promised Land. At the end, Joshua told them, "Now therefore fear the LORD, and serve him in sincerity and in truth: and put away the gods which your fathers served."

Joshua told the people that they needed to choose which god they would serve. But no matter what they decided, he and his house were going to serve the LORD. The people answered, "God forbid that we should forsake the LORD, to serve other gods; for the LORD our God, he it is that brought us up and our fathers out of the land of Egypt."

The Israelites remained faithful until the death of Joshua and all the leaders who had worked with him.

A. ANSWERS FROM THE BIBLE

Israel Finishes the Conquest

By the end of six years, the Israelites had conquered much of the land of Canaan. God had told them that He would not drive out all the inhabitants at once, so that the land would not go to waste. He would help them to conquer the rest of the land as they needed it. After Joshua divided the land, each tribe was to drive out any Canaanites that remained in its section.

Joshua 11:21–23

The Anakims were the last people that the Israelites conquered before Joshua divided the land among the tribes.

1. a. Who had been afraid of the Anakims (sons of Anak)? Read Numbers 13:30–33 if you have

   forgotten. <u>the ten spies who gave an evil report</u>

   b. Why did these people think the Anakims would be hard to conquer? _____

   <u>The Anakims were giants.</u>

2. What did Joshua do to the Anakims? _____

   <u>He cut them off and destroyed them utterly with their cities.</u>

- Joshua 14:10 states that Caleb waited forty-five years after spying out the land before he received his possession. Moses had sent out the twelve spies about one year after Israel left Egypt (compare Exodus 16:1 with Numbers 10:11), so Caleb waited about thirty-nine years in the wilderness. Apparently Joshua's conquest of Canaan took at least six years (the "long time" of Joshua 11:18).

Lesson 25

Oral Review

1. What are five ways (from Lesson 1) that God wants us to use the Bible? [1] **read, hear, study, believe, obey**
2. Why did Sarah want to send Hagar and Ishmael away? [9] **Sarah saw Ishmael mocking Isaac.**
3. Why did the Israelites have to wander in the desert for forty years? [20] **When God wanted them to enter Canaan, they rebelled and wished they were back in Egypt.**
4. Why did Joshua set up twelve stones at Gilgal? [22] **to serve as a memorial of how God helped Israel cross the Jordan River**
5. What were the Israelites commanded to do with the silver, gold, brass, and iron that they found in Jericho? [22] **They were to put them into the LORD's treasury.**
6. When did Achan confess his sin? [23] **after Joshua already knew he was the guilty one**
7. What were the Gibeonites required to do? [24] **They were to become servants of the Israelites.**
8. Why did Joshua not kill the Gibeonites for their dishonesty? [24] **The Israelites had sworn an oath to spare their lives.**

178   Chapter Five   Israel Conquers Canaan

3. What did Joshua do with the whole land of Canaan? _____

   He took the whole land and gave it to the tribes of Israel.

Caleb Claims His Inheritance

Caleb was a man of faith. Because of this, he and Joshua were the only men older than sixty that God allowed to enter Canaan. Now, at eighty-five, he was still ready to prove his faith in God by asking for land that was inhabited by the Anakims, the foes that the Israelites had dreaded most. Caleb had an important part in the victory over these giants.

Joshua 14:6–14

4. Forty-five years before this, Caleb was one of the men that Moses had sent to _____

   spy out the land of Canaan   .

5. a. What had Moses promised to Caleb after he returned? _____

      the land where he had walked

   b. Why? Caleb had wholly followed the LORD.

6. What did Caleb ask for now, as a fulfillment of the promise that Moses had made to him? _

   a mountain (Hebron)

7. Caleb was sure that he would be able to drive the Anakims out of his inheritance if _____

   the LORD would be with him   .

8. Because of his faithfulness, Caleb was given the region around Hebron for his inheritance.

   a. Who else had lived at Hebron? (See Genesis 35:27.) _____

      Abraham, Isaac, and Jacob

   b. In what way was Caleb like these men? _____

      (Sample answers) He was faithful. He believed that God would keep His promises.

- The name *Hebron* evidently referred to the region around the city as well as to the city itself. The city was one of the cities of refuge given to the Levites, but the surrounding region was given to the descendants of Caleb. (See Joshua 21:11–13.)
- This was part of the land that the twelve spies had explored.
- The cave of Machpelah, where Abraham, Sarah, Isaac, Rebekah, Jacob, and Leah were buried, was near Hebron. So the area that Caleb asked for was rich in heritage for the Israelites.

Joshua Gives His Last Words

Joshua knew that he was growing old. He was afraid that the Israelites would stop serving God when he died, so he called them together to talk with them one more time. In his talk, he challenged the Israelites to follow his example and continue to serve the Lord.

Joshua 23:1, 2

9. Joshua called for the Israelites to come before him when
   a. the last of the Canaanites were killed.
   b. he was old and stricken in age.
   c. he heard that they were worshiping idols.

10. Joshua called for
    a. all Israel, with their leaders.
    b. the older men of Israel.
    c. the Israelites who served the LORD.

In This Lesson

Scope: Joshua 11–24

Main Events

- Joshua and the Israelites conquer the Anakims.
- Caleb gains Hebron as a reward for his faithfulness.
- Before his death, Joshua challenges the Israelites to serve the LORD.
- The tribes receive their inheritance in Canaan.

Objectives

- Students should know
  —what Caleb did in his old age. (He asked for the mountain [Hebron] where the Anakims dwelled, and he had an important part in the victory over them.)
  —when Joshua challenged the people to choose whom they would serve. (near the end of his life)
  —which tribes received their inheritance east of the Jordan, and who commanded them to help conquer Canaan. (Reuben, Gad, and half the tribe of Manasseh; Moses)

Joshua 23:6; 24:14, 15

11. Joshua encouraged the people to
    a. work hard on their new farms.
    (b.) keep the Law of Moses.
    c. love one another.

12. Joshua asked the people to choose between
    a. serving him or serving the LORD.
    b. serving the LORD or serving one another.
    (c.) serving false gods or serving the LORD.

13. Joshua and his family set a good example for the Israelites. He had decided to do right, even

    if the rest of them chose the wrong way. He declared, "As for me and my house, _____

    <u>we will serve the LORD</u> ."

Israel Makes a Solemn Promise

Joshua 24:16–21

14. The people told Joshua that they would also serve the LORD because (choose three)
    (a.) He had brought them up out of Egypt.
    (b.) He had preserved them in the desert.
    c. He was the God of their fathers.
    (d.) He had driven out the people of Canaan.

15. Joshua challenged the Israelites by telling them,
    (a.) "The LORD is a holy and jealous God."
    b. "The LORD is very angry with you."
    c. "The LORD has forsaken you."

16. The Israelites answered his challenge by saying, "Nay; _____

    <u>but we will serve the LORD</u> ."

Where Is It Found?

17. Which two chapters of Joshua give his last message to the Israelites? <u>Joshua 23, 24</u>

B. BIBLE WORD STUDY

★ *Write a word from the verse given to fit each definition. All references are from Joshua.*

    <u>espy</u>   1. To view; search (14:7)
    <u>wholly</u>   2. Completely; entirely (14:8)
    <u>stricken</u>   3. Troubled, as by sickness or old age (23:1)

—what happened when they built an altar near the Jordan. (See Part C, numbers 2, 3.)
—what the purpose of the cities of refuge was, and how the Law protected an innocent manslayer. (See Part D, "The Cities of Refuge.")

Truths to Instill

• Caleb asked for a mountain. In his old age, he was still vigorous and eager for new territory to conquer, confident that he would be as victorious as he had been earlier. What was the key to his success? It was his unshaken confidence that God could work through him to conquer. "If so be the LORD will be with me, then I shall be able." He did not believe in Caleb; he believed in the LORD.

• The story of the eastern tribes building their altar shows the peril of forming opinions based on hearsay. Joshua 22:11 says, "And the children of Israel *heard say.*" Even though the report they heard was true, they had not heard the whole story. They immediately formed false conclusions and prepared for war. How much better it would have been had they trusted the eastern tribes and refused to believe the worst until they had no alternative.

___courageous___   4. Brave and strong; having no fear (23:6)

___serve___   5. To obey and respect; to worship (24:14)

___jealous___   6. Demanding complete faithfulness (24:19)

___nay___   7. No (24:21)

C. THINKING ABOUT BIBLE TRUTHS

The Israelites conquered the land east of the Jordan River before Moses died. Moses gave this land to the tribes of Reuben, Gad, and half the tribe of Manasseh. The Jordan River was a barrier between these tribes and the rest of the Israelites. This soon led to a misunderstanding that almost caused war between these tribes and the rest of the Israelites.

1. Read Deuteronomy 3:18–20.

   a. What had Moses commanded the armed men of the eastern tribes to do? __He told them to cross the Jordan River and help the other Israelites conquer the rest of the land.__

   b. Where did he say they should leave their wives and children? _____
      __in the cities east of Jordan__

2. Read Joshua 22:9–12.

   a. What did the men from the eastern tribes build after Joshua had sent them back home?
      __a great altar near the Jordan River__

   b. The rest of the tribes thought that the eastern tribes were turning away from God. What did these other tribes prepare to do to the eastern tribes? _____
      __The rest of the tribes prepared to fight against the eastern tribes.__

3. Read Joshua 22:21–30.

   a. The eastern tribes said they had not built their altar to offer sacrifices, but rather to serve as __a witness that they were part of God's people, so that their children would not forget__.

   b. How did the rest of the tribes feel when they learned why the altar had been built? ____
      __pleased__

4. What should people do to avoid misunderstandings like this?
   (a.) They should make sure that they know all the facts about a situation before judging someone else.
   b. They should not pay attention to the things that other people do.
   c. They should never build an altar without asking permission from the rest of God's people.

D. LEARNING MORE ABOUT THE BIBLE

The Cities of Refuge

The Israelites set aside six cities of refuge, three on either side of the Jordan River. Levites lived there and cared for the fields and gardens around them.

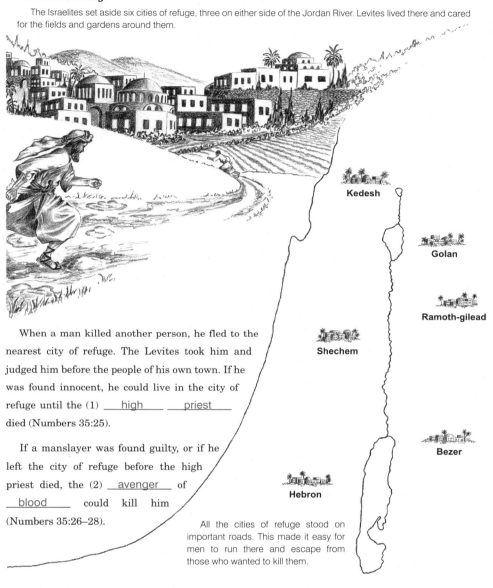

When a man killed another person, he fled to the nearest city of refuge. The Levites took him and judged him before the people of his own town. If he was found innocent, he could live in the city of refuge until the (1) __high__ __priest__ died (Numbers 35:25).

If a manslayer was found guilty, or if he left the city of refuge before the high priest died, the (2) __avenger__ of __blood__ could kill him (Numbers 35:26–28).

All the cities of refuge stood on important roads. This made it easy for men to run there and escape from those who wanted to kill them.

Map labels: Kedesh, Golan, Ramoth-gilead, Shechem, Bezer, Hebron

- People of ancient times thought that whenever one man killed another, intentionally or not, the dead man's nearest relative (the avenger of blood) was duty bound to kill the slayer. This is the reason for the cities of refuge. Historically, it was perhaps the first time that recognition was given for the motive in a killing—that there is a difference between an accidental slaying and a murder.

The Twelve Tribes in Canaan

The Mediterranean Sea

(The Great Sea)

N
W — E
S

- The map showing how Canaan was divided among the twelve tribes of Israel is only approximate, since some boundaries are difficult to determine. Also note that this map shows the areas given to the tribes, not those they actually controlled. Some of the tribes failed to drive out all the Canaanite inhabitants, as the map in Lesson 27 shows.

★ *Study the map "The Twelve Tribes in Canaan" to find answers for the following questions.*

1. Which tribes settled east of the Jordan River?

   __Reuben__ , ___Gad___ , and half of _Manasseh_

2. Which tribe settled within the boundaries of another tribe (Joshua 19:1)? __Simeon__

3. Which tribe received large sections of land on both sides of the Jordan River? _Manasseh_

4. Which tribe had a small section of land in the north besides their land farther south?

   ___Dan___

5. Which tribes settled around the tribe of Zebulun? ___Asher___ , __Naphtali__ , __Issachar__ ,

   and _Manasseh_

6. If you compare the names on the map with the names of Jacob's sons, you will notice that
   two names are missing.

   a. Ephraim and Manasseh were the sons of ___Joseph___ , but they each received a section
      of land because Jacob had adopted them (Genesis 48:3–5).

   b. The tribe of ___Levi___ (Deuteronomy 18:1, 2) did not receive an inheritance of land,
      because they were in charge of the tabernacle. Joshua gave them cities scattered
      throughout the other tribes.

184

Chapter Five Review

A. ORAL REVIEW

★ *Be sure you know the answers to these questions. Give as many answers as you can without looking back. If you need help, turn to the Bible reference or the lesson given in brackets.*

★ *In the first two sections, tell whether each statement is true or false. Also tell how the false statements should be corrected.*   In the rewritten sentences for numbers 1–8, the corrections are in italics. The pupil's sentences may vary somewhat.

Who >>

1. After David killed some Gibeonites, the LORD sent a famine for three years. [2 Samuel 21:1]
2. Adonizedec was king of Jerusalem in Joshua's time. [Joshua 10:1]
3. Caleb was afraid of the Anakims. [Joshua 14:12]
4. The tribes of Reuben, Gad, and part of Manasseh lived east of the Jordan River. [Lesson 25]
5. Achan waited to confess his sin until after Joshua knew he was guilty. [Joshua 7:16–21]

Where >>

6. Joshua commanded the sun to stand still upon Gibeon. [Joshua 10:12]
7. Jerusalem was located in the coastal plain of Canaan. [Lesson 21]
8. The Israelites had three cities of refuge on each side of the Jordan River. [Lesson 25]

★ *Give answers for the following questions.*

What >>

9. What happened to Rahab and her family when Jericho was destroyed? [Joshua 6:25]
10. What did Joshua build on Mount Ebal? [Joshua 8:30]
11. What did Caleb ask for in his old age? [Joshua 14:12]
12. What did Joshua say he and his house would do, even if the other Israelites did not? [Joshua 24:15]
13. What is the meaning of *valour*? [Lesson 22]

Why >>

14. Why was Canaan a good place for Jesus to live and teach? [Lesson 21]
15. Why were the Israelites defeated at Ai? [Joshua 7:1, 10–12]
16. Why did Joshua use the lot? [Joshua 7:16–18]
17. Why did men start using metal to make weapons? [Lesson 23]

How >>

18. How did Rahab help the spies? [Joshua 2:6, 15]
19. How did the Israelites conquer Ai? [Joshua 8:18–21]

1. false; After *Saul* killed some Gibeonites, the LORD sent a famine for three years.
2. true
3. false; Caleb was *ready to fight* the Anakims.
4. true
5. true
6. true
7. false; Jerusalem was located in the *central mountains* of Canaan.
8. true
9. The two spies brought them out of the city.
10. an altar
11. the mountain on which the Anakims lived (Hebron)
12. He said, "We will serve the LORD."
13 courage; bravery
14. Many people passed through Canaan and heard His teaching.
15. God did not help them, because Achan had sinned.
16. to find out who had sinned
17. Metal weapons were lighter and sharper, and they lasted longer.
18. Rahab hid the spies and helped them escape from Jericho. She also gave them important information.
19. Some of the Israelites hid, while others got the soldiers of Ai to leave the city and pursue them. Then the hidden Israelites entered Ai and set fire to the city.

B. WRITTEN REVIEW

★ *Write answers to the following questions. If you need help, use the Bible reference or the lesson given in brackets.*

Where

1. Where would you find a city if a Bible atlas index gave its location as D2—6? [Lesson 21]
   on Map 6, column D, row 2

What

2. What were the Israelites commanded to do with the silver, gold, brass, and iron that they found in Jericho? [Joshua 6:19]
   They were to put them into the LORD's treasury.

3. What did the Israelites force the Gibeonites to do? [Joshua 9:21]
   They forced them to cut wood and carry water.

4. What did Moses command the armed men of the eastern tribes to do? [Deuteronomy 3:18–20]   He commanded them to help conquer all of Canaan before settling down in their own inheritance.

When

5. When did Adonizedec decide to fight Joshua? [Joshua 10:1–4]
   after the Gibeonites made peace with Israel

6. When did Joshua make a long speech to the Israelites? [Joshua 23:1, 2]
   when he was old

7. When could a man find safety in a city of refuge? [Lesson 25]
   when he had accidentally killed someone

8. When could an innocent manslayer leave a city of refuge? [Numbers 35:25; Lesson 25]
   after the high priest died

Why

9. Why did the Syrians think it would be easier to fight the Israelites in the valleys than in the mountains? [Lesson 21]   The Syrians could use their chariots in the valleys. (They also thought Israel's God was a God of the hills but not of the valleys.)

10. Why did the main roads through Canaan follow the shore of the Mediterranean Sea? [Lesson 21] <u>It was easier to travel on the level plain along the sea than through the mountains.</u>

11. Why did Joshua set up twelve stones at Gilgal? [Joshua 4:19–24] <u>so that the Israelites would not forget how God had helped them to cross the Jordan River</u>

12. Why did Joshua not kill the Gibeonites for their dishonesty? [Joshua 9:20] <u>He and the princes had promised to let the Gibeonites live.</u>

How

13. How did the Israelites cross the Jordan River? [Joshua 3:14–17] <u>They walked across on dry land after God parted the water.</u>

14. How did the Israelites conquer Jericho? [Joshua 6:3–5] <u>They followed God's instructions by walking around the city each day for seven days. On the seventh day they shouted and the walls fell down. Then they burned the city.</u>

15. How did the Gibeonites deceive Joshua? [Joshua 9:4–6] <u>They took old food, clothes, and goods, and pretended to be ambassadors from a far country, who were seeking peace.</u>

16. How did God help the Israelites defeat the five Amorite kings? [Joshua 10:11–13] <u>He made the sun and moon stand still, and He sent a great hailstorm.</u>

Bible Outline

★ *Match these chapters with the events they record.*

<u>g</u> 17. Joshua 1, 2   a. God helps the Israelites conquer Jericho.

<u>i</u> 18. Joshua 3–5   b. The Israelites make a league with the Gibeonites.

<u>a</u> 19. Joshua 6   c. Joshua appoints cities of refuge; the eastern tribes build an altar.

<u>d</u> 20. Joshua 7, 8   d. Achan sins; Israel fights against Ai; Joshua builds an altar on

<u>b</u> 21. Joshua 9   Mount Ebal.

<u>h</u> 22. Joshua 10–12   e. Caleb asks for Hebron; Joshua divides the land of Canaan.

<u>e</u> 23. Joshua 13–19   f. Before he dies, Joshua challenges Israel to serve the LORD.

<u>c</u> 24. Joshua 20–22   g. God calls Joshua; Rahab helps the spies.

<u>f</u> 25. Joshua 23, 24   h. Adonizedec attacks Gibeon; Joshua commands the sun to stand

still; God helps Israel defeat five Amorite kings.

i. The Israelites cross Jordan and camp at Gilgal.

Map Review

★ *Label these places on the map: Central Mountains, Coastal Plain, Eastern Mountains, Hebron, Jericho, Jerusalem, Jordan River Valley. [Lesson 21]*

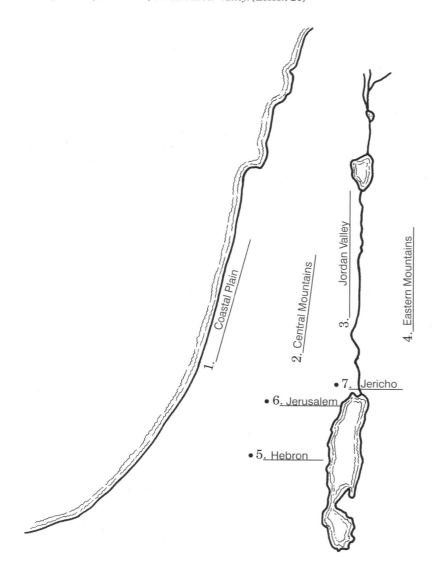

CHAPTER SIX

Israel in the Days
of the Judges

But the path of the just is as the shining light, that shineth more and more unto the perfect day. Therefore turn thou to thy God: keep mercy and judgment, and wait on thy God continually. And let us not be weary in well doing: for in due season we shall reap, if we faint not. (Proverbs 4:18; Hosea 12:6; Galatians 6:9)

TIME LINE OF THE JUDGES—Chapter Six

480 years from the Exodus to the building of the temple (1 Kings 6:1)

About 300 years from the conquest to the Ammonite oppression (Judges 11:26)

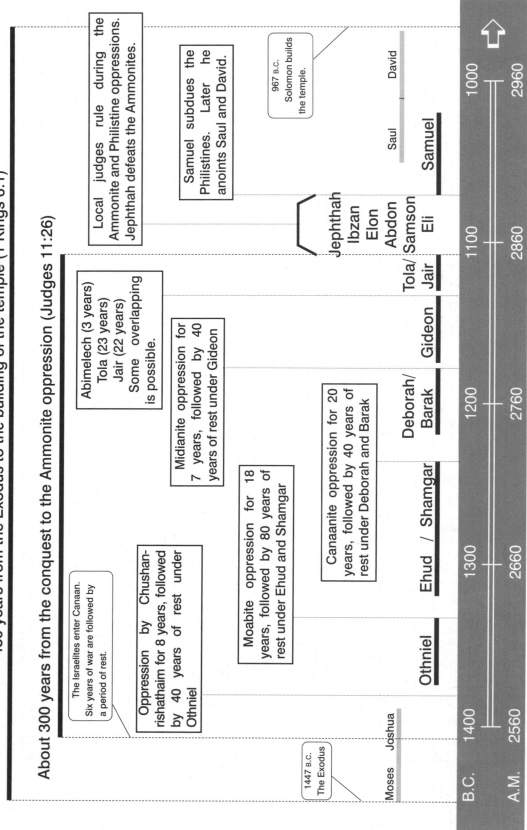

The Israelites enter Canaan. Six years of war are followed by a period of rest.

Oppression by Chushan-rishathaim for 8 years, followed by 40 years of rest under Othniel

Moabite oppression for 18 years, followed by 80 years of rest under Ehud and Shamgar

Canaanite oppression for 20 years, followed by 40 years of rest under Deborah and Barak

Midianite oppression for 7 years, followed by 40 years of rest under Gideon

Abimelech (3 years)
Tola (23 years)
Jair (22 years)
Some overlapping is possible.

Local judges rule during the Ammonite and Philistine oppressions. Jephthah defeats the Ammonites.

Samuel subdues the Philistines. Later he anoints Saul and David.

1447 B.C. The Exodus

967 B.C. Solomon builds the temple.

Moses   Joshua

Othniel   Ehud / Shamgar   Deborah/ Barak   Gideon   Tola/ Jair   Jephthah Ibzan Elon Abdon Samson/ Eli   Samuel

Saul   David

B.C.	1400	1300	1200	1100	1000
A.M.	2560	2660	2760	2860	2960

NOTE: The dates for individual judges are approximate. Other arrangements of overlapping are possible. Some scholars avoid the need for most overlaps by adding 114 years to the 480-year period. (See The Wonders of Bible Chronology, by Philip Mauro.) This raises other questions, however.

191

Lesson 26. Divisions of the Old Testament

The Bible has two main parts, the Old Testament and the New Testament. Both parts are libraries of shorter books. Like any library, the Bible contains different kinds of books. The books of the Old Testament can be divided into five sections.

In Chapters 1–4 of this Bible course, you briefly studied Genesis, Exodus, Leviticus, Numbers, and Deuteronomy. These books make up the first section of the Old Testament. In Genesis, you studied how God created the earth and how He spoke to men such as Adam, Noah, and Abraham. In Exodus and Numbers, you saw how God delivered His people from Egypt and cared for them in the wilderness. The Book of Leviticus gives details about the Law, and the Book of Deuteronomy records Moses' last words to the Israelites. These five books cover about 2,600 years of history!

In Chapters 5 and 6, you are studying the Books of Joshua and Judges. These two books begin the second section of the Old Testament library. This second section tells the story of God's chosen family as a nation in their own land.

A. ANSWERS FROM THE BIBLE

The books of the Old Testament can be divided into five groups, or "shelves," as illustrated in this drawing. You will study each shelf of books in the following sections.

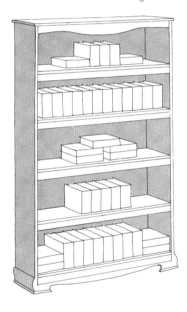

The Books of Moses

The Books of History

The Books of Poetry

The Major Prophets

The Minor Prophets

- It seems likely that Moses compiled the Book of Genesis from written records that were passed down from earlier generations. See *The Genesis Record,* by Henry Morris.

- Some students may wonder why we include the small Books of Lamentations and Daniel with the Major Prophets rather than with the Minor Prophets. In the Masoretic Hebrew text, the writings of the twelve "minor" prophets are all in one book. Later this book was divided into twelve books, but they are still grouped together. Since Daniel and Lamentations were separate books in the Masoretic text, they are grouped with the Major Prophets. (See *The New Unger's Bible Dictionary*, p. 205, and *Halley's Bible Handbook*, p. 26.)

Lesson 26

Oral Review

1. Name the things God created on each day of Creation. [2] *First day*: **light (also heaven and earth);** *Second*: **firmament;** *Third*: **dry land, seas, and plants;** *Fourth*: **sun, moon, and stars;** *Fifth*: **sea animals and birds;** *Sixth*: **land animals and man**

2. What do the abbreviations *A.M., B.C.,* and *A.D.* mean when they are used with dates? [6] **A.M.—in the year of the world, B.C.—before Christ, A.D.— in the year of our Lord**

3. What two things did God tell Rebekah about her sons before they were born? [9] **They would become two manner of people, and the elder would serve the younger.**

4. What well-known river flowed through Canaan? [11] **the Jordan River**

5. Why did Moses need to flee from Egypt? [14] **Moses was afraid because he had killed an Egyptian and now Pharaoh wanted to kill him.**

6. Why did Joshua set up twelve stones at Gilgal? [22] **He set them up to serve as a memorial of how God had helped the Israelites cross the Jordan.**

7. What commandment did Achan disobey? [23] **God's command forbidding the Israelites from taking any treasures from Jericho for themselves**

★ *Study the Bible passages given. Fill in the short blanks with words, using exact words from the Bible whenever possible. Write complete answers for the questions with long blanks. For multiple choice questions, circle the letter of the correct answer or underline the correct word in parentheses.*

The Books of Moses

We call the first five books of the Old Testament the Books of Moses, since Moses wrote them. These books tell about man's beginning and record the laws God gave to the Israelites.

★ *Write the title of each Book of Moses on its back. (Genesis has been done for you.) Then fill in the blank following the shelf.*

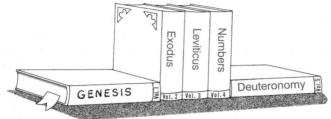

Number of books: _5_

1. Read Mark 12:26. Here Jesus taught a lesson from the Book of Exodus, which He called the

   Book of _____Moses_____. He was probably referring to the complete set of books that

   Moses wrote.

★ *For each shelf of books, write the title of each book on its back, as you did above. Then fill in the blanks following the shelf.*

The Books of History

After the Books of Moses come the twelve Books of History. They tell the story of God's people from their entrance into Canaan until their captivity in Babylon.

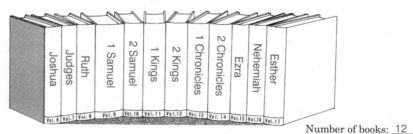

Number of books: _12_

2. Read Matthew 12:3, 4. Here Jesus taught a lesson from the life of _____David_____,

   as it is given in the Old Testament Books of History.

8. What did Joshua say that he and his house would do, even if no one else did? [25] **Joshua and his house would serve the LORD.**

In This Lesson

Main Points
- The five divisions of the Old Testament include
  —the Books of Moses (5 books).
  —the Books of History (12 books).
  —the Books of Poetry (5 books).
  —the Major Prophets (5 books).
  —the Minor Prophets (12 books).

- God expects us to learn from Old Testament examples.
- Bible concordances can help us find Bible verses and Bible stories.

Objectives
- Students should know
  —the five divisions of the Old Testament from memory. (the Books of Moses, the Books of History, the Books of Poetry, the Major Prophets, the Minor Prophets)
  —which books are in each division. (See Part A.)

The Books of Poetry

After the Books of History come the five Books of Poetry and wise sayings.

Number of books: __5__

3. Read Mark 12:10, 11. Here Jesus quoted from Psalms, one of the Books of Poetry. These verses refer to Jesus, comparing Him to a _____stone_____ that was rejected by the builders.

The Major Prophets

God told some men in Old Testament times what would happen in years to come. These men, the prophets, wrote the messages they received from God.

Because several of these books are large, they are known as the Major Prophets.

Number of books: __5__

4. Read Luke 4:18, 19. Here Jesus read from Isaiah, one of the Major Prophets. These verses also talk about Jesus. The Spirit of the Lord had __anointed__ Jesus to preach the Gospel and to do the other works that He did while He lived on the earth.

Truths to Instill

- God cares for the Bible. The Bible was written over a period of at least 1,500 years by about forty different authors, yet it is one unified book. This is a marvelous testimony to God's inspiration.

The Minor Prophets

The last twelve books of the Old Testament record the messages that God gave to twelve more prophets. Because these books are small, they are known as the Minor Prophets.

12

5. Read Acts 2:16, 17. Here the apostle Peter quoted from the Book of _____Joel_____, one of the Minor Prophets. These verses were fulfilled on the day of Pentecost.

★ *Add together the number of books in each section to find the total number of Old Testament books.*
Total number of books in the Old Testament: _39_

★ *Memorize the name of each "shelf" of books in the Old Testament: the Books of Moses, the Books of History, the Books of Poetry, the Major Prophets, and the Minor Prophets. Also memorize the names of the first seventeen Old Testament books in the correct order, and remember which "shelf" they belong on.*

The Purpose of the Old Testament

Why do we study the Old Testament? The Old Testament is more than just a collection of stories, poems, and wise sayings. We can learn many things by reading it.

1 Corinthians 10:11

The first ten verses of this chapter tell about the Israelites in the wilderness. They list some of the sins that the Israelites committed, and the punishments that they received for them.

6. The Old Testament accounts were written for our _admonition_.

7. This means that these stories were written
   a. so that we can avoid making the same mistakes the people in the stories made.
   b. so that we can see how much better we are than the people who lived long ago.
   c. so that we can pray for the people in the stories.

Where Is It Found?

8. The story of the Flood is found in the Book of _____Genesis_____.

9. The life story of Abraham is found in the Book of _____Genesis_____.

10. The story of the ten plagues is found in the Book of _____Exodus_____.

11. Moses' parting words to the Israelites are found in the Book of _Deuteronomy_.

If your students have time, it would be good to require them to memorize all the books of the Old Testament, even though this is not included in the test for this chapter.

B. BIBLE STUDY BOOKS

Bible Concordances—Finding Verses and Stories

In Lesson 6 you learned to find references for Bible words by using a Bible concordance. You can also use a Bible concordance to find specific verses and Bible stories. First you must decide which word to look for. Suppose you want to find the verse, "In every thing give thanks." Which word would you look for in a concordance? The words *every*, *thing*, and *in* are used very often in the Bible. Many Bible concordances do not list words that are used so often. Even if your concordance does list them, it would take a long time to find the right verse by using these words. The word *thanks* would be the best choice because it is not used as often, and it also gives the main idea of the verse. You could also try *give*, but that is a very common word too.

If you wanted to find the story of Daniel in the lions' den, you could try looking up *Daniel*, *lions*, or *den*. Try to think which one is probably used the fewest times in the Bible. Sometimes you will need to try several different words, since the word you are thinking of may not actually be used in the Bible. For instance, which word could you look up to find the story of the wise men who came to worship the baby Jesus: *wise*, *men*, *baby*, *Jesus*, or *star*? If you look in your concordance, you will see that the word *baby* is not used in the Bible. You will need to look up one of the other words to find the story.

★ *Use a concordance to find the following Bible verses and phrases. For each one, write (a) which word you looked up and (b) the book, chapter, and verse where it is found.*

	Word you looked up		Reference
1. "The LORD had respect unto Abel."	a. ___Abel___	b.	___Genesis 4:4___
2. "Jesus wept."	a. ___wept___	b.	___John 11:35___
3. "In every thing give thanks."	a. ___thanks___	b.	___1 Thessalonians 5:18___

★ *Use a concordance to find the following Bible stories. For each story, write the word you looked up, and the book and chapter where it is found.* (Any one)

4. Aaron's rod grows buds	a. ___buds, rod___	b.	___Numbers 17___
5. Daniel is thrown into the lions' den	a. ___lions', den___ Daniel	b.	___Daniel 6___
6. Jacob dreams about a ladder that reaches heaven	a. ___ladder___ reached, dreamed	b.	___Genesis 28___

★ *In Chapter 5 you read about Joshua and how he led the Israelites in conquering Canaan. Use a concordance to find the following verses about Joshua. Write the reference of the verse in the blank.*

7. Joshua fights with Amalek while Moses, Aaron, and Hur watch from a hill. ___Exodus 17:8–16___

8. Moses calls Joshua and tells him to be strong and of a good courage. ___Deuteronomy 31:7___

9. Joshua meets the captain of the LORD's host. ___Joshua 5:13–15___

Take time to review the use of a Bible concordance before the students start this section, to make sure that they still remember how to use one efficiently.

Lesson 27. Israel's Great Mistake

The Israelites were glad to be settled in Canaan. They had lived in the wilderness for forty years, and then they had spent six more years conquering Canaan. Now they lived in their own houses and farmed their own fields. They could have received God's blessings year after year and generation after generation. But the Israelites made a serious mistake.

God had commanded the Israelites to completely drive out the wicked Canaanite nations. He had told them to destroy all their idols and to tear down all their places of worship. God had warned them not to make any covenants with the people of the land.

At first the Israelites tried to follow God's directions. Only the Gibeonites were able to escape, by pretending to be from a far country. But after several years, the Israelites grew tired of fighting. Instead of driving out all the heathen, the Israelites made some of them work as slaves. Others were not conquered, because the Israelites did not have enough faith in God.

The Lord was not pleased with this. He knew that if these people were left in the land, they would lead His chosen family into sin. Soon God's people would be worshiping idols, marrying heathen wives, and living wickedly.

Do you know what happened?

A. ANSWERS FROM THE BIBLE

The Broken Covenant

Judges 1:18–21
  These verses give only two examples of the Israelites' disobedience. Many of the other tribes did not drive out all the heathen from their lands either. The rest of this chapter gives a long list of people that the Israelites failed to expel.

1. The tribe of Judah drove out the inhabitants of the mountains but not the inhabitants of the valley.

   a. Why could Judah not drive out the people who lived in the valley? _____
      The people of the valley had chariots of iron.

   b. What should the tribe of Judah have done?   (Sample answer) They should have
      trusted in the LORD for complete victory over their enemies.

2. Which city did the Benjamites fail to conquer? _____ Jerusalem _____

Judges 2:1–5
  These verses record that a heavenly messenger spoke directly to a large group of Israelites. This Bible account is very unusual. In most cases, angels brought messages to one person or to a small group. Perhaps at this time there was no man that God could trust to give His message to the Israelites. Or perhaps God used a heavenly messenger to show the people how serious their sin was.

- The Hebrew word translated *angel* in Judges 2:1–5 is *mal'ak*. (See number 4397 in the Hebrew dictionary in *Strong's Exhaustive Concordance*.) This word is often translated *messenger* and can refer either to men or to heavenly messengers. However, in almost every passage where the expression "*mal'ak* of the LORD" is used, it obviously refers to a heavenly messenger. In this case, the context does not clearly indicate whether the messenger was earthly or heavenly, but the Bible translators followed the standard usage of the term by using *angel*. (In some cases, such as Genesis 48:16, *mal'ak* apparently refers to an appearance of the LORD Himself.)

Lesson 27

Oral Review
1. How did Noah prove that he had faith in God? [4] **He obeyed all of God's commandments.**
2. What did God compare Abraham's descendants to? [7, 8] **the dust of the earth, the stars of the heaven, the sand of the seashore**
3. How did the Israelites know that God was pleased with the tabernacle? [19] **God filled the tabernacle with His glory.**
4. How did God help the Israelites defeat five Amorite kings? [24] **He sent a great hailstorm, and He made the sun and the moon stand still.**
5. What did Caleb ask for in his old age? [25] **the mountain of Hebron (and the privilege of conquering it)**
6. What did Joshua say that he and his house would do, even if the other Israelites did not? [25] **Joshua and his house would serve the LORD.**
7. Name the five divisions of the Old Testament. [26] **the Books of Moses, the Books of History, the Books of Poetry, the Major Prophets, the Minor Prophets**
8. Name the five Books of Moses. [26] **Genesis, Exodus, Leviticus, Numbers, Deuteronomy**

3. God and the Israelites had promised to be faithful one to another. This was a covenant. Who broke the covenant? _____ the Israelites _____

4. What two commands from the Lord had the Israelites disobeyed?
   a. Ye shall make no league with them.
   b. Ye shall throw down their altars.

5. What did the angel say that the LORD would do because of Israel's disobedience? The LORD would not drive out Israel's enemies, but they would be as thorns and snares to Israel.

6. How did the children of Israel respond to this warning from God? _____
   They wept.

The Results of Disobedience

The Israelites had a serious problem. Whenever they had a good leader, they followed God; but when the leader died, they forgot God. Often God needed to punish them before they were ready to listen to Him again.

Judges 2:6–13

7. Joshua was ___ 110 ___ years old when he died.

8. What did the people do as long as Joshua lived? _____
   They served the LORD.

9. What did the people do after Joshua and the elders of his generation died?
   a. They served the Philistines.
   b. They served the Lord.
   c. They served Baal and Ashtaroth.

10. The people who lived after Joshua
    a. did not know the Lord and the great things He had done for Israel.
    b. did not know how to divide the land fairly among the tribes.
    c. did not know how to serve the gods of the Canaanites.

Judges 3:5–11

11. What happened to the Israelites when they started living among the Canaanites?
    a. They learned better ways of farming.
    b. They taught the Canaanites how to follow God's commandments.
    c. They married Canaanites and served false gods.

12. How did the Lord cause the Israelites to return to Him?
    a. He let their enemies mistreat them.
    b. He spoke to them from Mount Sinai.
    c. He offered to make them rich and happy.

13. The first king that God used to punish Israel was Chushan-rishathaim (koo shan rihsh uh THAY ihm). Who delivered the Israelites from this king?
    a. Kenaz, the brother of Caleb
    b. Othniel, the son of Kenaz
    c. Caleb, the son of Jephunneh

In This Lesson

Scope: Judges 1–3

Main Events
- The Israelites break their covenant with God.
- God stops driving out Israel's enemies.
- God allows the Israelites to be mistreated by their enemies so that His people will return to Him.
- God raises up judges to deliver Israel.

Objectives
- Students should know
  —how Israel changed after Joshua's death. (They did not continue to follow God's command to drive out all the Canaanites.)
  —why Israel was unable to conquer more territory. (They did not have enough faith; then, after they disobeyed, God said He would not drive out their enemies.)
  —why Israel suffered oppression. (They served other gods.)
  —who Chushan-rishathaim was. (the first king that God used to punish Israel)

Ehud Delivers Israel

Forty years after they defeated Chushan-rishathaim, the Israelites fell into sin again. This time God used Eglon, king of Moab, to punish them. The Israelites served Eglon for eighteen years.

Judges 3:15–23, 29, 30

14. Most men carried their weapons on the left thigh, where they could quickly draw them out with their right hand. Ehud carried his on his right thigh and was therefore able to hide it from Eglon's servants. Why could Ehud use his dagger easily, even though he carried it on the wrong side?   Ehud was left-handed.

15. What happened to the Moabites after Ehud killed Eglon, their king?
    a. The Moabites fled to Egypt.
    (b) Ten thousand Moabites were killed.
    c. Ehud made peace with the Moabites.

Where Is It Found?

16. Which chapter of Judges tells the story of Ehud?   Judges 3

B. BIBLE WORD STUDY

★ *Match these definitions with the Bible words on the right. Read the verses given or use a dictionary if you need help. All references are from Judges.*

  b   1. The people who live at a place (1:19)   a. gird
  g   2. To force out (1:20)   b. inhabitants
  c   3. A trap; something that entangles (2:3)   c. snare
  e   4. A group of people born at about the same time (2:10)   d. subdue
  a   5. To fasten on (3:16)   e. generation
  f   6. Vigorous; healthy (3:29)   f. lusty
  d   7. To conquer or bring under control (3:30)   g. expel

C. THINKING ABOUT BIBLE TRUTHS

The Israelites quite likely thought of many excuses for not driving out the Canaanites. You have seen some of these already as you worked on this lesson. But no excuse is ever good enough to justify disobeying God. In the end, the Israelites had to reap a bitter harvest for their disobedience.

1. Read Exodus 23:27–30.
    a. Did God plan to drive out Israel's enemies in one year?   no
    b. Why or why not?   God planned to drive out their enemies slowly so that the land would not become desolate and so that the wild beasts would not take over the land.

—who delivered Israel from Chushan-rishathaim. (Othniel)
—how Ehud delivered Israel. (See Part A, numbers 14, 15.)
—who lived in Jerusalem during the time of the judges. (Jebusites)

Truths to Instill

• The Israelites' success in driving out the inhabitants of Canaan did not depend on their fighting skills. The LORD drove out their enemies for them. Joshua told them that the LORD would continue to help them if they continued to obey and love Him (see Joshua 23:5–13). But they quickly departed from God, and they failed to keep their part of the covenant they had made at Shechem (Joshua 24:19–28).

• Moses had warned Israel, "When thou shalt have eaten and be full; then beware lest thou forget the LORD" (Deuteronomy 6:11, 12). In times of plenty, we face the same danger. Does God need to send adversity to bring us back to Him?

• The Israelites' toleration of the Canaanites in their land illustrates the danger of allowing ourselves to be in a place of temptation. It is not wrong to be tempted, and God does promise to make a way of escape if we do our part. But we cannot expect Him to help us if we deliberately put ourselves in the path of temptation. It is good to say no to temptation, but it is better to avoid it entirely if possible.

2. Read Joshua 23:9–13. Joshua gave this warning before he died.

   a. Why did the Israelites have victories over their enemies when they first entered the land?
   The LORD drove their enemies out.

   b. Why were they unable to finish conquering the land?   The LORD stopped driving
   out their enemies because the Israelites had broken the covenant.

The Book of Jeremiah was written many years after the events in this lesson took place. It shows the final results of the way that the Israelites lived in Canaan. Because of their continued disobedience, God finally took their land away and allowed foreigners to move them far away from their homes.

3. Read Jeremiah 11:8. This verse says that the Israelites would not obey God or listen to Him. Instead, they "walked every one in the imagination of their evil heart." This means that they disobeyed God because
   (a) they thought their own ideas about right and wrong were more important than God's laws. So they ignored God and did whatever they wanted to do.
   b. they spent so much time daydreaming that they had no time to listen to God's Word. So they did not know what God wanted them to do.
   c. God did not tell them exactly what He wanted them to do. So it was not really their fault that they were disobedient.

4. Read Jeremiah 15:6. In this verse, God was telling the Israelites that because of their disobedience, He would ____stretch out His hand against____ them and __destroy__ them. This is the final result of disobedience to God.

HABITS

A habit is a sticky thing;
Much good or evil it can bring;
It binds a victim, holds him fast,
And keeps him in a viselike grasp.

Bad habits grow with extra speed,
Much like a healthy, growing weed.
The roots grow deep, the stem grows stout;
How difficult to pull it out!

Good habits are a little slow;
They need a lot of care to grow;
If tended well, they grow more fair
Than any bloom a plant can bear.

Good habits help us all through life;
Bad habits bring us pain and strife;
Our habits, whether right or wrong,
Each day will grow more firm and strong.

200   Chapter Six   Israel in the Days of the Judges

D. LEARNING MORE ABOUT THE BIBLE

The Unfinished Conquest

This map shows which areas of Canaan the Israelites usually controlled, and which areas their enemies often controlled. When the Israelites were strong, they pushed their enemies back; but when their enemies were strong, the Israelites lost some of their land.

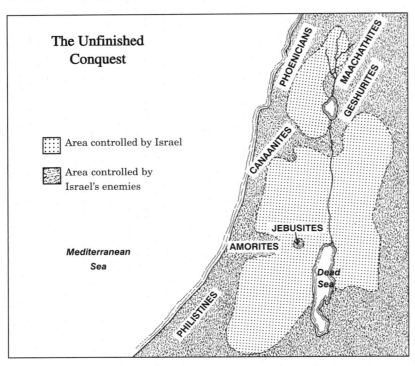

- This map shows the general areas that Israel controlled during the time of the judges. They had trouble keeping possession of the valleys and plains, where their enemies could use chariots. Because of the Israelites' unfaithfulness, God allowed these nations to remain in the land.

★ *Use the map and your Bible to answer these questions.*

1. Who lived in Jerusalem during the time of the judges (Judges 1:21)? _____
   Jebusites _____

2. Who controlled most of the coastal plain: Israel or the enemies of Israel? _____
   the enemies of Israel _____

3. Who forced the tribe of Dan into the mountains (Judges 1:34)? ___ Amorites _____

4. Which two groups of enemies lived east and northeast of the Sea of Galilee (Joshua 13:13)?
   Geshurites and Maachathites _____

201

Lesson 28. God Sends Deliverers

God is patient. He is long-suffering and merciful. How do we know that He is patient and merciful? One way we can know what God is like is by reading what He did for His people long ago.

After Joshua died, the Israelites departed from God, and He allowed their enemies to overrun their land. The Midianites were one group of Israel's enemies. Every year, just after the Israelites' crops were up and shining green in the sun, the Midianites would come up from the desert region where they lived. They would bring their cows and sheep and goats and camels and wives and children. They would set up whole villages of tents wherever they pleased. Their animals would trample the fields of the Israelites and eat up the plants. Then the Midianites would move on, and the poor Israelites would have little to eat.

This went on for seven years. The Israelites had to plant crops in secret places and thresh their grain where no one could see them. Finally they became so miserable that they cried to God for help. God heard and answered their prayer.

God is always ready to help His people when they want Him to and ask for His help.

A. ANSWERS FROM THE BIBLE

In the last lesson, you read about Chushan-rishathaim, Othniel, Eglon, and Ehud. This lesson deals with two more occasions when the Israelites sinned and God allowed their enemies to oppress them. They should have learned from the lessons of the past, but they failed to do so.

Barak and Deborah

After Ehud died, the Israelites sinned again. This time the Lord let them suffer for twenty years before He sent a deliverer. The Bible says that they were "mightily oppressed" during this time.

Judges 4:1–9

★ *What job or position did each of these persons have?*

1. Jabin ___king of Canaan_____

2. Sisera ___captain of Jabin's host_____

3. Deborah ___prophetess (and judge)_____

4. Lapidoth ___Deborah's husband_____

5. Barak ___captain of the Israelite army_____

Judges 4:15–24

Deborah encouraged Barak to fight against Jabin. When Sisera, the captain of Jabin's army, heard that Barak was coming, he gathered a multitude of men and nine hundred iron chariots. Barak had only ten thousand men, but God was with him.

6. Verse 15 says, "The Lord discomfited Sisera, and all his chariots, and all his host, with the edge of the sword before Barak." This tells us that

   a. God did all the fighting for Barak. He and his men did not need to fight at all in this battle.

   (b.) Even though Barak and his men did the fighting, it was God's power that defeated the enemy.

   c. God made Sisera and his men feel so uncomfortable that they all ran away from Barak's army.

Lesson 28

Oral Review

1. How did Joseph show that he had forgiven his brothers? [13] **He treated them kindly and took care of them.**

2. Say the Ten Commandments from memory. [18]
   (1) Thou shalt have no other gods before me.
   (2) Thou shalt not make unto thee any graven image.
   (3) Thou shalt not take the Name of the LORD thy God in vain.
   (4) Remember the Sabbath Day, to keep it holy.
   (5) Honour thy father and thy mother.
   (6) Thou shalt not kill.
   (7) Thou shalt not commit adultery.
   (8) Thou shalt not steal.
   (9) Thou shalt not bear false witness.
   (10) Thou shalt not covet.

3. Which two Old Testament commandments did Jesus say are the greatest? [18] **"Thou shalt love the Lord thy God with all thy heart, and with all thy soul, and with all thy mind, and with all thy strength." "Thou shalt love thy neighbour as thyself."**

202 Chapter Six Israel in the Days of the Judges

7. Sisera fled to Jael's tent to hide because there was ___peace___ between Jael's husband and ___Jabin___, the king of Hazor.

8. List three things that Jael did to make Sisera think she was his friend.

   a. ___(Any three)___

   b. ___She went out to meet him.___   ___She invited him into her tent.___

   c. ___She covered him with a mantle.___   ___She gave him milk to drink.___

9. What did Jael do while Sisera slept? _____

   ___She killed him with a tent nail.___

God Speaks to Gideon

After the victory of Barak, the Israelites had rest for forty years. Then they found themselves in trouble again.

Judges 6:1

10. The Lord delivered Israel into the hand of the Midianites because _____

    ___they did evil in His sight_____.

Judges 6:11, 16

After seven years of Midianite invasion, the Israelites were very poor. They cried to the Lord, and He sent a prophet who told them they were suffering because of their sin. Then God sent an angel to talk to Gideon, the man He had chosen to deliver Israel.

11. Gideon was threshing wheat by the winepress. Why was he doing it there? _____

    ___to hide it from the Midianites_____

12. The Lord told Gideon that he was to ___smite the Midianites_____.

Judges 6:25, 26

13. God tested Gideon to see if he was really willing to follow Him. He told Gideon to destroy his father's false gods. Then he was to build an altar to the Lord and offer his father's second ___bullock___ for a burnt sacrifice.

Judges 6:36–40

Gideon passed God's test, but he wanted to be sure that he understood God's call. He asked God to give him a sign that He would help him defeat the Midianites. Then, to be absolutely sure, he asked God for a second sign.

14. What were the two signs that Gideon asked God to give him?

    a. ___One night he asked God to send dew only on a fleece that he put down.___

    b. ___The next night he asked God to let the fleece be dry and the ground wet.___

4. Why did Joshua not kill the Gibeonites for their dishonesty? [24] **The Israelites had sworn an oath that they would let them live.**

5. Name the twelve books of history in the Old Testament. [26] **Joshua, Judges, Ruth, 1 Samuel, 2 Samuel, 1 Kings, 2 Kings, 1 Chronicles, 2 Chronicles, Ezra, Nehemiah, Esther**

6. Who delivered Israel from Chushan-rishathaim? [27] **Othniel**

7. Who delivered Israel from Eglon, king of Moab? [27] **Ehud**

In This Lesson

Scope: Judges 4–8

Main Events

- Israel sins after Ehud's death, and God allows the Canaanites to oppress them for twenty years.
- God uses Deborah, Barak, and Jael to deliver Israel from the Canaanites.
- After forty years of rest, the Israelites sin, and God delivers them into the hand of Midian for seven years.
- God uses Gideon and three hundred men to deliver Israel from the Midianites.

Judges 7:2, 7

15. Why did God want Gideon to take only a few soldiers? _____

    God did not want the Israelites to boast that they had saved themselves.

16. How many men did God choose? _____ three hundred _____

The Midianites Defeated

Gideon still had doubts about being able to win a battle against the great army of his enemies. But God told him to go down to the Midianite camp and listen to what they were saying. There Gideon overheard a Midianite man telling about a dream in which Gideon triumphed over them. When Gideon heard this, he worshiped. Now he knew that God would give the Israelites the victory.

Judges 7:15–23

17. When Gideon's men broke their pitchers and blew their trumpets, they cried, "_____

    The sword of the LORD, and of Gideon   ."

18. What did the Lord do to the host of the Midianites when Gideon's men blew the trumpets?

    He set every man's sword against his fellow. (He caused them to become so confused
    that they began killing one another.)

There were about 135,000 soldiers in the host of the Midianites, but almost all of them were destroyed in this battle. The Israelites were so impressed by the victory that they asked Gideon to be their king. He refused, however, because he knew that God wanted to be their king. The children of Israel followed God for forty years after this, until Gideon died.

Where Is It Found?

19. Write which chapters in Judges tell the stories of these people.

    a. Deborah and Barak _____ Judges 4, 5 _____   Judges 2, 3

    b. Gideon _____ Judges 6–8 _____   Judges 4, 5

                                                                 Judges 6–8

B. BIBLE WORD STUDY

★ *Write a word from the verse given to fit each definition. All references are from Judges.*

_____ oppress _____	1. To rule over in a harsh, cruel way (4:3)
_____ light _____	2. To get down, as from a vehicle (4:15)
_____ pertain _____	3. To belong to (6:11)
_____ fleece _____	4. The woolly coat of a sheep (6:37)
_____ vaunt _____	5. To boast (7:2)
_____ watch _____	6. A period of time when one group of guards is on duty (7:19)

Objectives

• Students should know
  —who Barak, Deborah, Jael, and Sisera were. (See Part A, numbers 1–9.)
  —what role Deborah and Jael played in defeating the Canaanites. (Deborah encouraged Barak to fight against Jabin, and went with him; Jael killed Sisera.)
  —what the Midianites did to the Israelites. (brought them into bondage and spoiled their crops)
  —how the LORD called Gideon, how Gideon made sure of his calling, and how he defeated the Midianites with three hundred men. (See Part A, numbers 11–18.)

Truths to Instill

• When men fail to carry out their responsibility, sometimes godly women need to fill an important place. Deborah and Jael were strong for the LORD, and they received the honor that Barak should have earned. (See Judges 4:8, 9.) Deborah's words seem to indicate that the course of action they were about to take was not ideal, but it was the best that could be done under the circumstances.

• Only a humble man could have faced the enemy as Gideon did. Even though an angel told him, "The LORD is with thee, thou mighty man of valour," Gideon did not trust in his own ability. After making sure the LORD was indeed with him, he carefully

C. THINKING ABOUT BIBLE TRUTHS

1. Read Judges 4:8. Why did Deborah go with the Israelite army when they fought against
   Sisera? _____Barak said that he would not go unless Deborah went with him._____

   _____

   _____

2. Read 1 Timothy 2:11, 12.
   a. Deborah filled an important place as a leader of the Israelites. Does the New Testament
      allow women to be leaders of God's people? _____no_____
   b. What do these verses tell women to do? _____to learn in silence, to be in subjection_____

      _____

3. Gideon laid out a fleece to find out what God wanted him to do. Today God leads His people
   in other ways. Read the following verses. For each reference, write a way that God leads His
   people today.
   a. Psalm 119:105 _____God leads through His Word._____

      _____

   b. Hebrews 13:17 _____God leads through those who are over us._____

      _____

   c. 1 Kings 12:6 _____God leads through good advice from others, especially from those
      older than we are._____

   d. James 1:5 _____God gives us wisdom if we ask Him for it._____

      _____

D. LEARNING MORE ABOUT THE BIBLE

The Cycles of the Judges

This diagram shows the cycles of sin and deliverance during the first three hundred years of the judges. The
tops of the cycles show the times of righteousness, deliverance, and rest. The bottoms of the cycles show the
times when the Israelites fell into sin and God allowed their enemies to oppress them.

*Discuss this diagram with
the students. (See the notes on
the following page.)*

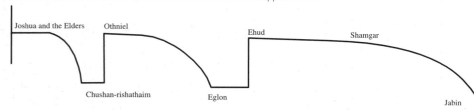

Joshua and the Elders   Othniel   Ehud   Shamgar

Chushan-rishathaim   Eglon   Jabin

followed God's instructions. He did not trust in his
valor, but in the LORD.

    Gideon's humility is also seen in his response to
the men of Ephraim (Judges 8:1–3) and to the offer
of kingship (Judges 8:22, 23).

F
L
A
X

Flax is the plant used to make linen cloth. Both flax and linen are mentioned a number of times in the Bible. Linen cloth has been discovered in some ancient Egyptian graves.

Flax, seeded in fields like wheat, grows about three feet tall. Its blue flowers turned the flat fields of Egypt into what seemed to be a reflection of the blue sky. After the stalks were harvested, they were soaked, crushed, and beaten to separate the fibers. Then the threads were woven into linen cloth.

Besides its use for clothing, flax fiber was used to make sailcloth, tent curtains, wicks for lamps, and thread. Flax has also been used to make paper. The oil pressed from flax seeds, called linseed oil, is still used in paints, varnish, printing ink, and linoleum.

Whom did God command to wear linen clothes? (Leviticus 6:10).

- "The Cycles of the Judges." This diagram illustrates the cycles of sin, oppression, supplication to God, deliverance, and rest that were repeated during this era. The diagram stops with Jephthah because the later cycles are not as clearly defined in the Scriptures. Many people believe that at times, two or more judges may have been active in different parts of Israel.

- Point out that most Israelites would have lived for only one or two complete cycles. Often a new generation forgot the lesson of the previous one and had to learn the consequences of sin all over again. Will the rising generation of today make the same mistake? "Now these things were our examples, to the intent we should not lust after evil things, as they also lusted" (1 Corinthians 10:6).

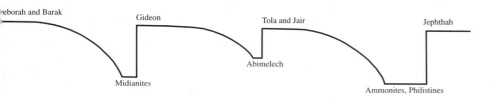

Deborah and Barak   Gideon   Tola and Jair   Jephthah

Midianites   Abimelech   Ammonites, Philistines

206   Chapter Six   Israel in the Days of the Judges

The Midianites

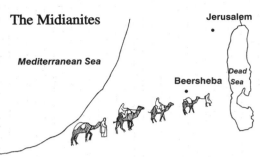

Some Midianites made their living by trading (1) __spicery__, (2) __balm__, and (3) __myrrh__. They carried their goods from place to place with camel caravans (Genesis 37:25).

After the Israelites lived in Canaan, the Midianites chased their animals onto the Israelites' fields and spoiled their crops. (5) __Gideon__ finally defeated them (Judges 7:15; 8:28).

Moses asked Hobab the Midianite (his brother-in-law) to travel through the wilderness with the Israelites. Since Hobab knew how to live in the desert, he was like (4) __eyes__ to them (Numbers 10:31).

The Midianites were descendants of Midian, a son of (6) __Abraham__ and (7) __Keturah__ (Genesis 25:1, 2). They lived beside the Gulf of Aqaba. With easily moveable tent villages, they followed their flocks in search of pasture.

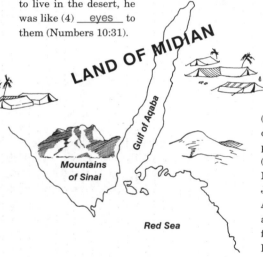

Moses married (8) __Zipporah__, the daughter of Jethro, a priest of Midian (Exodus 2:21). Some Midianites worshiped Jehovah, the God of Abraham. But they also worshiped a false god, Baal of Peor.

207

Lesson 29. Judges Who Misjudged

You have seen the cycle of the Book of Judges. The Israelites served God when they had a good leader, but as soon as the leader died, they fell into sin. Then God had to punish them to bring them back to Him again. When they repented, God sent another new leader for them; but when that leader died, they sinned again. Thus it went, on and on and on.

The men that God used to lead Israel back to Him and deliver them from their enemies were called judges. After he drove the enemies from the land, the judge sat and judged any problems that arose among the Israelites. When one man killed another man, the judge decided who was guilty. When one person's cows got into another man's fields, the judge decided who would pay the damages. But

sometimes the judges made mistakes.

Jephthah was one judge who misjudged. Before going to battle, he made a foolish vow. He promised to offer to the Lord as a burnt offering the first thing that met him after he returned from battle. This turned out to be his own daughter! Now Jephthah wished he had not been so quick to make a vow. But he fulfilled it because it was a vow.

Samson was another judge who misjudged. God gave him superhuman strength that enabled him to fight a lion or an army by himself, yet he failed to control his own desires. He loved the heathen daughters of the Philistines. Because of his careless relationships with them, he lost everything he had—his freedom, his eyesight, and finally even his life. What a costly misjudgment!

A. ANSWERS FROM THE BIBLE

The Israelites Sin Again

After Gideon died, one of his sons, Abimelech, killed all his brothers except the youngest one. Abimelech reigned as king for three years. Then the Lord caused the Israelites to turn against Abimelech and kill him.

Next Tola and Jair judged Israel. After Jair died, the children of Israel turned away from the Lord again and served the gods of the heathen nations around them. The LORD's anger burned against His people.

Judges 10:6–8

1. Which two groups of people did the Lord send to punish Israel?
   a. the Philistines
   b. the Ammonites (children of Ammon)

2. How long did this punishment continue? eighteen years

Judges 10:10–14

3. What did the Israelites tell God? "We have sinned against thee."

4. Where did God tell the Israelites to go for deliverance? to the other gods that they had chosen

- Jephthah's vow. The Bible seems to indicate that Jephthah fulfilled his rash vow by offering his daughter as a burnt sacrifice to the LORD. However, some people argue that Judges 11:31 could read, "Shall surely be the LORD's, *or* I will offer it up for a burnt offering." If this wording is correct, Jephthah might have fulfilled the vow by consecrating his daughter to God as a Nazarite virgin for life. But considering Jephthah's sorrow, his background, and the low level of spirituality in Israel at this time, an actual sacrifice seems likely. This view is supported by the ancient Jewish authorities.

- In a day when many are lightly disregarding marriage and baptismal vows, and when a person's word often changes with circumstances, we should emphasize the importance of fulfilling promises. According to Psalm 15:4, God honors the man "that sweareth to his own hurt, and changeth not."

Although Jephthah is to be commended for taking his vow seriously, his action raises questions. Use discretion in discussing his vow in

Lesson 29

Oral Review

1. How did Joseph become a blessing to many people? [12] **by storing up food in Egypt to prepare for a seven-year famine**

2. Why did Moses make a serpent of brass? [20] **so that the people who had been bitten by serpents could look at the brass serpent and be healed**

3. Name the five divisions of the Old Testament. [26] **the Books of Moses, the Books of History, the Books of Poetry, the Major Prophets, the Minor Prophets**

4. What did the Israelites do after Joshua and the elders of his generation died? [27] **They served Baal and Ashtaroth. (They forsook the LORD and did evil in His sight.)**

5. What woman led Israel as a judge? [28] **Deborah**

6. Where did Sisera go to hide himself? [28] **into Jael's tent**

7. What tests did Gideon use to make sure God wanted him to fight the Midianites? [28] **He laid out a fleece and asked God to make it wet with dew and to keep the ground dry one night and to make the ground wet and keep the fleece dry the next night.**

208   Chapter Six   Israel in the Days of the Judges

The Israelites put away their false gods and served the Lord in spite of what He had told them. They were truly sorry for their sin. God saw this and was grieved because of their afflictions. So once again He sent someone to deliver them.

Jephthah Delivers Israel

Jephthah was an outcast. After his brothers drove him out of his father's house, he became the leader of a gang of "vain men." Probably he was considered an outlaw. But when his relatives were in trouble, they turned to him for help.

Judges 11:4–6

5. What did the men of Gilead ask of Jephthah? _____
   They asked him to be their captain.

Judges 11:29–36

Before leading his army into battle, Jephthah made a very foolish vow to the LORD. Afterward he was sorry, but he fulfilled the vow anyway. During the time of the judges, the Israelites often forgot how God wanted them to live. Perhaps Jephthah thought the LORD would be pleased with his vow. We should think carefully before we make promises.

6. Jephthah vowed that if God would _____deliver the Ammonites into his hands_____
   _____, then he would _____offer up to God whatever came out of his_____
   house to meet him when he returned_____.

7. What did the Lord do for Jephthah? _____
   The LORD delivered the Ammonites into his hands.

8. What did Jephthah's daughter tell her father to do after she learned of his vow? _____
   She told him to do what he had vowed.

Jephthah judged Israel six years. After him Ibzan, Elon, and Abdon judged Israel. Then the Lord delivered the Israelites into the hands of the Philistines because they were doing evil again.

Samson Fights the Philistines

Samson was the strangest of the judges. He was probably the strongest man that ever lived, yet in some ways he was very weak. He judged Israel during the Philistine oppression, but he did not completely drive out the Philistines or give the Israelites much spiritual help. Yet in spite of his weaknesses, God used him; and Hebrews 11:32 mentions him as one of the Old Testament heroes of faith.

★ *Fill in the blanks. All references are from Judges.*

9. An (a) _____angel_____ of the Lord told Manoah's wife that she would have a son (13:3). Manoah and his wife were not to cut their son's hair, because he was to be a (b) _____Nazarite_____ from his birth (13:5).

10. Manoah's wife named her son (a) _____Samson_____ (13:24). As he grew older, the (b) _____Spirit_____ of the Lord began to move him in the camp of Dan (13:25).

class. If a person cannot fulfill a vow or promise without sinning, he must repent of his careless or sinful intentions and be willing to suffer loss to make reparation for his wrong. He might also reap consequences for his carelessness. For example, a student who has promised to help a classmate cheat might earn a bad reputation, even if he repents before he actually cheats. Making a vow that one cannot keep is a very serious matter.

- Samson's weaknesses should not be ignored, but detailed discussion of them is not appropriate at the fifth-grade level. Considering Samson's moral weakness, it is hard to understand how God could have used him. However, he is mentioned in Hebrews 11, so we should not be too hard on him. Remember that he lived during a very degenerate period in Israel's history. Nevertheless, God could have done much more with him if he had been willing to allow the LORD to control his whole life.

8. Why did God want Gideon to take only three hundred men to fight the Midianites? [28] **so that the Israelites would not boast that they had saved themselves**

In This Lesson

Scope: Judges 10–16; Ruth

Main Events

- God punishes the Israelites when they sin against Him.
- Some of the judges make foolish mistakes.
- The judges who misjudge suffer because of their mistakes.
- Ruth leaves her country and trusts in the LORD.

Objectives

- Students should know
  —what foolish promise Jephthah made. (He promised that if God gave him victory over the Ammonites, he would offer up to God whatever came out of his house to meet him when he returned.)
  —how Samson's birth was announced, how he treated the Philistines, how he lost his strength, and how he ended his life. (See Part A, numbers 9–16.)
  —the names of five Philistine cities and four Phoenician cities. (See Part D, "Settlements Along the Sea.")

11. Later, Samson wanted to marry a daughter of the (a) __Philistines__ (14:2). His parents were (b) __displeased__ with his choice. But Samson said, (c) "_____Get her for me_____;
(sad, disappointed)
for she pleaseth me well" (14:3). On his way to see the Philistine woman, Samson killed a (d) __lion__ (14:5, 6).

12. Samson made a big marriage feast. He asked his friends a (a) __riddle__ (14:12), but his wife told them the answer. Because of this, Samson became (b) __angry__ (14:19), and his wife was given in marriage to his (c) __companion__ (14:20).
(friend)

13. When Samson learned that his wife had been given to another man, he caught (a) __three hundred foxes__ and used them to burn the Philistines' standing (b) __corn__, their shocks, their (c) __vineyards__, and their olive groves (15:3–5).

14. The Philistines came up to the land of Judah to (a) __bind__ __Samson__ (15:10). The men of Judah took new ropes, bound Samson, and delivered him to the Philistines. But when Samson stood among them, the cords became as (b) __flax__ that was burnt with fire. He picked up a (c) __jawbone of an ass__ and killed a (d) __thousand__ men (15:14–16).

15. Sometime later, Samson loved a woman named (a) __Delilah__, who lived in the valley of Sorek (16:4). This woman found out the secret of Samson's strength by pressing him (b) __daily__ with her words (16:15–17). When the Philistines discovered Samson's secret, they put out his (c) __eyes__, took him to (d) __Gaza__, and made him grind in a (e) __prison house__ (16:21).

16. While Samson was there, his hair began to grow back. The Philistines made a great feast to (a) __Dagon__, their god, to celebrate because they had captured Samson (16:23). Samson prayed, "O Lord God, (b) __remember__ me, I pray thee, and (c) __strengthen__ me, I pray thee, only this once" (16:28). Samson killed (d) __more__ people at his death than he had killed during his life (16:30). He had judged Israel for (e) __twenty__ years (16:31).

In spite of Samson's feats, the Philistines continued to trouble Israel. The Israelites drove them out during Samuel's leadership, but Saul and David also had to deal with them. Finally, many years after Samson died, David completely subdued them.

Where Is It Found?

17. a. Which chapter of Judges tells about Jephthah's foolish vow? ____Judges 11____

   b. Which chapters tell about Samson? ____Judges 13–16____

- Samson as a man of faith (Hebrews 11:32). Some people consider Samson a type of Christ. Matthew Henry gives the main points of this belief in his commentary. Dirk Philips, an Anabaptist bishop and co-laborer with Menno Simons, also taught it in his book (*Dietrich Philip Hand Book*). You may want to study this for your own interest. The type is not necessarily accurate, but it is an interesting study that is still taught by some Mennonites.

—what a Nazarite vow included. (A Nazarite vowed to keep himself holy unto the Lord. He did not cut his hair or eat grapes or drink their juice in any form.)

Truths to Instill

- "For whatsoever a man soweth, that shall he also reap" (Galatians 6:7). Both Jephthah and Samson suffered because of their mistakes. Jephthah refused to help Israel until he had been promised he could be chief, in contrast to Gideon, who turned down an offer of kingship. Jephthah apparently promised a human sacrifice if victorious, probably showing the influence of his heathen relatives. Samson's willful and undisciplined moral life brought him much grief. How much greater would the lives and works of both men have been if they had walked more closely with God!

- We should think seriously *before* we make vows or promises.

- We should also note the positive things about Jephthah and Samson. Both are listed among the heroes of faith in Hebrews 11:32.
  —Jephthah courageously moved ahead against the enemy, even when others failed to come to his aid. (Judges 12:2,3). He also took seriously his responsibility to keep his vow. (Avoid using Jephthah as an example to follow, however. See further in the second teacher note in this lesson.)

B. BIBLE WORD STUDY

★ *Match these definitions with the Bible words on the right. Read the verses given or use a dictionary if you need help. All references are from Judges.*

__i__	1. To bring trouble to (10:8)	a. avenge
__h__	2. Much trouble or distress (10:14)	b. expound
__c__	3. To go after and bring back (11:5)	c. fetch
__b__	4. To explain (14:19)	d. fetters
__e__	5. A piece of burning wood; torch (15:4)	e. firebrand
__f__	6. A plant with fibers that are used to make linen (15:14)	f. flax
__d__	7. Rings or bands placed around the ankles to hold a prisoner (16:21)	g. lord
__a__	8. To punish or get back at someone who has done wrong (16:28)	h. tribulation
__g__	9. A person having authority; a leader (16:30)	i. vex

C. THINKING ABOUT BIBLE TRUTHS

Many sad events took place during the time of the Judges. The Bible says, "In those days there was no king in Israel, but every man did that which was right in his own eyes." The Lord wanted to be their King, but His people turned away from Him time after time.

Not everyone turned away from the Lord, however. Ruth, a woman from Moab, left her country, her home, her family, and her heathen gods to move to Bethlehem. She learned to trust in the Lord God of Israel, and God blessed her for her faithfulness. Ruth became one of the ancestors of Jesus.

1. Why did Elimelech and his family move to the country of Moab (Ruth 1:1, 2)? _____
   There was a famine in Israel.

2. Why did Naomi decide to return to her own country after her husband and sons were dead
   (Ruth 1:6)?   She heard that the LORD had blessed His people and given them bread.
   _____

3. When Naomi told Ruth to return to her own home, Ruth answered, "Intreat me not to
   (a)   leave   thee, or to return from following after thee: for whither thou goest,
   (b)   I will go   ; and where thou lodgest, (c)   I will lodge   : thy people
   shall be (d)   my people   , and thy God (e)   my God   : where thou diest,
   (f)   will I die   , and there will (g)   I be buried   " (Ruth 1:16, 17).

4. For what two things did Boaz appreciate and respect Ruth, even though she was a stranger
   in Israel (Ruth 2:10–12)?
   a. Ruth had helped her mother-in-law.
   b. She had left her home and learned to trust in the LORD.

—In a time of Philistine infiltration of Israel, with obvious economic advantages (Judges 15:11), Samson's one-man campaign should have helped Israel to see the danger of accommodation. "Out of weakness [he was] made strong," and he sacrificed his life to destroy Israel's enemy.

5. Boaz married Ruth, and the Lord blessed them with a son (Ruth 4:13–17, 22).

a. What name was given to Boaz and Ruth's son?   __Obed__

b. What was the name of their grandson?   __Jesse__

c. What was the name of their well-known great-grandson?   __David__

D. LEARNING MORE ABOUT THE BIBLE

Settlements Along the Sea

Sea-traveling merchants lived in the cities of Phoenicia. They made long trips to trade, buy, and sell their wares. The cities of Tyre and Sidon were given to the tribe of (1) __Asher__ (Joshua 19:24, 28, 29), but the Israelites never conquered them.

A widow who lived near Sidon fed the prophet (2) __Elijah__ during a famine (1 Kings 17:8–16). Hundreds of years later, Jesus visited the region of (3) __Tyre__ and (4) __Sidon__ (Matthew 15:21).

Byblos
(Gebal)

Beirut
(Berytus)

Sidon
(Zidon)

Tyre
(Tyrus)

PHOENICIA
LEBANON

The Philistines lived on the lowlands between the hills of Judah and the Mediterranean Sea. The land of the Philistines was part of Judah's inheritance, but the Israelites did not subdue them until the reign of King (8) __David__ (1 Chronicles 18:1). The five main cities of Philistia were ruled by the five (9) __lords__ of the Philistines (1 Samuel 5:8).

Great trees grew in the mountains of Lebanon. Hiram, a Phoenician king, supplied Solomon with (5) __cedar__ __trees__ and (6) __fir__ __trees__, and with (7) __gold__ to build the temple in Jerusalem (1 Kings 9:11).

Ashdod

Ekron

Ashkelon

Gath

Gaza

PHILISTIA

Nazarites

A Nazarite could be either a man or a woman. A person became a Nazarite by making a vow to keep himself (1) __holy__ unto the LORD (Numbers 6:8).

Nazarites were not allowed to cut their hair. Their uncut hair was a sign that they were set apart for God's service.

During the time of his separation, a Nazarite could not drink (2) __wine__ or (3) __strong drink__. He could not even eat moist or dried (4) __grapes__ (Numbers 6:3).

Most Nazarites separated themselves for shorter periods of time. After their separation ended, they brought sacrifices to the tabernacle or temple. While their sacrifices burned on the altar, they cut off their hair and put it into the fire (Numbers 6:17, 18).

Parents sometimes gave their children to God to be Nazarites all their lives. Name three men who were given to God by their parents.

(5) __Samson__ Judges 13:5, 24

(6) __Samuel__ 1 Samuel 1:11, 20

(7) __John the Baptist__ Luke 1:15, 57–66

213

Lesson 30. Samuel Judges Israel

The Book of Judges covers the history of God's people between the time of Joshua and the time of Samuel. As you have seen, much of this history is the sad story of what happens to God's people when they forget Him or disobey Him. But during this time there were also many people who were faithful to God. One of them was Ruth, whom you read about in the last lesson. In this lesson you will meet another woman who was faithful to God at a time when many Israelites were not following Him.

Hannah was a godly woman married to a good husband, but she had no children. This made her very sad. In Bible times it was considered a disgrace for a married woman not to have children. One year when Hannah

went with her husband to the tabernacle to bring offerings to the Lord, she earnestly prayed that God would give her a son. She promised God that she would give her son back to Him if He granted her request. God in His great kindness heard Hannah's prayer and gave her a baby boy.

Hannah was overjoyed with her baby, but she remembered her promise. When Samuel was old enough to leave her, she took him to Eli to help serve God in the tabernacle. The Lord was pleased with Hannah's unselfishness, and He gave her five more children.

Hannah's little boy became the greatest judge that Israel ever had. Samuel walked with God all the days of his life. Who can measure the joy that unselfishness brings!

A. ANSWERS FROM THE BIBLE

God Prepares Samuel for His Work

God had a work for Samuel to do. He started preparing him for this work at a very young age. Probably Samuel was no more than five or six years old when his mother brought him to Eli.

1 Samuel 1:2, 10–13

1. Hannah was an unhappy woman because __she had no children__.

2. Eli thought Hannah was drunk because _____
   __she moved her lips but prayed silently__.

1 Samuel 1:19, 20, 24–28

3. Hannah became the mother of a little boy because_____
   __the LORD remembered her (she asked him of the LORD)__.

4. Hannah gave Samuel, her son, to the Lord because _____
   __she had promised that if the LORD gave her a son, she would give her son back to Him__
   _____.

1 Samuel 2:18, 19

5. Hannah showed her love for her son by making him a __coat__ every year.

- Before presenting Samuel to Eli, Hannah would have taught him to care for himself and to follow instructions. It seems reasonable to assume that he was at least three or four years old when she took him to the tabernacle, but he could hardly have been more than five or six.

Lesson 30

Oral Review

1. What was the purpose of the cities of refuge? [25] **to provide a place of safety for someone who killed another person accidentally**
2. Name the five Books of Moses. [26] **Genesis, Exodus, Leviticus, Numbers, Deuteronomy**
3. Name the twelve books of history in the Old Testament. [26] **Joshua, Judges, Ruth, 1 Samuel, 2 Samuel, 1 Kings, 2 Kings, 1 Chronicles, 2 Chronicles, Ezra, Nehemiah, Esther**

4. How did Gideon's army frighten and confuse the Midianites? [28] **They blew trumpets, broke pitchers, held up lamps, and shouted, "The sword of the LORD, and of Gideon."**
5. What vow did Jephthah make to God? [29] **He vowed that if God would give him victory, he would sacrifice the first thing that came out of his house to meet him when he returned.**
6. Who lost his strength and his eyes because of his love for heathen women? [29] **Samson**
7. Who lived in Ekron, Ashdod, Gath, Ashkelon, and Gaza? [29] **the Philistines**

God Gives His Message to Samuel

1 Samuel 3:1–4, 11–13

It seems from this context that Samuel was still very young when God first spoke to him. He may have been about twelve years old, but no one knows this for sure.

6. Samuel got up one night because ___the LORD called him___.

7. God told Samuel that He would judge the house of Eli because
   (a) Eli did not stop his sons from sinning against God.
   b. Eli helped the Philistines when they fought against the Israelites.
   c. Eli would not let Samuel be a prophet of the Lord.

The Philistines Capture the Ark

God was with Samuel, and soon all Israel knew that Samuel was a prophet of the Lord. But the Lord was not with Eli and his sons. When the Philistines came up against Israel, Eli's sons took the ark of the covenant out to the battle. They thought that the Lord would surely help them if they had the holy ark with them. But Eli's sons were slain in the battle, and the ark of God was taken. When Eli heard this terrible news, he fell down and died.

★ *Match these passages from 1 Samuel with the events on the right.*

   _c_   8. 4:1–11   a. The Philistines return the ark to Israel.
   _b_   9. 4:12–22   b. Eli and his daughter-in-law die.
   _f_   10. 5:1–5   c. The Philistines capture the ark and kill Eli's sons.
   _e_   11. 5:6–12   d. God smites the men of Bethshemesh for looking into the ark.
   _a_   12. 6:1–18   e. God smites the Philistines.
   _d_   13. 6:19–21   f. Dagon falls down before the ark.

The ark never returned to Shiloh. After the Philistines sent it back to Israel, it was kept at Kirjath-jearim. Many years later, King David moved it to Jerusalem.

Samuel Leads Israel Back to God

1 Samuel 7:3–11

The Israelites wanted to return to God. Samuel told them to put away their strange gods and serve only the Lord. When they did this, he asked them to gather at Mizpah. Here Samuel prayed for them, and the Israelites fasted and declared their sorrow for their sins. During this time, the Philistines heard that the Israelites were gathered together and decided to attack them.

14. How did the Israelites show that they really wanted to serve God? ___They put away their idols, fasted, and confessed that they had sinned against the LORD.___

15. The Israelites won the battle with the Philistines because ___the LORD heard Samuel's prayer and thundered with a great thunder upon the Philistines___.

- Twelve was the age at which a child was considered accountable to God under the Old Testament covenant. While Samuel may have been younger, it seems reasonable to think that God might have made this first approach at a time when he was considered personally accountable to God.

8. What customs of the Nazarites set them apart from others? [29] **They did not cut their hair, they drank no wine or strong drink, and they ate no grapes.**

In This Lesson

Scope: 1 Samuel 1–12

Main Events

- Hannah prays for a son and returns him to the LORD.
- God speaks to Samuel.
- God punishes Eli and his sons.
- Samuel warns the people of their folly in asking for a king.

Objectives

- Students should know
  —what Hannah promised the LORD. (If the LORD gave her a son, she would give him back to Him.)
  —what happened to the ark of the LORD. (See Part A, "The Philistines Capture the Ark.")
  —who was Israel's last judge. (Samuel)
  —why God was displeased with Israel's desire for a king. (They were rejecting God as their King.)

The Israelites Ask for a King

The Israelites were tired of the up-and-down cycle in which they were caught. They thought that if they had a king as other nations did, things would go better for them. They were so sure this would solve their problems that they did not ask God what He thought of their plans.

1 Samuel 8:4–7, 19, 20

16. The Israelites wanted Samuel to make them a king because Samuel was ___old___, and his sons ___did not walk in his ways___.

17. Samuel was unhappy with the people's request, but the Lord told him that they had really rejected ___the Lord___ instead of ___Samuel___.

18. The people did not listen to Samuel's warnings, because they wanted to be like _____ ___the other nations___.

1 Samuel 12:16–19

19. Samuel called on the Lord, and a great thunderstorm broke over the Israelites because ___ ___they had sinned by asking for a king___.

Where Is It Found?

20. Which chapter of 1 Samuel tells

    a. about Hannah's prayer for a child? ___1 Samuel 1___

    b. about God calling the boy Samuel? ___1 Samuel 3___

    c. what happened to the Philistines and their god while they had the ark? ___1 Samuel 5___

B. BIBLE WORD STUDY

★ *Underline the words below the sentences that mean the same as the words in italics. All references are from 1 Samuel.*

1. God heard Hannah's *petition* (1:27).
    a. thanksgiving   b. complaint   c. <u>request</u>

2. Samuel *ministered* unto the Lord before Eli (2:11).
    a. instructed   b. worshiped   c. <u>served</u>

3. Samuel was *girded with a linen ephod* (2:18).
    a. <u>wore a linen ephod</u>
    b. was tired of his linen ephod
    c. got trapped in his linen ephod

4. Samuel spoke to Eli about his sons' *iniquity* (3:13).
    a. wealth   b. <u>sin</u>   c. disease

5. Eli's sons were *vile* (3:13).
    a. <u>evil</u>   b. rich   c. curious

Truths to Instill

- Hannah's unselfishness brought her joy. Hannah must have missed her son, but her testimony was, "My heart rejoiceth in the LORD" (1 Samuel 2:1). She learned the truth of Jesus' words, "It is more blessed to give than to receive" (Acts 20:35).
- Samuel showed proper respect for Eli as God's high priest, even though Eli had failed in his responsibility. Samuel promptly responded to what he thought was Eli's call. After God spoke to him, he was reluctant to tell Eli the distressing news.
- God would not honor the Israelites' vain worship of the ark, nor would He tolerate the Philistines' disrespect toward it. "The LORD is righteous in all his ways, and holy in all his works" (Psalm 145:17). Someday everyone will bow before him and honor His Name.
- God's will for the Israelites was a theocracy, in which they would depend directly on Him for protection and guidance. In asking for a king, the Israelites really asked for a more visible protection, which would require less faith. For this reason, God told Samuel, "They have not rejected thee, but they have rejected me, that I should not reign over them."

6. The Philistines cried, "Be strong, and *quit yourselves like men*," when they heard that the ark of God was in the camp of Israel (4:9).

    a. stop acting like men   b. <u>act like men</u>   c. surrender like men

7. God sent a great rain so that the people would *perceive* their wickedness (12:17).

    a. get rid of   b. hide   c. <u>understand</u>

C. THINKING ABOUT BIBLE TRUTHS

★ *You will find the answers to these questions in the verses you read for the previous sections. Try to write the answers without looking back.*

1. Why did Samuel run to Eli when the Lord called him the first three times? <u>Samuel thought that Eli was calling him (because he had never heard God's voice before).</u>

2. a. Did Samuel run to Eli as soon as the Lord had finished speaking to him? <u>no</u>

    b. Why or why not? <u>Samuel was afraid to tell Eli the bad news.</u>

3. When the Israelites fought the Philistines, they took the ark of God with them. However, that did not mean that God was with them. What should the Israelites have done that would have helped them much more than taking the ark into battle? <u>(Sample answer) They should have repented of their sins and prayed to God for help.</u>

4. In what two ways did the Lord show the Philistines that He is strong, even when His people are defeated? (See 1 Samuel 5:3, 6.)

    a. <u>The LORD caused Dagon to fall down before the ark.</u>

    b. <u>The LORD brought a severe disease upon the Philistines.</u>

5. Why was God displeased with the Israelites' desire for a king? <u>God wanted to lead them and to be their king.</u>

D. LEARNING MORE ABOUT THE BIBLE

Israel and Her Enemies

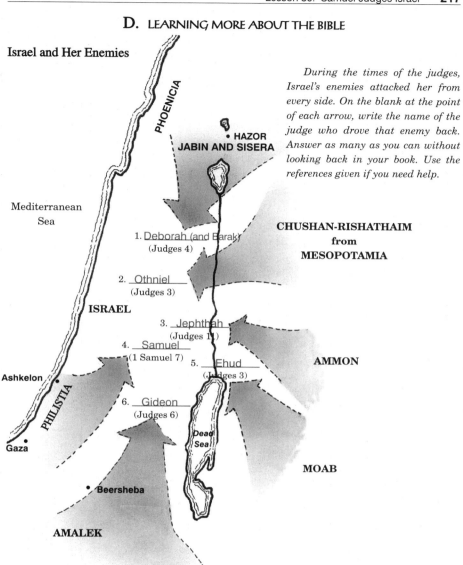

During the times of the judges, Israel's enemies attacked her from every side. On the blank at the point of each arrow, write the name of the judge who drove that enemy back. Answer as many as you can without looking back in your book. Use the references given if you need help.

PHOENICIA

• HAZOR
JABIN AND SISERA

Mediterranean Sea

1. Deborah (and Barak)
(Judges 4)

CHUSHAN-RISHATHAIM
from
MESOPOTAMIA

2. Othniel
(Judges 3)

ISRAEL

3. Jephthah
(Judges 11)

4. Samuel
(1 Samuel 7)

5. Ehud
(Judges 3)

AMMON

Ashkelon •

PHILISTIA

6. Gideon
(Judges 6)

Dead Sea

Gaza •

MOAB

• Beersheba

AMALEK

MIDIAN

218 Chapter Six Israel in the Days of the Judges

Anointing With Oil

Many areas of the Middle East have a hot, dry climate like that of Arizona or Mexico. In such a climate, people's skin cracks and becomes rough from the wind and burning sunlight. Today people use hand lotion to help with this problem, but in Bible times they could not buy modern lotions. Instead, they used olive oil.

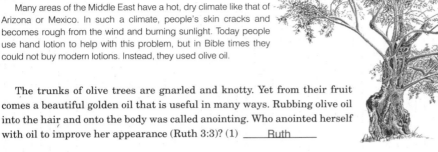

The trunks of olive trees are gnarled and knotty. Yet from their fruit comes a beautiful golden oil that is useful in many ways. Rubbing olive oil into the hair and onto the body was called anointing. Who anointed herself with oil to improve her appearance (Ruth 3:3)? (1) _____Ruth_____

The Israelites used olive oil for a medicine and as a symbol of God's power to heal. Who anointed the sick with oil (Mark 6:7, 13)? (2) _Jesus' twelve disciples_

Servants rubbed visitors' heads, hands, or feet with olive oil. Sometimes the oil was mixed with spices or perfume to make ointment. Who failed to anoint an important guest (Luke 7:44–46)? (3) Simon (a Pharisee)

The Israelites thought of olive oil as a gift from God. Since the Holy Spirit is also a gift from God, olive oil became a symbol of the Holy Spirit. The Israelites anointed their kings and priests with olive oil to show that the Spirit of God rested upon them. The name *Messiah* (used for *Jesus*) means "The Anointed One."

Name two men whom Samuel anointed (1 Samuel 9:27; 10:1; 16:13). (4) _____Saul_____ (5) _____David_____

Many people of the Middle East had black, curly hair. They anointed their hair with olive oil to make it sleek and shiny. Oil made their skin smooth. When people stopped anointing themselves with oil, what did it mean (2 Samuel 14:2)? (6) _It meant that they were mourning._

219

Chapter Six Review

A. ORAL REVIEW

★ *Be sure you know the answers to these questions. Try to answer as many as you can from memory.*

Who

★ *Give a name for each description. If you need help, match with the list on the right. To study for the test, cover the list.*

1. Delivered Israel from Chushan-rishathaim   Othniel   Barak
2. Delivered Israel from Eglon, king of Moab   Ehud   Deborah
3. Refused to go to battle without the help of a woman   Barak   Ehud
4. A woman who judged Israel   Deborah   Hannah
5. Made a thoughtless vow to God   Jephthah   Jephthah
6. Left her country and served the LORD   Ruth   Othniel
7. Gave her son back to the LORD   Hannah   Ruth

★ *If you need help with the questions below, turn to the Bible reference or the lesson given in brackets.*

What >>

8. What did the Israelites do as long as Joshua lived? [Judges 2:7]
9. What did the Israelites do after Joshua died? [Judges 2:10–13]
10. What was Gideon doing when the LORD called him? [Judges 6:11]
11. What are the five main divisions of Old Testament books? [Lesson 26]
12. What can we use to find references of Bible verses and Bible stories? [Lesson 26]

Where >>

13. Where in Canaan did the Philistines live? [Lesson 29]
14. Where were the Phoenician harbors of Tyre and Sidon? [Lesson 29]
15. Where did Sisera go to hide himself? [Judges 4:17]

When >>

16. When did Samson's father-in-law decide to give Samson's wife to another man? [Judges 15:2]
17. When did Samson kill the most Philistines at one time? [Judges 16:30]
18. When did the Philistines capture the ark? [1 Samuel 4:1–11]

Why >>

19. Why did Ehud carry his sword on the right? [Judges 3:15; Lesson 27]
20. Why did Jael give Sisera milk to drink? [Judges 4:18–21; Lesson 28]
21. Why could the Midianites easily move from place to place? [Lesson 28]
22. Why was anointing with oil necessary in the Middle East? [Lesson 30]

8. They served the LORD.
9. They served Baal and Ashtaroth. (They forsook the LORD and did evil in His sight.)
10. He was threshing wheat by the winepress to hide it from the Midianites.
11. the Books of Moses, the Books of History, the Books of Poetry, the Major Prophets, the Minor Prophets
12. a concordance
13. on the lowlands between the hills of Judah and the Mediterranean Sea
14. north of Israel along the Mediterranean Sea
15. into Jael's tent
16. after Samson became angry that his riddle had been solved
17. at his death
18. during the battle when Eli's sons were killed
19. He was left-handed.
20. She wanted to make him think she was his friend.
21. They lived in tents.
22. The hot, dry climate caused people's skin to crack and become rough.

B. WRITTEN REVIEW

★ *Match the descriptions with the names on the right. If you need help, use the Bible reference or the lesson given in brackets.*

Who

_d__ 1. Lived in Jerusalem during the time of the judges [Lesson 27]   a. Moses

_a__ 2. Married the daughter of a Midianite priest [Exodus 2:21]   b. Samuel

_c__ 3. Lost his strength and his eyes because he told the secret of his   c. Samson
strength [Lesson 29]   d. Jebusites

_f__ 4. Lived in Tyre, Sidon, Beirut, and Byblos [Lesson 29]   e. Philistines

_e__ 5. Lived in Ekron, Ashdod, Gath, Ashkelon, and Gaza [Lesson 29]   f. Phoenicians

_b__ 6. A faithful Nazarite who anointed two kings [Lesson 30]

★ *Write the answers to the following questions. If you need help, use the Bible reference or the lesson given in brackets.*

What

7. What did the angel tell Manoah's wife about the son they would have? [Lesson 29] _____
He said that their son would be a Nazarite from his birth.

8. What customs of the Nazarites set them apart from others? [Lesson 29] __They did not__
cut their hair, they drank no wine or strong drink, and they did not eat grapes.

Why

9. Why did Samson burn the Philistines' grain? [Judges 15:2–5] _____
He was angry that his wife had been given to another man.

10. Why did Eli think Hannah had been drinking? [1 Samuel 1:13] _____
He saw her mouth moving while she was praying silently.

11. Why was God displeased with Israel's desire for a king? [1 Samuel 8:7] _____
They were rejecting God as their king.

How

12. How did God punish the Israelites for not driving the Canaanites from Canaan? [Judges 2:3]
God did not drive out all the heathen nations, but left some in Canaan, where they
were as thorns and snares to Israel.

Chapter Six Review **229**

13. What two tests did Gideon use to make sure God wanted him to fight the Midianites? [Judges 6:36–40] ___ He laid out a fleece and asked God to make it wet with dew and to keep the ground dry one night and to make the ground wet and keep the fleece dry the next night.

14. How did Gideon's army frighten and confuse the Midianites? [Judges 7:20] ___ They blew trumpets, broke pitchers, held up lamps, and shouted, "The sword of the LORD, and of Gideon."

15. How did the Philistines find out the secret of Samson's strength? [Judges 16:5, 16] ___ They paid Delilah to get the secret from Samson.

Bible Outline

★ *Match these chapters with the events they record.*

___d___ 16. Judges 1–3
___e___ 17. Judges 4, 5
___b___ 18. Judges 6–10
___g___ 19. Judges 11, 12
___a___ 20. Judges 13–16
___c___ 21. Ruth 1–4
___f___ 22. 1 Samuel 1–16

a. God gives Samson strength to fight the Philistines; Samson loses his strength and his eyes because of his weaknesses.

b. Gideon, Abimelech, Tola, and Jair lead Israel.

c. A young woman from Moab leaves her home and her gods to serve the LORD.

d. The Israelites sin after Joshua's death; God allows enemies to oppress them; Othniel, Ehud, and Shamgar defeat the enemies.

e. Deborah and Barak deliver Israel.

f. God blesses Hannah with a son and punishes Eli's family; Samuel serves God faithfully.

g. Jephthah, Ibzan, Elon, and Abdon judge Israel.

Bible Books

★ *Label the divisions of Old Testament books, and number the books within each group in the proper order. You may look back to Lesson 26 if you need help. Be sure you know the divisions of the Old Testament, and the names of the first seventeen books in their proper order.*

Books of ____Moses____

- 4 Numbers
- 3 Leviticus
- 1 Genesis
- 5 Deuteronomy
- 2 Exodus

Books of ____History____

- 5 2 Samuel
- 1 Joshua
- 7 2 Kings
- 3 Ruth
- 11 Nehemiah
- 2 Judges
- 4 1 Samuel
- 9 2 Chronicles
- 12 Esther
- 6 1 Kings
- 10 Ezra
- 8 1 Chronicles

Books of ____Poetry____

- 2 Psalms
- 5 Song of Solomon
- 3 Proverbs
- 4 Ecclesiastes
- 1 Job

Books of Major Prophets

- 4 Ezekiel
- 5 Daniel
- 2 Jeremiah
- 1 Isaiah
- 3 Lamentations

Books of Minor Prophets

- 2 Joel
- 5 Jonah
- 6 Micah
- 1 Hosea
- 7 Nahum
- 4 Obadiah
- 12 Malachi
- 10 Haggai
- 3 Amos
- 11 Zechariah
- 8 Habakkuk
- 9 Zephaniah

223

Reviewing What You Have Learned

★ *This exercise reviews some of the important facts that you have studied this year. Be sure you know the answers to these questions before taking the final test. Try to answer as many as you can from memory. If you need help, you may check the Bible reference or the lesson given in brackets.*

Chapter One—The Dawn of Human History >>

1. What are five ways that God wants us to use the Bible? [Lesson 1]
2. How long had Timothy known the Scriptures? [2 Timothy 3:15]
3. Where can we find the meanings of difficult Bible words? [Lesson 1]
4. Name the things God created on each day of Creation. [Genesis 1]
5. How did God create light and many other things? [Genesis 1:3; Lesson 2]
6. What lie did Satan tell Eve? [Genesis 3:4]
7. How did Noah prove that he had faith in God? [Hebrews 11:7; Genesis 6:22]
8. Why did men start to build the Tower of Babel? [Genesis 11:4]

Chapter Two—The Patriarchs >>

9. What do the abbreviations *A.M.*, *B.C.*, and *A.D.* mean when they are used with dates? [Lesson 6]
10. What did God compare Abraham's descendants to? [Lessons 7, 8]
11. How did Abraham show that he had faith in God? Give at least two specific examples. [Lessons 7, 8]
12. Why did Abraham not want his servant to take Isaac back to Haran? [Lesson 9; Genesis 24:7]
13. What two things did God tell Rebekah about her sons before they were born? [Genesis 25:23]
14. What is the meaning of (a) the name *Jacob*; (b) the name *Israel*? [Lesson 10]

Chapter Three—God's Chosen Family in Egypt >>

15. What well-known river flowed through Canaan? [Lesson 11]
16. Why did Joseph's brothers hate him? [Genesis 37:4]
17. Why did Pharaoh choose Joseph as the one to gather food during the seven good years? [Genesis 41:38–40]
18. How did Joseph know that his brothers had changed? [Genesis 44:33, 34; Lesson 13]
19. How did Joseph show that he had forgiven his brothers? [Genesis 45:4–15]
20. Why did Moses need to flee from Egypt? [Exodus 2:11–15]
21. What did Pharaoh say when the LORD commanded him to let His people go? [Exodus 5:2]
22. What did the ten plagues prove about the gods of Egypt? [Lesson 15]

Final Review

This review is intended for class discussion or as a self-study review before the final test. It could also be used for extra review throughout the school year.

1. read, hear, study, believe, obey
2. since he was a child
3. in a Bible dictionary
4. First day: light (also heaven and earth); Second: firmament; Third: dry land, seas, and plants; Fourth: sun, moon, and stars; Fifth: sea animals and birds; Sixth: land animals and man
5. He said, "Let there be . . ."
6. He said that she would not die if she ate the forbidden fruit.
7. He obeyed all of God's commands.
8. They wanted to make a name for themselves, and to keep from being scattered.
9. A.M.—in the year of the world; B.C.—before Christ; A.D.—in the year of our Lord
10. (Any one) the dust of the earth, the stars of the heaven, the sand of the seashore
11. (Sample answers) Abraham left his home without knowing where God would lead him. Abraham believed God's promise even before he had a son. Abraham was willing to sacrifice his promised son.
12. Isaac was to receive the promise of the land of Canaan, and Abraham's relatives at Haran worshiped idols.
13. They would become two manner of people, and the elder would serve the younger.
14. Jacob—heel catcher, supplanter; Israel—having power with God
15. the Jordan River
16. They were jealous that their father loved him better than the rest of them. (They also hated him because of his dreams, his special coat, and the evil report of them that he gave their father.)
17. Pharaoh saw that the Spirit of God was in Joseph and that no one else was as discreet and wise as he.
18. He could see that they loved Benjamin.
19. He treated them kindly and took care of them.
20. Moses had killed an Egyptian, and now Pharaoh wanted to kill him.
21. "Who is the LORD, that I should obey his voice?"
22. They proved that the LORD was more powerful than any of Egypt's gods.

224   Final Review

Chapter Four—Israel in the Wilderness >>

23. Why is God's written Word often better for us than God's spoken word? Give three reasons. [Lesson 16]
24. How did God guide the Israelites through the wilderness? [Exodus 13:21]
25. Say the Ten Commandments from memory. [Exodus 20:1–17]
26. Which two Old Testament commandments did Jesus say were the greatest? [Mark 12:30, 31]
27. What three pieces of furniture were in the holy place of the tabernacle? [Lesson 19]
28. What was in the holy of holies of the tabernacle? [Lesson 19]
29. How did the Israelites know that God was pleased with the tabernacle? [Lesson 19]
30. Which two of the twelve spies gave a good report of Canaan? [Numbers 14:6–9]
31. Why did the Israelites have to wander in the desert for forty years? [Numbers 14:26–33]

Chapter Five—Israel Conquers Canaan >>

32. Why was Canaan a good place for Jesus to live and teach? [Lesson 21]
33. Why did Joshua set up twelve stones at Gilgal? [Joshua 4:20–24]
34. What commandment did Achan disobey? [Joshua 6:17–19; 7:1]
35. Why did Joshua not kill the Gibeonites for their dishonesty? [Joshua 9:20]
36. How did God help the Israelites defeat the five Amorite kings? [Joshua 10:11–13]
37. What did Caleb ask for in his old age? [Joshua 14:12]
38. What did Joshua say that he and his house would do, even if the other Israelites did not? [Joshua 24:15]
39. What was the purpose of the cities of refuge? [Lesson 25]

Chapter Six—Israel in the Days of the Judges>>

40. Name the five divisions of the Old Testament. [Lesson 26]
41. What did the Israelites do after Joshua and the elders of his generation died? [Judges 2:10–13]
42. Who delivered Israel from Chushan-rishathaim? [Judges 3:8, 9]
43. Who delivered Israel from Eglon, king of Moab? [Judges 3:15, 30]
44. What woman led Israel as a judge? [Judges 4:4]
45. Why did God want Gideon to take only three hundred men to fight the Midianites? [Judges 7:2]
46. What vow did Jephthah make to God? [Judges 11:30, 31]
47. Who lost his strength and his eyes because of his love for heathen women? [Judges 16:16–21]
48. What customs of the Nazarites set them apart from others? [Lesson 29]
49. Who was Israel's last judge? [Lesson 30]
50. Why was God displeased with Israel's desire for a king? [1 Samuel 8:7]

23. (Sample answers) We can remember it better, since we can reread it often. We can make copies of it to give to others. We can read it, even though we live many years after God gave it.
24. with a pillar of cloud by day and a pillar of fire by night
25. (1) Thou shalt have no other gods before me.
    (2) Thou shalt not make unto thee any graven image.
    (3) Thou shalt not take the Name of the LORD thy God in vain.
    (4) Remember the Sabbath Day, to keep it holy.
    (5) Honour thy father and thy mother.
    (6) Thou shalt not kill.
    (7) Thou shalt not commit adultery.
    (8) Thou shalt not steal.
    (9) Thou shalt not bear false witness.
    (10) Thou shalt not covet.
26. "Thou shalt love the Lord thy God with all thy heart, and with all thy soul, and with all thy mind, and with all thy strength." "Thou shalt love thy neighbour as thyself."
27. the golden candlestick, the altar of incense, and the table of shewbread
28. the ark of the covenant
29. God filled the tabernacle with His glory.
30. Caleb and Joshua
31. When God wanted them to enter Canaan, they rebelled and wished they were back in Egypt.

32. Many people passed through Canaan and heard His teachings.
33. for a memorial of how God helped them cross the Jordan
34. God's command forbidding them to take any treasures from Jericho for themselves
35. The Israelites had sworn an oath that they would let them live.
36. He sent a great hailstorm, and He made the sun and the moon stand still.
37. for the mountain of Hebron (and for the privilege of conquering it)
38. They would serve the LORD.
39. to provide a place of safety for someone who accidentally killed another person
40. the Books of Moses, the Books of History, the Books of Poetry, the Major Prophets, the Minor Prophets

41. They served Baal and Ashtaroth. (They forsook the LORD and did evil in His sight.)
42. Othniel
43. Ehud
44. Deborah
45. God did not want the Israelites to boast that they had saved themselves.
46. Jephthah vowed that if God gave him victory, he would offer to the LORD whatever came from his house to meet him.
47. Samson
48. They did not cut their hair, they drank no wine or strong drink, and they did not eat grapes.
49. Samuel
50. They were rejecting God as their king.

God Chooses A Family

Chapter One Test

Name _____ Date _____ Score _____

A. *Match.*   *(7 points)*

   _c_   1. First day   a. land animals and man

   _f_   2. Second day   b. sun, moon, and stars

   _g_   3. Third day   c. light (also heaven and earth)

   _b_   4. Fourth day   d. God rested.

   _e_   5. Fifth day   e. sea animals and birds

   _a_   6. Sixth day   f. firmament

   _d_   7. Seventh day   g. dry land, seas, and plants

B. *Write* true *or* false.   *(8 points)*

_____true_____ 8. After Adam and Eve sinned, they were afraid of God.

_____true_____ 9. Satan told Eve she could disobey God and not die.

_____false_____ 10. The story of Adam and Eve's sin is told in the first chapter of Genesis.

_____true_____ 11. Everyone has received Adam's sinful nature.

_____true_____ 12. By the time of Noah, God was sorry He had made man.

_____true_____ 13. The Flood covered the highest mountain peaks.

_____false_____ 14. The men who built the Tower of Babel had planned to move to many places around the world.

_____false_____ 15. Bible dictionaries tell how many times each word in the Bible is used.

C. *Fill in the blanks.*   *(5 points)*

16. God made light and many other things by saying, "____Let____ ____there____ ____be____ . . ."

17. _____Jesus_____ was with God in the beginning and helped to create all things.

18. Because of Adam's sin, God cursed the _____ground_____.

19. During the Flood, it rained _____forty_____ days and _____forty_____ nights.

20. God's _____Word_____ will stand true forever.
    (Scriptures, Bible)

D. *Complete these sentences.*   *(10 points)*

21. The word *sanctify* means ___to set apart for holy use_____.

22. God clothed Adam and Eve by ___killing animals and using their skins for coats___
    _____.

23. Cain killed Abel because ___he was envious (jealous) of Abel_____
    _____.

24. A covenant is ___a binding agreement_____.

25. God wants us to _____read_____, _____hear_____, _____study_____,
    _____believe_____, and _____obey_____ the Bible.

E. *Write complete answers.*   *(10 points)*

26. Why did God accept Abel's sacrifice? _____
    ___Abel showed that he had faith in God by offering the best that he had._____
    _____

27. How did Noah prove that he had faith in God? _____
    ___Noah obeyed God and built the ark._____
    _____

28. What covenant did God make with Noah? _____
    ___God promised that He would not destroy the earth again with a flood._____
    _____

29. Why was God displeased with the building of the Tower of Babel? _____
    ___The people were becoming proud._____
    _____

30. How did the men who wrote the Bible know what to write? _____
    ___The Holy Spirit told men what to write._____
    _____

Total Points: 40

God Chooses A Family
Chapter Two Test

Name _____ **Date** _____ **Score** _____

A. *Circle the letter of the best ending.*   *(7 points)*

1. Abram first lived in
   a. the land of Egypt.   ⓒ Ur of the Chaldees.
   b. southern Canaan.   d. Beersheba.

2. When Abram left his homeland,
   a. Ishmael was fourteen years old.
   b. his wife stole some idols to take along.
   ⓒ he did not know where God would lead him.
   d. he was looking for better pastures for his herds.

3. During a famine in Canaan, Abram went to
   ⓐ Egypt.   b. Mount Moriah.   c. Ur of the Chaldees.   d. Haran.

4. Lot chose
   a. the hills of Canaan.   c. to live like the wicked people of the plain.
   ⓑ the plain of Jordan.   d. to leave his children behind in the burning city.

5. When God said that Sarah would have a son, she
   a. prayed.   b. smiled.   ⓒ laughed.   d. cried.

6. Sarah sent Hagar and Ishmael away because Ishmael
   a. was younger than Isaac.   c. became an archer.
   b. began to worship idols.   ⓓ made fun of Isaac.

7. Which of these men had only one wife?
   a. Abraham   ⓑ Isaac   c. Jacob

B. *Write* true *or* false.   *(5 points)*

____false____ 8. The abbreviation A.M. means "in the year of our Lord."

____false____ 9. Isaac moved to Haran when he married Rebekah.

____false____ 10. Isaac took back the blessing he had given to Jacob and gave it to Esau.

____true____ 11. An heir is a person who receives the property of someone who dies.

____true____ 12. Jacob's crafty ways brought him many troubles.

C. *Fill in the blanks.*   *(8 points)*

13. To find a certain word or verse in the Bible, use a __concordance__ .

14. Terah was Abram's ____father____ .

15. Lot was Abram's _____nephew_____.

16. ____Ishmael____ was Abram's oldest son.

17. God provided a _____ram_____ to take Isaac's place as a sacrifice.

18. ____Jacob____ wanted the birthright more than his brother did.

19. When Jacob saw his vision at Bethel, the _____LORD_____ was standing above the ladder.

20. ____Leah____ was Jacob's first wife.

D. *Complete these sentences.*   *(10 points)*

21. About 6,000 years have passed since ___the Creation_____.

22. Dates labeled A.D. are counted from ___the birth of Christ_____.

23. God said Abraham's descendants would be as the _____
    _stars in the sky, or dust of the earth, or sand on the seashore_____.

24. Abram wanted the Egyptians to think that Sarai was his sister because _____
    _he was afraid other men would kill him to marry her_____.

25. Before Jacob and Esau were born, God told Rebekah that the elder would _____
    _serve the younger_____.

E. *Write complete answers.*   *(10 points)*

26. How did Abraham show that he had faith in God? Give at least two specific examples. ____
    (Any two) He left his home without knowing where God would lead him. He believed that God would
    keep His promises, even though he had no children until he was old. He believed God would give him
    Canaan, even though he lived in tents. He prepared to offer his son when God commanded him to.

27. What did Rebekah do for Abraham's oldest servant? _____
    _She drew water from the well for him and his camels._____

28. What trouble did the herdsmen of Gerar cause Isaac? _____
    _They strove with his herdsmen for his wells._____

29. List four things Jacob did to deceive his father into blessing him.
    A. _(Answers may vary somewhat.) He put on Esau's clothes._____
    B. _____ _He wore goat skin on his hands and neck._____
    C. _____ _He took goat meat instead of venison._____
    D. _____ _He told his father lies._____

30. Why did God change Jacob's name? ___Jacob had changed from a deceiver to a_
    _prince who had power with God. (His old name no longer described him.)_____

Total Points: 40

God Chooses A Family
Chapter Three Test

Name _____ Date _____ Score _____

A. *Match.*   *(10 points)*

__h__ 1. Went with Moses to speak to Pharaoh   a. discreet

__g__ 2. Place where the Israelites settled in Egypt   b. Reuben

__e__ 3. Large sea west of Canaan   c. Judah

__b__ 4. Persuaded his brothers to throw Joseph into a pit   d. hyssop

__d__ 5. A bushy, sweet-smelling plant   e. Mediterranean

__c__ 6. Begged Joseph to let him take Benjamin's place as a servant   f. Joseph

__j__ 7. Land to which Moses fled   g. Goshen

__a__ 8. Careful in speech and action   h. Aaron

__f__ 9. Interpreted Pharaoh's dream   i. surety

__i__ 10. A guarantee against loss or damage   j. Midian

B. *Write* true *or* false.   *(8 points)*

_____false_____ 11. Egypt received more rain than Canaan did.

_____true_____ 12. Joseph's brothers hated him.

_____true_____ 13. For many years, Jacob thought Joseph was dead.

_____true_____ 14. Jacob was afraid to let Benjamin go to Egypt.

_____true_____ 15. The new pharaoh was afraid that the Israelites would rise up against the Egyptians.

_____false_____ 16. Moses was pleased to call himself the son of Pharaoh's daughter.

_____false_____ 17. Moses fled from Egypt because he had killed an Israelite.

_____true_____ 18. Pharaoh refused to let the Israelites go until after the tenth plague.

C. *Fill in the blanks.*   *(10 points)*

19. The _____Jordan_____ River flows through Canaan.

20. The _____Nile_____ River flows through Egypt.

21. Joseph's dream came true when his brothers came to Egypt and _____bowed_____ _____down_____ before him.

22. Jacob traveled to Egypt in _____wagons_____ that Joseph had sent for him.

23. Pharaoh told his people to throw all the Israelites' baby _____boys_____ into the river.

24. While Moses lived in Midian, he worked as a _____shepherd_____.

25. God spoke to Moses from out of a _____burning_____ _____bush_____.

26. _I AM [THAT I AM]_ is the name God called Himself.
    (Jehovah)

27. God told the Israelites to put the _____blood_____ of the Passover lamb on the _____doorposts_____ of their houses.

28. Before the Israelites left Egypt, they asked the _____Egyptians_____ for silver, gold, and clothes.

D. *Write complete answers.*   *(12 points)*

29. What was meant by Pharaoh's dream about the cows and the ears of grain? _____
    There would be seven years of plenty in Egypt, and then seven years of famine.

30. In what way did Joseph's life become a blessing to many? _____
    Joseph sold corn (grain) to many during the famine.

31. How could Joseph see that his brothers' hearts had changed? _____
    Joseph saw their love and concern for Benjamin.

32. How did Joseph show that he had forgiven his brothers? _____
    Joseph treated his brothers kindly.

33. What did Pharaoh answer when the LORD commanded him to let the Israelites go? _____
    "Who is the LORD, that I should obey his voice?"

34. When did Pharaoh and the Egyptians urge the Israelites to leave? _____
    Pharaoh and the Egyptians urged the Israelites to leave after the death of their first-born sons.

Total Points: 40

God Chooses A Family
Chapter Four Test

Name _____ Date _____ Score _____

A. *Write the Ten Commandments.*   *(10 points)*

1. Thou shalt have ___no___ ___other___ ___gods___ ___before___ ___me___ .

2. ___Thou___ ___shalt___ ___not___ ___make___ ___unto___ ___thee___ ___any___ ___graven___ ___image___ .

3. Thou shalt not ___take___ ___the___ ___Name___ ___of___ ___the___ ___LORD___ ___thy___ ___God___ ___in___ ___vain___ .

4. Remember ___the___ ___Sabbath___ ___Day___ , ___to___ ___keep___ ___it___ ___holy___ .

5. ___Honour___ ___thy___ ___father___ ___and___ ___thy___ ___mother___ .

6. ___Thou___ ___shalt___ ___not___ ___kill___ .

7. ___Thou___ ___shalt___ ___not___ commit ___adultery___ .

8. ___Thou___ ___shalt___ ___not___ ___steal___ .

9. Thou shalt not bear ___false___ ___witness___ .

10. ___Thou___ ___shalt___ ___not___ ___covet___ .

B. *Write* true *or* false.   *(8 points)*

___true___ 11. God did not allow the Israelites to take the shortest route to Canaan.

___false___ 12. The Israelites rejoiced when they heard the voice of God speaking from Mount Sinai.

___false___ 13. Moses, Aaron, and the elders of Israel were on Mount Sinai when the Israelites worshiped the golden calf.

___false___ 14. An ephod was a special hat worn by the high priest.

___true___ 15. Ten of the spies were afraid of the sons of Anak.

___false___ 16. Moses destroyed the serpent of brass after the people began to worship it.

___true___ 17. No man knows where Moses was buried.

___false___ 18. The Bible was first written in the English language.

C. *Underline the correct words or phrases.*   *(9 points)*

19. When the Israelites saw Pharaoh's army, Moses told them to (flee to the Red Sea, turn back and fight the Egyptians, <u>stand still and see how God would save them</u>).

20. God used the Red Sea to (frighten the Israelites, keep back the Egyptians, <u>destroy Pharaoh's army</u>).

21. Moses stayed on Mount Sinai for (four months, forty weeks, <u>forty days</u>) while God gave him the Law.

22. The first tables of stone were (<u>broken</u>, ground to powder, placed in the ark).

23. The people gave (<u>more than enough</u>, barely enough, just the right amount of) things to build the tabernacle.

24. The (altar, <u>ark</u>, candlestick) stood in the holy of holies.

25. When the tabernacle was finished, God (sprinkled it with blood, thanked the people for it, <u>filled it with His glory</u>).

26. Moses recorded the Ten Commandments in the Book of (Genesis, <u>Exodus</u>, Numbers).

27. Today God usually gives His message to man through (His spoken words, <u>His written Word</u>, dreams).

D. *Place a check (√) in front of the things that belonged to the tabernacle.*   *(5 points)*

28. _√_ a table   _√_ a golden candlestick

    _√_ an altar of incense   ____ six chairs

    ____ a bookcase   _√_ the ark of the covenant

    ____ Joseph's coffin   _√_ a covering of rams' skins dyed red

    ____ the brazen serpent   ____ the Dead Sea Scrolls

E. *Write complete answers.*   *(12 points)*

29. Name the food that God sent from heaven, and tell what the name means. _____
    <u>The food was called manna, which means "What is it?"</u>

30. With what did God guide the Israelites through the desert by day and by night? _____
    <u>a pillar of cloud by day and a pillar of fire by night</u>

31. Why did God wait forty years before leading the Israelites into Canaan? _____
    <u>God waited until the people who had rebelled were dead.</u>

32. How did Caleb and Joshua show that they had faith in God? <u>Caleb and Joshua were
    ready to enter Canaan when God wanted them to. (They gave a good report of the land.)</u>

33. Which two commandments did Jesus say are the greatest? _____

"Thou shalt love the Lord thy God with all thy heart, and with all thy soul, and with all

thy mind, and with all thy strength." "Thou shalt love thy neighbour as thyself."

_____

34. What do the Dead Sea Scrolls show about the Old Testament we use today? _____

They show that the Old Testament we use is a good copy of God's Word.

F. *Match the letters on the map with the places listed below.*   *(6 points)*

___A___ 35. Nile River

___D___ 36. Red Sea

___C___ 37. Mount Sinai

___F___ 38. Mediterranean Sea

___B___ 39. Egypt

___E___ 40. Canaan

Total Points: 50

God Chooses A Family
Chapter Five Test

Name _____ Date _____ Score _____

A. *Match the clues with the names on the right. Each name may be used more than once.*
(10 points)

__g__ 1. Sheltered the two spies   a. Achan

__h__ 2. Stood in the Jordan while the Israelites crossed   b. Adonizedec

__a__ 3. Stoned for disobeying the LORD   c. Caleb

__e__ 4. Built an altar on Mount Ebal   d. Gibeonites

__d__ 5. Forced to chop wood and draw water   e. Joshua

__b__ 6. Gathered an army to attack Gibeon   f. Moses

__e__ 7. Commanded the sun to stand still   g. Rahab

__b__ 8. Was king of Jerusalem   h. priests carrying the ark

__f__ 9. Told the eastern tribes to help their brethren conquer the rest of Canaan

__c__ 10. Asked for a mountain where giants lived

B. *Write* true *or* false.   *(9 points)*

____false____ 11. The two Israelite spies escaped from Jericho by slipping out through the gate.

____false____ 12. The LORD helped the Israelites defeat Jericho by sending fire from heaven.

____true____ 13. Rahab and her family were saved when Jericho was destroyed.

____false____ 14. The LORD told the Israelites to completely destroy the gold, silver, brass, and iron that they found in Jericho.

____true____ 15. Jerusalem was situated in the central mountains of Canaan.

____false____ 16. The LORD told Joshua to kill the Gibeonites for lying to the Israelites.

____true____ 17. Joshua had decided to serve the LORD, even if the rest of the Israelites chose to serve other gods.

____true____ 18. The Israelites found it easier to defend the cities in the mountains than the cities in the plains and valleys.

____false____ 19. A city marked A4—11 in a Bible atlas index would be found on Map A, column 4, row 11.

C. *Fill in the blanks or underline the correct word.*   *(5 points)*

20. The Israelites marched around Jericho once each day for _____six_____ days. On the last day, they marched around the city _____seven_____ times.

21. If a man accidentally killed someone, he could flee to a city of _____refuge_____.

22. An innocent manslayer could return home safely after the _____high_____ _____priest_____ died.

23. The tribe of (Judah, Manasseh, Levi) received large sections of land on both sides of the Jordan River.

24. The main roads through Canaan followed the (central mountains, Jordan River, Mediterranean Sea).

D. *Write complete answers.*   *(10 points)*

25. Why did the LORD tell Joshua to set up twelve stones at Gilgal? _____
    The LORD wanted the Israelites to remember how He had helped them to cross the Jordan River.

26. Why were the Israelites defeated at Ai? _____
    God did not help them, because Achan had sinned.

27. How did the Gibeonites deceive Joshua and the men of Israel? _____
    They took old food, clothes, and goods, and pretended to be ambassadors from a far country, who were seeking peace.

28. What shows that Achan probably did not repent of his sin, even though he confessed it? ___
    Achan waited to confess his sin until he was chosen by lot. If he had not been caught, he probably would never have confessed it.

29. Why was Canaan a good location for Bible events to take place? _____
    Many people passed through Canaan and heard about the true God.

E. *Match the letters on the map with the places listed below.*   *(6 points)*

   __E__ 30. Jordan Valley
   __B__ 31. Central Mountains
   __F__ 32. Eastern Mountains
   __A__ 33. Coastal Plain
   __C__ 34. Jerusalem
   __D__ 35. Jericho

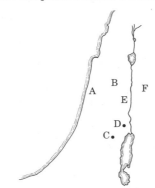

Total Points: 40

God Chooses A Family
Chapter Six Test

Name _____ **Date** _____ **Score** _____

A. *Match.*   *(5 points)*

  d   1. Lived on the lowlands between the hills of Judah and the   a. Gaza

              Mediterranean Sea   b. Jebusites

  b   2. Lived in Jerusalem during the time of the judges   c. Midianites

  c   3. Lived in tents and moved from place to place   d. Philistines

  a   4. One of the five main Philistine cities   e. Tyre

  e   5. A harbor on the Mediterranean coast

B. *Write* true *or* false.   *(7 points)*

_____true_____ 6. After Joshua died, the Israelites began to serve other gods.

_____false_____ 7. The Israelites conquered all the land of Canaan in one year.

_____true_____ 8. Sisera thought Jael would help him.

_____false_____ 9. The Philistines found out the secret of Samson's strength by giving him money.

_____false_____ 10. Of all the judges of Israel, only Samson was a Nazarite.

_____true_____ 11. The Philistines captured the ark of the LORD during a battle.

_____true_____ 12. Gideon made sure that God was calling him by laying out a fleece.

C. *Fill in the blanks.*   *(8 points)*

13. _____Ehud_____ wore his sword on his right side.

14. Barak helped _____Deborah_____ defeat the Canaanites.

15. _____Gideon_____ was threshing wheat by a winepress when the LORD called him.

16. _____Samson_____ killed more Philistines at his death than he had killed during his life.

17. Nazarites were not allowed to cut their _____hair_____, drink wine or strong drink, or eat moist or dried _____grapes_____.

18. _____Ruth_____ left her people and her heathen gods to serve the God of Israel.

19. _____Samuel_____, Israel's last judge, anointed the first two kings of Israel.

20. A _____concordance_____ can be used to find Bible verses and Bible stories.

D. *Write complete answers.*   *(10 points)*

21. Why did God allow the enemies of Israel to oppress them? _____
    <u>The Israelites had not obeyed God's command to drive out all the Canaanites. (It was</u>
    <u>a way of bringing the people back when they departed from God.)</u>

22. Why did God want Gideon to take only three hundred men to fight against the Midianites?
    <u>God did not want the Israelites to boast that they had saved themselves.</u>

23. What foolish vow did Jephthah make? _____
    <u>He vowed that if God helped him win the battle, he would offer up the first thing that</u>
    <u>came out of his house to meet him when he returned home.</u>

24. What did Hannah promise to do if the LORD gave her a son? _____
    <u>She promised to give her son back to the LORD.</u>

25. Why was God displeased with the Israelites' desire for a king? _____
    <u>They were rejecting God as their king.</u>

E. *List the main divisions of the Old Testament in the correct order.*   *(5 points)*

26. <u>the Books of Moses</u>
27. <u>the Books of History</u>
28. <u>the Books of Poetry</u>
29. <u>the Major Prophets</u>
30. <u>the Minor Prophets</u>

F. *List the five Books of Moses in the correct order.*   *(5 points)*

31. <u>Genesis</u>
32. <u>Exodus</u>
33. <u>Leviticus</u>
34. <u>Numbers</u>
35. <u>Deuteronomy</u>

Total Points: 40

God Chooses A Family

Final Test

Name _____ Date _____ Score _____

A. *Match. Some names are not needed.*   *(10 points)*

__l__	1. Learned the Scriptures when he was a child	a. Caleb
__i__	2. Saved his family by obeying all of God's instructions	b. Deborah
__b__	3. Led Israel to battle with Barak's help	c. Israel
__e__	4. Made a foolish vow before going to battle	d. Jacob
__g__	5. Commanded the sun to stand still	e. Jephthah
__j__	6. Lost God's presence and power within him because	f. Jordan River
	he told the secret of his strength	g. Joshua
__k__	7. Was Israel's last judge	h. Nile River
__a__	8. Asked for a mountain where giants lived	i. Noah
__c__	9. Means "having power with God"	j. Samson
__f__	10. Flows through the land of Canaan	k. Samuel
		l. Timothy

B. *Write* true *or* false.   *(5 points)*

__false__ 11. Moses fled from Egypt because one of the Israelites wanted to kill him.

__true__ 12. Before Esau and Jacob were born, God told their mother that the elder would serve the younger.

__false__ 13. The abbreviation A.D. means "in the year of the world."

__false__ 14. Jesus said that the greatest commandment is, "Remember the sabbath day, to keep it holy."

__true__ 15. The Israelites could not kill the Gibeonites because of the league they had made with them.

C. *Complete these sentences.*   *(6 points)*

16. God created light by saying, " __Let there be light__ ."

17. God told Abraham that he would have as many descendants as the _____
__(Any one) dust of the earth, stars of the heaven, sand of the seashore__.

18. Joseph knew that his brothers had changed because _____
    he saw that they loved Benjamin   .

19. In the holy of holies of the tabernacle stood the ___ark (of the covenant)___ .

20. The Israelites had to wander in the desert for forty years because ___when God wanted
    them to enter Canaan, they rebelled and wished that they were back in Egypt___ .

21. God was displeased with Israel's desire for a king because _____
    they were rejecting Him as their king   .

D. *Write complete answers.*   *(8 points)*

22. How did Abraham show that he had faith in God? Give two specific examples. ___(Any two)___
    He left his home without knowing where God would lead him. Even before he had a son, he believed
    God's promise that he would have many descendants. He was willing to sacrifice his promised son.

23. Why is God's written Word often better for us than God's spoken word? Give at least two reasons. ___(Any two) We can remember it better, since we can reread it often. We can mak___
    copies of it to give to others. We can read it, even though we live many years after God
    gave it.
    _____

24. What commandment did Achan disobey? _____
    Achan disobeyed God's command forbidding them to take any treasures from Jericho
    for themselves.

25. How did Gideon make sure that God was calling him? _____
    He laid out a fleece and asked God to make it wet with dew and to keep the ground dry
    one night and to make the ground wet and keep the fleece dry the next night.

E. *Name the things God made on each day of Creation.*   *(6 points)*

26. First day: ___light (also heaven and earth);___
    Second day: ___firmament;___
    Third day: ___dry land, seas, and plants;___
    Fourth day: ___sun, moon, and stars;___
    Fifth day: ___sea animals and birds;___
    Sixth day: ___land animals and man___

F. *Name the five divisions of Old Testament books.* (*5 points*)

27. Books of __Moses__
28. __Books of History__
29. __Books of Poetry__
30. __Books of Major Prophets__
31. __Books of Minor Prophets__

G. *Write one word in each blank to complete the Ten Commandments.* (*10 points*)

1. Thou shalt have __no__ __other__ __gods__ __before__ me.
2. Thou shalt not __make__ __unto__ thee __any__ __graven__ __image__.
3. Thou shalt not __take__ __the__ __Name__ of the __LORD__ __thy__ __God__ in __vain__.
4. __Remember__ the __Sabbath__ __Day__, __to__ __keep__ __it__ __holy__.
5. __Honour__ __thy__ __father__ and __thy__ __mother__.
6. Thou shalt not __kill__.
7. Thou shalt not __commit__ __adultery__.
8. Thou shalt not __steal__.
9. Thou shalt not __bear__ __false__ __witness__.
10. Thou shalt not __covet__.

Total Points: 50

Index of Special Features

Miscellaneous Special Features